Shro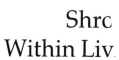
Within Liv.

WITHIN LIVING MEMORY SERIES

Other Counties in this series include:

Bedfordshire
Buckinghamshire
Cheshire
Cumbria
Devon
Hampshire
Herefordshire
Hertfordshire
Isle of Wight
East Kent

Leicestershire & Rutland
Northamptonshire
Oxfordshire
Somerset
Staffordshire
Suffolk
Surrey
West Sussex
Warwickshire
Wiltshire

Shropshire Within Living Memory

Compiled by the Shropshire Federation
of Women's Institutes from notes sent by
Institutes in the County

Published jointly by
Countryside Books, Newbury
and the S.F.W.I. Shrewsbury

COUNTRYSIDE BOOKS
3 Catherine Road
Newbury, Berkshire

ISBN 1 85306 203 0

The cover photograph shows Alice Rickus at six years of age,
and was supplied by Lawley WI.

Designed by Mon Mohan
Produced through MRM Associates Ltd, Reading
Printed in England by J.W. Arrowsmith Ltd, Bristol.

Contents

Acknowledgements

Shropshire Federation of Women's Institutes would like to thank all W.I. members who supplied material for this project through their local Institutes. We are grateful also to the Ironbridge Gorge Museum Trust Social History Group for material on Coalbrookdale.

Special thanks is due to Mrs Barbara Hampson for providing the delightful sketches.

Unfortunately we were not able to include extracts from every submission; to do so would have meant some duplication of content, and of course we had to take into account the total amount of space available in the book.

But all the contributions, without exception, were of value: deciding the shape and content of the book. We are grateful for them all.

Betty Carlyle
Co-ordinator

Foreword

Shropshire is a large land-locked rural county which had no large conurbation, only the county town of Shrewsbury, situated almost centrally with a handful of market towns scattered around. The main road in the county is the Roman Road – Watling Street or A5, which carries the traffic in a south easterly and north westerly direction across Shropshire.

After the Second World War the new town of Telford was built, incorporating Coalbrookdale, Dawley, Madeley, Oakengates and Shifnal and designated as an overspill town for the industrial Midlands. New road links were built to the main motorways of the Country, bringing traffic from the industrialised Midlands to the factories of Telford and holiday traffic across the county to the coasts of Mid and North Wales.

This book, 'Within Living Memory', describes what life was like during the first part of the century, when a trip outside the county was still a great adventure, either by train to a large city or an annual Sunday school charabanc trip to the sea-side.

The first part of this century has seen the greatest ever change in the life of rural women with the coming of electricity and modern household appliances, mechanisation on the farms and the family car making isolated villages more easily accessible. The Women's Institute has played an important part in the countryside during these changing times.

We often hear people say 'If only I could remember all that my Grandparents told me', so this book has given the members of Shropshire Federation of Women's Institutes the chance to record some of their stories and memories for future generations to enjoy, and have an insight of rural life in the first half of the 20th century.

We are grateful to all those members who provided the collection of memories and to Mrs Betty Carlyle and Mrs Anne Pipkin who co-ordinated the project.

Kathleen E Jones
County Chairman

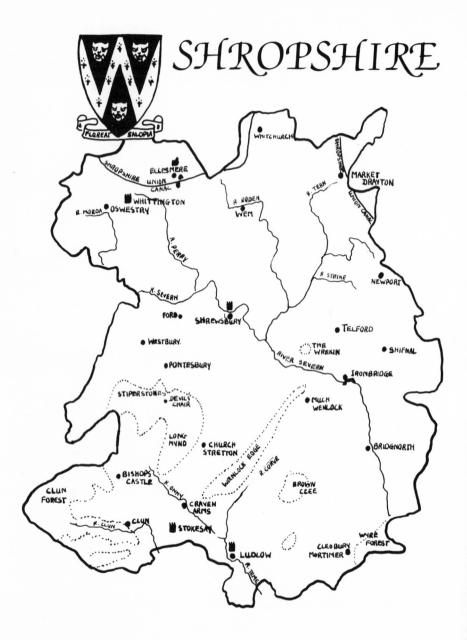

TOWN
& COUNTRY LIFE

TOWN AND VILLAGE REMEMBERED

'The countryside,' remembered one lady born in the early years of the century, 'was very beautiful. The hedges met overhead from the sides of the lanes, all sweet briar and honeysuckle and the roads were green in the middle because there wasn't a lot of traffic.' Shropshire's countryside is still beautiful, but the way of life in her towns and villages has changed almost beyond recognition since the beginning of the century, and even since the end of the Second World War.

SHREWSBURY PAST

'Aromatic Shrewsbury! Was it "aromatic"? Oh yes, terrible – especially after the sheep, more than the cows and I remember the West Mid Show when cattle and bulls were walked from the railway station to the showground. Shrewsbury had nice and nasty aromas. If you went down Frankwell you'd come across the Skin Yard where the skins were cured – that was terrible, that was. Then you'd go up Mardol and you'd pass Charlie Beddard's "Pork Pie Shop" that wasn't so bad. Then on up Gullet Passage there was a coffee grinder's; that was lovely. Go into Barker Street and there was the Tan Yard where they used to tan the hides; but you got used to these smells. Passing Philips in Mardol you had all the lovely grocery smells and Morris the bakers on Welsh Bridge gave out mouthwatering, tempting smells. I remember the baker's boy arrived in the street at about 7.00am ringing his bell and carrying a tray of rolls "All hot, all hot!" he would shout.'

'Shrewsbury was bursting at the seams in the 1920s and 1930s. The slum clearances started in the 1920s and continued until the outbreak of war, giving rise to numerous new housing estates on the then periphery of the town. In the 1930s there were still large numbers of mean little houses, without water or sanitation. Each area would have one or two community middens, community laundry and washing facilities. Inhabitants sat outside these houses as long as possible during the summer months. The houses, which consisted of one small room downstairs and one above, were bug infested and grossly overcrowded. This led to many disturbances. When quarrels

10

occurred, leading to fighting, it often resulted in one or other of the aggressors being knocked through a very fragile wall and landing in the neighbouring dwelling. The law often came down very heavily on some of these people. Barker Street in particular was a hive of humanity dominated by the smelly tannery at the bottom of Claremont Bank.

The majority of the shops, which were diverse, were run by local people. Many were very small businesses and were run from the shuts and alleyways in the minimum of space.

My brother-in-law Jack tells the story of his time as an errand boy for a local butcher in Mardol. Also in Mardol in an alleyway behind the present baker's shop was a carpenter who, among furniture and other items, often made coffins. A young boy had drowned by the Welsh Bridge and his body was in the mortuary on Smithfield Road; an order had been placed with the carpenter for a coffin for the boy. The carpenter requested a loan of the butcher's errand boy, Jack, whom he estimated to be the same size as the drowned boy. Jack was sent to the carpenter where he was obliged to lie in several coffins until an agreed size was arrived at!

The old Victorian market was a thriving centre in its own right. It held the well patronised pannier market with dozens of country ladies hiring one or two yards of bench to display their baskets of fresh produce. These could be anything from the odd bunch of herbs, a dozen eggs, a few fresh vegetables, to small portions of home-made butter and cheese, the odd rabbit, duck or chicken, and bunches of flowers. It was essential to arrive at the market very early in order to acquire a yard or two of selling space, all spaces being occupied within ten minutes of opening time. Thus the surrounding streets would be full of ponies and traps, and many of the accompanying drivers would spend some hours in one of the many pubs. For the non-drinkers there was the working men's hall in Princess Street. There they received a very cheap lunch and could indulge in several activities in the games room.

The pubs themselves did a thriving business on market days and it was often said that the pony, with its passengers, would find its own way home.

Poultry was not then an everyday item and on high days and holy days, especially Christmas Eve, there would be an auction of live poultry, ducks and geese. There was no refrigeration so people often preferred to buy their product "in their feathers". We would go with my father about nine o'clock on Christmas Eve in order to get a bargain as the remaining produce would be sold off cheaply.

A large wholesale cheese market also occurred at intervals, the cheese having been made on surrounding farms. There were enormous whole, assorted cheeses auctioned to buyers from as far afield as Birmingham, Liverpool, Manchester and other cities.

The cattle market in Smithfield Road was also a hive of activity and brought great business into the town. Cattle and sheep would be brought in by the farmers and drovers, often from quite long distances. The streets of Shrewsbury would be full of animals making for the Smithfield on cattle market days. The publicans around the Smithfield, many of whom closed down when the market went out of the town, would be preparing for the influx from a very early hour. After business transactions the pubs would be overflowing with farmers, drovers and drink. The drovers returning the animals at the end of the day were often under the influence.

The abattoir was situated where the Raven Meadows precinct now stands and that also was busy on market days.'

'When my parents brought me to live in Shrewsbury in 1936 the by-pass had only recently been opened and houses were springing up all around the new road and the green fields fast disappearing. A postman once told me that Shelton Road was known as "Lovers Lane" before the by-pass was built. The road was quiet then with very few cars about, and cattle were driven on foot along Shelton Road on their way to the cattle market, then in Smithfield Road. On one occasion I was woken at about 6am by the bleating of a flock of a sheep which had strayed into a neighbour's garden, and on another occasion I was ordered indoors by a farmer whose bull was running amuck in the opposite garden. Quite often there were reports in the *Shrewsbury Chronicle* of cows on their way to the cattle market having escaped and run into one of the nearby shops.

Of course, during the war the road became busier as the convoys of gun carriers and army lorries clattered along. There was very little other traffic apart from a few horse-drawn vehicles delivering groceries, etc. I believe part of the by-pass was closed to the public, as I had to obtain a pass from the Army authorities in order to cycle from Meole Brace to Sutton Road on my way to school.

As a small girl I enjoyed rowing on the Severn with my father – boats were available for hire from the Boat House Hotel, who also owned the "Lady Sue", a larger boat which took parties out on the river. Near Port Hill Bridge were the remains of the ferry which ran across the river from Beck's Field to The Quarry. Up river near the Welsh Bridge at the bottom of Mardol there were several old buildings which had been part of the wharf used when goods were brought by river from Bristol.'

'The tiny hamlet of Nox was just two farm cottages and two larger houses, but in that little place there was my father's butcher's shop. We were able to slaughter our own animals in those days. Father would buy cattle and sheep in the auction at Shrewsbury and bring them home to keep until he needed them for killing. We as children used to watch this process and help with the making of sausages, pressed beef, brawn, black puddings and lard. I loved going with my father to farms to cut up the pig which most families kept in those days.

Opposite our shop was Mr Goode's, who was injured in the First World War and was trained to repair shoes. He had been provided with a wooden hut and all the equipment to carry on his trade. He had to walk two miles each day because of the injuries to his legs so he was found a home at Cruckmeole. We spent many exciting hours trying on all the shoes he had to repair. We watched him cut the shapes from a large piece of leather, dip it in water to soften it, then stitch the soles on to the shoes with thread which he rubbed through a block of beeswax.

Next to Mr Goode was another wooden shed where Mr Stubbs the carpenter worked. He made coffins. We watched him saw and shape the wood and put the lovely soft padding and lining on the inside, and shiny handles to complete it.

The next building was Price the blacksmith's, another very interesting place. The steel for the horseshoes came in long lengths which were cut to the size of the shoes needed when the massive horses arrived. It would take almost all day to fit the four shoes. Cart wheels were also fitted with iron hoops, which had to be heated red hot in a fire in the open and then quickly knocked onto the wooden wheel and cooled by throwing water over before the wood was burnt; very hot, hard work.

Mr Price also kept a sweet shop, where we spent our pocket money on a penny's worth of sweets or chocolate. Working out which to have gave us the most for our money. Mrs Price also made soap in a large bath, which she would then cut into blocks for sale.

In Yockleton I remember a very old man called John Evans who lived in a cottage behind the village, across fields, and was a wonderful carpenter. My father ordered a chopping block from him and it took three years for him to "pickle" the wood. It was made from blocks of wood little larger than a brick, all joined together and bound with more wood. It was a wonderful piece of work.'

ASH VILLAGE

'When I was growing up in Ash in the 1940s the character of the village was quite different to the present day.

At that time the village was centred on agriculture and most people either worked on farms or had jobs associated with them. The process of modernisation was still in its early days and only the centre of the village had electricity and mains water. There were three pumps for water and the outskirts of the village did not get electricity until 1960.

The corn in those days was all cut with a binder and the threshing box used to travel from farm to farm, the farmers helping each other with labour. In the early days after the war two or three land girls travelled round with the threshing box. Most of the hay was harvested loose and it was some years later than balers became common. Most of the farms had tractors but many still kept and worked one or two carthorses and I remember one of the features of the annual fete being a carthorse race. Several farms in the village made Cheshire cheese and most killed a pig each year.

There were two blacksmiths in Ash then. Frank Barlow had the smithy next to the parish room and Ralph Bateman still shod horses from his home on Brown Moss. He also kept goats which I remember him tethering on the Moss.

Bill Hollowood had his shoe repairing kiosk next to the village smithy, where all the locals took their shoes for repair. One of his main jobs was re-soling men's hobnailed boots.

There was no village shop as such but Bill Chesworth kept a few groceries in a shed attached to his house which was next to the White Lion pub. There you could buy a loaf of bread etc and we children used to go across from the village school to buy pop and crisps.

Just after the war, while petrol was on ration, we used to go to Whitchurch on market day in the horse-drawn trap. The horse was used for riding as well as driving. One day we were going out when the hounds were drawing the Springs (a small wood at New Woodhouses) and the horse was so eager to join them and pulled so hard that we drove all the way to Whitchurch on the reins without the traces tightening.

James Farnell was the local builder, wheelwright and undertaker, working from his Pride Hill workshop. He was a true craftsman and could turn his hand to most jobs, apart from being a keen gardener. When all the farm carts had wooden wheels he used to have one day each week hooping wheels. He also made coffins of best oak. He did all the building work for the Wynne-Corvie estate and at one time had over 20 men working for him. When the panelling was installed in Ash church to commemorate the church's centenary in 1936 he made

14

and fitted it all. There is a chair in the chancel of the church which he designed and made himself.

Jim Farnell was a fount of knowledge and did not mind in the least spending time answering the questions of an inquisitive youngster. He told me that he remembered the last reaping team coming to Ash. They were moving a field of corn at Edgeley Hall. The men cut the corn with sickles and the women followed them with bands tying the sheaves.

He also recalled an old man named Joseph Dykes who lived in Catteralls Lane and could remember Ash Church being built in 1836, the bricks being brought to church by mule train.'

WHEN THE SQUIRE RULED

Life on a country estate or in a village where the Squire and his lady headed the social hierarchy could be almost feudal, even well into the 20th century. Many landowners, however, accepted the responsibilities which went with their position and when the system worked well, it provided a degree of security unknown to those outside.

ON THE ESTATE

'My grandparents John and Martha Ralphs were tenants on the Hawkestone Estate, my grandfather being a waggoner at the Home Farm. Work was from six in the morning to dark, remuneration twelve shillings a week. As grandfather got older he said to the bailiff: "You know, I don't think I'm worth twelve shillings now." "No," the bailiff replied, "No, John, you binna", and reduced his wage to ten shillings.

The waggoners always tried to be at work well before six to groom their horses and get an extra feed of oats for them.

My father (born in 1877) remembered going to the Hall kitchen on Saturday mornings with a can for soup, along with all the other children from the estate. What joy there was the week when there had been a party and there would be goodies in the way of cakes, or sometimes a bread pudding.

At Christmas each tenant was given three items. One was a load of coal, another a joint of beef. Father said this was the only "butcher's meat" of the year; rabbits, boiling hen and of course, the cottager's pig, being the yearly meat intake. The third item was a length of flannel or suiting. Grandmother having six sons, she always chose the suiting and made all her boys suits, laboriously hand stitched. She never wore glasses but at night sewing the dark stuff she was very extravagant and burnt two candles. There was not time to waste on sewing in daylight hours, with so much else to do, including cultivation of her "potato field" at Darliston two miles away.

Uncle Ambrose acted as postilion to Lord Hill who was crippled with rheumatism. He had a sort of invalid carriage with a step on the back on which Ambrose rode ready to open and shut the many gates as his lordship perambulated his vast estate. Uncle Albert was employed to sweep all the paths on the landscaped estate, along the terrace to the obelisk and right through to Hodnet Lodge.'

'My father was the Clerk of Works on Lord Barnard's estate, the heart of which was the estate yard and offices at Uppington. He had moved there from Northamptonshire in 1911 and remained in charge until he died in 1945, when my brother took it over.

It was the old style village, with a Squire in Colonel Sowerby, who was Lord Barnard's agent. He ruled with a rod of iron and decreed that all front doors on the estate should be grey! He and his family went to church every Sunday and woe betide any tenant farmers who did not attend – he would want to know the reason why.

There was no pub in the village, anyone who wanted a drink would have to walk a couple of miles to the Horseshoe Inn at Uckington or The Grove at Walcot which was about three miles away. Walcot was also our nearest railway station.

All the people in the village were either employed at the estate yard or by the two farms in the village, and in addition there was a blacksmith, a postmistress and, of course, a parson.

My father was in charge of all the estate, which stretched from the Wrekin to Wenlock Edge in those days. In the estate yard there were joiners, painters, plumbers etc. Power for the machinery came from a magnificent steam engine which was the pride and joy of Mr Griffiths who kept its brass bands gleaming. It broke his heart when electricity came to the village and made his beloved engine redundant.'

'Fred Sillitoe left Sherrifhales school in 1915. His memories were recorded prior to his death and paint a vivid picture of life in the first part of the century.

The Duke of Sutherland lived at Lilleshall Hall. As his name suggests his family were from Scotland at Dunnlodie Castle. He also owned Trentham Hall in Staffordshire. In 1900 it was decided to dismantle Trentham because of the smell of the filthy river which ran through the potteries. The stable yard and the coach houses were left so Fred's father used to have to travel over there to sort out any problems. Eventually these were sold to the Staffordshire Steel and Iron Company. On his 21st birthday in 1909, the duke came into his title.

All the farmland around the area was owned and rented from the duke. The big wood was patrolled by nine gamekeepers. Horses were kept to work on the property, 32 at one time, to pull carriages and for leisure. The Duke's sister Rosemary used to ride around the village on horseback. Polo ponies were brought to and fro from London. The children from the village could earn a halfpenny if they were lucky by running to open a gate for the gentry on horseback. That was if you were lucky, if you weren't you could receive a flick of the whip!

To rent seven and a half acres cost £3 17s 6d. Many of the village people therefore used to find it hard to make ends meet. Fred's father, the estate plumber, used to have both his own smallholding and to start work daily at 6am on the Duke's estate. The Duke himself was not interested in farming and got his supplies from the Home Farm. It supplied all the meat, turkeys and dairy produce. Abbey Farm was rented out too, as was Littlehales Farm. On Fred's father's smallholding were kept two cows, three calves, a pony, several pigs and about 2,000 fowl. These used to roam freely throughout the Big Wood behind the farm.

Life for the ordinary villager was very poor. Many children went to school in the village in bare feet, in snow and all weathers. Fred was fortunate. He had both shoes and stockings and also bread and dripping for his lunch. There was no school dinners. The children had water to drink and that was all. There were two taps, one each for the boys and girls. There were three fires in the school for heating, one in the infants room and two in the larger room. The children stayed at the village school for the whole of their education. Fred left school at 13 in 1915 but he nevertheless had to work out of school hours and at weekends. The family who lived on one side of Fred were from Ireland. They had no furniture at all and only a frying pan to cook with. Straw was used to lie on and food consisted mainly of a big fat cake cooked in the pan made of flour and other stuff which they called cakebread. On the other side was another poor family too. Some houses had only two bedrooms and about seven children. Food was rationed out to them and they never had new clothes. These were all farmworkers with jobs such as pigmen, shepherds, waggoners or cowmen. All the village boys were trained to touch their hats to the ladies and the girls to curtsey. Each Christmas the village children would be presented with a small present by the duchess and would be trained to say "Thank you, your Grace". Politeness was also stressed at school as well as at home. Both mother and teacher told Fred always to be polite and he would never lose by it.

Shopping in the village could be at the village shop and in the outlying areas. Bakers used to call daily with fresh bread. Lloyds of Shifnal used to come in a van to bring groceries. There has never been a pub in the village itself but the duke would sometimes provide beer or the villagers could walk to three pubs nearby. There was a lot of drunkenness at times with the men of the village. Outings were rare except once a year when everyone went to Shifnal for the "Duff" festival.

In 1918, the First World War had taken its toll of the lives of many of the village's young people. Lilleshall Hall was sold and the remaining young people left for work elsewhere. The farmland was bought by the council and broken up into smallholdings for rent so that the people who came into them after the war were mostly ex-servicemen who could not afford to pay for help.'

THE MEMORIES OF LADY MORE

'My name is Clare Mary More and I'm aged 80; and I'm going to tell you, if I can remember, the things that happened to me in my youth. *(Lady More, as Miss Clare Hope-Edwards, inherited Netley Hall, Dorrington in 1933.)*

I was told that my great-grandmother (in the 1880s) used to drive round the village at Christmas time with a large roll (a "bolt" I think it was called), and at every house that had any young, she used to snip off a large bit of red flannel to make a nightdress for all the children. When my great-aunts and great-uncles died their funerals used to be like this: a farm-cart used to come to the house and they used to walk with horses from the house to the church, which is about a mile, with the relations and farm employees and tenants all walking behind, and that was the last time that that happened. When my mother died she went in the ordinary motor-car.

(She inherited a very aged staff, including an old man called Mr Benn, who came to dig the garden.) And Benn used to wear, on his left wrist, five strands of rather dirty wool; and I said to him "Benn, why do you wear that wool on your wrist?" "Oh, miss", he said, "it's for me wrisseses – bang in the pos'seses, I can't do it without it!".

He was an amazing old man, and he used to lodge with a widow lady in the village. He used to go down to the pub very often for rather longer than was necessary and when he came back, if he wasn't absolutely sober, she used to lock him in the coal-shed all night, and the next day he didn't come to work. I always used to say, "Flu again, Benn?" "Yes, miss, flu again" but I knew exactly what had happened – he'd been in the coal-shed all night.

(In 1944 she married Mr Jasper More.) Because my husband had to go to the war and was called up very suddenly, we had to do the whole thing in four days. I had nothing – no wedding dress, so I was lent one. He had his uniform, just made – very uncomfortable as all new things are. We had no food but we rang round (of course we were heavily rationed) and all the farmers, bless their hearts, all came and they brought everything: like chickens and ham – they ate what they brought – plus! I managed to get some wine, which was some champagne – two bottles; six bottles of "white wine sherry" (as it was known in those days); and a barrel of beer; and we had our wedding in the village, the school had a holiday and they all came in the choir and sang. The church was absolutely filled with people and I had a lovely wedding. But I was told that the last thing that was found was my friend Mr Benn, over the barrel of beer, lying back and saying: "Bless 'em all, I say, bless 'em all, bless 'em all!"

In war-time I worked for nine months in the Royal Salop Infirmary in Shrewsbury as a VAD (lowest form of animal life in the hospital!) and for three months I was allowed off to farm. We had a very small holding of 48 acres round the house and I was in charge of the farm plus the gardener, who was left behind. I went to the market and I bought some animals, some cows. I paid £28 for a short-horn cow and £32 for an Ayrshire cow: I remember the prices well and they were two of the most wonderful cows! They produced milk, milk, milk. I was the dairymaid – I made the butter in an old fashioned churn that went round and round and round, and sometimes it would "come" and sometimes it wouldn't. I used to cheat and put a little warm water in. And if it looked very white, the butter, I used to put a tiny little bit of saffron in to make it look yellow and more attractive! Anyhow, it was a great boon, I can tell you.

But milking was *not* a boon. The gardener said to me "Milking will come to you as barking comes to a dog" – but no dog would ever bark if he was true! I used to sit and pull and pull – I *could* milk but I could never absolutely get the cows dry – I used to think I had and I used to say to Maddox: "I've done it! at last, she won't give any more milk at all." He'd say "Let me have a look, miss", and he'd bend down, turn his head towards me (to see that I was looking at him!) and it would go swish, swish, swish, into the bucket – I used to scream with rage, because I didn't think there was a drop left – he always used to find that extra drop. . .

19

Every single thing we grew and didn't eat went to market. And I had a horse, an Arab, and we used to drive him, in harness, to market – and he was a beautiful Arab stallion but he didn't like the traffic lights, so whenever we got to the traffic lights I used to have to leap out of the trap and hold his head and talk to him, and then he was all right. And then when they changed, I'd jump back and into market we went and we used to sell our stuff and come back. That was fun – I enjoyed that, but we were very rationed with any kind of fuel at all, petrol and so on, then.

And the other thing that we did, we kept hives – bees. And Maddox, the head gardener and farmer and everything he was then – he knew a lot about bees. And we used to go to sales of bees and he was very particular and very superstitious about bees. And if he saw a bee on the floor, walking on the grass, he'd say "No miss, we won't buy these, they're wrong", and back we used to go. If they were wild bees – no he wouldn't have those either: he liked his bees to be tame bees. And another thing he insisted on was, when I bought bees, I bought from a willing seller, always – and it was a fair do, and I hadn't done the man down, or he'd done me down, otherwise the bees would go wrong, he was sure about that. And of course, *everything* that happened in the house – my engagement, my marriage, my mother's death – he went straight off and told the bees, *always*.

Well, the bees were all right as far as I was concerned, except when it meant that the honey had to be taken. And poor Maddox had one sting and his face used to blow up like a balloon, and so I said "Well, Maddox, you can't go on, I shall have to do it". I used to cover myself from top to bottom, but I was frightened and of course bees know when you're frightened and I always got stung. Once I was stung seven times and I was hopping about like a scalded cat, and old Maddox said "It's good for your rheumatism, miss, it's good for your rheumatism!".

Anyhow, the bees were a great help, and we were able to give honey away and we used honey in food, and the sugar; and in the autumn we used to take the bees to the Anchor Inn for the heather honey and that was very, very delicious – much nicer than any other honey.

But of course the bees used to swarm. And who had to take the swarm? It was me, because poor Maddox was allergic to bee-stings! And that used to terrify me: but he said "I'll hold the branch and give it a good BANG!" Bang! and down it would come. But I remember I was frightened and I don't like bees now. I don't like being stung by bees! And of course when they swarm, they used to fly all over the place, out of the garden, into the field and we used to have to rush after them with cans I remember, and sit, banging cans till we got a box to put the swarm in. . .

I've lived a very curious life, when I look back on it, but it was fun, and I enjoyed it, and then I was young.

(In 1954 Mr & Mrs More moved to his home at Linley, More; in 1960 he became MP for Ludlow – like his grandfather – and was knighted on his retirement in 1979.) Linley in those days was in a very bad way; it had no light, it had no heating, it had no water: the whole house stank of paraffin. It was on three floors and you had to bring your food from downstairs in the kitchen, to the scullery, up 14 stairs, into an ante-room and then into the dining room. Jasper was absolutely marvellous, he sold half the Linley estate and he spent the money on modernising this house and making it into a reasonably easy house that we could live in.'

ROWTON CASTLE

'The kitchen at Rowton Castle was very big and rows and rows of copper pots in all shapes and sizes hung from the ceiling. A black range was used for all cooking. Indoor staff consisted of cook, kitchen maid, scullery maid, head housemaid, second housemaid, butler (who had every afternoon off), parlour maid who used to "do" teas and lady's maid.

Meals were a cooked breakfast of bacon, eggs, black pudding, etc; lunch; afternoon tea – in the winter toast was made on the open fire; dinner in the evening. Every morning the lady of the house discussed with cook the menu for the nursery, dining room and servants' hall.

Most of the fruit (including grapes, melons, peaches, nectarines, figs, etc) and vegetables were grown in the kitchen garden. Milk, butter, cheese and poultry came from the Home Farm, and game in season from the estate. Any surplus was sold in Shrewsbury market.

Pheasants were reared in hen coops and fed, amongst other things, on hard boiled eggs and chopped onions. If certain local children visited the keeper at known times he would give them sufficient mixture to make a sandwich for their own tea.

Stopping was also popular with children. This meant standing at given points on the outskirts of woods and if the pheasants began to fly out, trees had to be tapped with sticks to "stop" them escaping. On cold winter days children often had a hot jacket potato in each pocket to warm the hands – and then ate the potato for lunch. A small payment was usually made to stoppers.

Visiting cards were used. If delivered by the lady herself, one corner was turned down; if delivered on her behalf the card was left intact.

Rents were paid at the Estate Office on specified dates. If anyone arrived on a cart horse, the horse had to be tied to a gate well away from the office. One young boy who was sent to pay the rent, and had about a four mile walk, had gold sovereigns placed in his waistcoat pocket. So that he did not lose them his mother then sewed his pocket up and gave him scissors to undo the stitching when he arrived so that he could hand the money to the agent.'

SHOWING PROPER RESPECT

'In the 1930s, life in Burlton village was almost feudal. The squire was revered by everyone and members of his family were treated with great respect. To the men of the village it was second nature to doff their cap to the gentry and to address them as "Sir" or "Madam" or "Miss". To be courteous and of general good character paid off when one wanted a job, or a house or a farm tenancy. In general workers on the estate were well treated and enjoyed a sense of security unknown to townsfolk during the Depression.

The Hunt was very much part of rural life and landowners could be very territorial. Squire Vaughan demonstrated this on one occasion when he foiled the Wynnstay Hunt; the fox they had been trailing for some time had gone to earth on the Squire's land. He had stood guard there all day waiting for just such an outcome and he would allow the Hunt no further. "My fox!" declared he, triumphantly, and neither pleas nor arguments would sway him.'

'My husband was born in Merrington, near Bomere Heath, which was then a very rural area. In the early 1930s, at the age of seven, he was sitting playing outside the gate of his home. Along came a lady, a member of a well known Shropshire family, in her carriage, which was being driven by a groom. My husband, like all small boys, stared with great interest at the passing carriage.

The following morning the groom arrived at the house with a letter from the said lady which he handed to my husband's mother. She complained that the boy had given her an insolent stare, that he had neither stood up nor doffed his cap. She sincerely hoped that the boy would be disciplined, that he would be taught his manners, and that, for his own sake, he would be taught to acknowledge and respect his betters.

This has left him with a very jaundiced view of his "betters"!'

'The mistress of one large house used to descend the staircase every morning with a snow white silk handkerchief in contact with the bannister. Any speck of dust meant the unleashing of tremendous rage on the staff waiting in great trepidation below.

This same lady helped to found the WI in the nearby village and used to journey there by car. If any of the staff – who all had to be members, of course – were unable, for reasons of weather, to walk, they would be carried in another vehicle.

One day the chauffeur took pity on one of the maids and gave her a ride in the mistress's car back to the house. The lady on hearing about this erupted in fury and ordered the whole car to be reupholstered.

Many years later when this lady died there was a hitch in providing a suitable chapel of rest before the funeral and many of the staff felt she had her "come-uppance" when her last night was spent in a local garage.'

SIGHTS AND SOUNDS OF EVERYDAY LIFE

The blacksmith's hammer on the anvil and the carpenter sawing and hammering away nearby, the postman off on his rounds from the local post office perhaps, or the baker loading up his horse-drawn vehicle with bread and cakes for home delivery – just some of the sights and sounds of everyday life along the village or town street up to the Second World War.

ALONG THE VILLAGE STREET

'In Cressage there was a blacksmith's shop where farmers brought their horses to be shod and iron gates and farm implements to be fashioned or repaired – a very skilled craft and the blacksmith often had a crowd of spectators to see him at work. Next to the blacksmith's was the carpenter's shop. Sometimes in passing we could see through the open door a cart, waggons or maybe a coffin, as the carpenter was also the undertaker.

For many years a cobbler lived in a little black and white cottage where people handed in their boots and shoes through the window and asked for them to be repaired. All these workshops have disappeared, only the bakehouse remains where bread and cakes have been baked for many years. In the old days the bread was delivered to the surrounding villages in a horse-drawn cart. There was also a general stores in the village.

23

There was a post office on the main road where collections were made twice daily and the mail bags were taken to the station to go on the train. Mail bags also came on the trains from Shrewsbury; twice a day they would be collected and taken to the post office for sorting by the postman and then taken round by bicycle to the farms and cottages over a large area of the countryside. Cressage post office was also the local telephone exchange.'

'Saturday nights in Wem before the Second World War were special. Ten grocery shops were open until nine o'clock, all on the High Street, and most of them baked their own bread and confectionery. They delivered twice weekly to the country folk and most days to the town folk. Locally owned buses brought people in from the surrounding villages at about seven o'clock and the pavements would be blocked by folk chatting together and catching up with the week's news. Shop workers finished at about a quarter to ten, after cashing up and putting all perishables, like cheese, butter, bacon etc, under muslin covers and generally tidying the shop. Early in the evening the Salvation Army would be singing and playing instruments on the street corners, the church bells would ring and sometimes we had the town brass band playing too.'

THE BUTCHER, THE BAKER

'We had our local butcher who lived nearby at East Wall. He had a slaughterhouse and would buy his animals off local farmers. When I remember him first he had a pony and trap. When he needed some lambs, he would come to fetch them in the trap, next time you saw him it would be loaded with meat. Later he had a motor van. When I was going to school he used to deliver meat into Cardington twice a week. There was always a bone for the dogs and they seemed to know which days he came and would be waiting for him. It was so funny to see these dogs going off home with a bone in their mouths.'

'In Meole Brace there was an ice factory in Mill Lane which stored meat and fish at weekends, and produced great blocks of ice.'

'My father, Charles Wright, came to Ifton Heath in about 1914 as the baker at the Co-op. Then he set up on his own on the Ellesmere Road opposite the Methodist chapel.

Everything was done by hand, no machinery. The dough was mixed overnight to be ready by half past five and started by six o'clock. My job was to start on the cake decorations and count them ready for distribution to the shops and for the van deliveries, which were by horse and cart in those days. All had to be ready by eight o'clock. I went delivering bread and cakes to all the outlying districts. When I went with my brother Eric, he never got wet when it rained. He always sat under the cover with the bread and cakes while I drove the horse and got soaked.'

'Annscroft was self-sufficient. We had Mr Bunn's farm where we bought our milk. I had to go over each morning before school and fetch milk for our family and some of our neighbours. Mr Bunn also had a bakery (very apt name!). The dough was kneaded by hand and the oven heated by coke fire. Mr Bunn would collect coke from the gas works after going to the cattle market on a Tuesday.

Bread was delivered by a horse-drawn van, the mare "Kit" took Mr Bunn's son Clarence on the bread round to most of the local villages. Hookagate, Nobold, Meole, Bayston Hill, Lythbank, Longden etc. When Clarence was on the Bayston Hill round he would reach Hookagate about the same time as we got out of school, so I went with him as delivery boy. Mother knew where I was and I was paid sixpence.

In all Mr Bunn had three bakers, first Mr Vicars, second Mr Peat and then Mr G Morris. On Saturday mornings as a boy I used to go into the bakery and help Mr Peat and watch him make Chelsea buns (oh they were lovely!), butter and sugar mixture poured over the pastry and rolled up, then cut into squares.

On Christmas mornings Mrs Bunn would cook the dinner birds for friends, she would have at least half a dozen in the oven. We always had to have the bird prepared and at the bakery by 9am and collected before 1pm. We always had a goose given to my father as part payment for his articles of local news written for the then *Shropshire and Border Counties Advertiser*. Mrs Bunn would pour the goose fat into a stone jar, this mother would keep and use it to rub on our chests when we had colds. Alas when my father died these Christmas geese ceased.

Mr Bunn was also the corn merchant delivering around the farms.'

'My father was a master baker and in 1921 my family went to live at a shop in Hadley. Mr Hale, who occupied this shop, asked my father if he would like to take it and my father agreed. One Saturday night they took stock, agreed a price and by Monday morning we were trading.

One of my earliest memories is of villagers bringing their Sunday joints to the bakehouse. For a small sum of money they were cooked in the bread oven, which was shut down at weekends. The tins were put into the oven with a long-handled peel (a baker's wooden shovel), big joints to the back and smaller ones to the front. These were then collected at lunchtime. The peel was quite difficult to handle but by the time I was nine I could draw an oven of bread.

We had a lot of house to house rounds and also supplied wholesale bread and cakes to shops in Ketley, Trench, Donnington, Horton, Preston and Kynnersley. Bread was delivered by horse and cart. The carts were loaded by the following method. Three people, one by the bread shelves, one outside and one inside the cart – two loaves were placed together then thrown to the next one, then they threw them to the one in the cart who packed them neatly away. Woe betide anyone who dropped one!

We had three horses, one of which my father had bought at a bargain price. He examined it but could find no fault. All went well until a man came in the square and played a bugle. The horse reared up, broke his traces, smashed the cart and galloped off. They caught it and discovered it had been in the front line in the war – when a bugle was sounded the horses charged. We now knew why it had been a bargain and if we saw anyone about to play a bugle, we would give them a donation to move on!'

THE WHEELWRIGHT AND THE BLACKSMITH

'From the late 19th century William Morris, who was later joined by his son John and then his grandson Harold, could be seen at Rodington building and repairing farm carts, making wheels and shoeing horses. The blacksmith's shop was in an old cottage about 400 years old and the wheelwright's shop was built around it.

An interesting sight which often attracted spectators was hooping a wheel. Usually several were done at one time. The iron hoops were carefully measured and joined, then laid on the ground, smallest in the centre and largest on the outside. A log fire was then built round the hoops and ignited. When the iron was red hot two or three men would lift a hoop with tongs and drop it over the wooden wheel. Cold water was thrown over to prevent the wood catching fire. As it cooled, the iron shrank and formed a tight fit.

Local horses were brought for shoeing and quite often left to be collected later. Certain horses would perhaps be given a pat and sent on their own way home – they always went straight back and, with little or no traffic about, were quite safe.'

'I came to live in Tong Norton in 1947 after I was married. We lived with my in-laws at the wheelwright's shop. My husband helped his

Three generations of the Morris family ran this smithy at Rodington. In those days Shropshire villages were self sufficient with their own blacksmith and wheelwright to service both horses and vehicles.

father to make coffins for the local people, also carts, trailers and wheelbarrows. They would go and measure the dead people, come back and make the coffin. Then they would bring it into the house and my mother-in-law would line the coffin and make a pillow. The undertaker always has to be present at the funeral. My husband did all the book keeping and we would go together on our bicycles and take the bills. Most people would save two shilling pieces and half crowns to pay for their coffin.

They often had to make new bell staves for the Tong church bells, and they made Tong church gates.'

GROCERS AND GENERAL STORES

'The village shop at Edgton was owned by Granny Davies. It was one room of a house but was full to bursting with everything besides clothes. There was just enough room to open the door and stand inside, and just enough room on the counter for your purchases to be put down and money exchanged. Everything was weighed on brass scales with brass weights. Sugar came in sacks to be weighed and put into blue bags. New Zealand butter came in a block and was cut as required. Cheese too came in a block to be cut with a thin wire with wood at the end to hold on to. Common salt was in blocks covered with brown paper, mostly bought by the farms for salting the pigs. Tea was in packets, loose. Brooke Bond tea was delivered in a red van and we used to shout at the driver "Brooke Bond tea, blooming rotten tea, Lyons tea, the best tea" and he would chase us, all in good fun. The van had solid tyres and was, I think, called a Trojan.

The small shop window had a shutter on the outside; if it was shut it was Thursday half day closing or after six o'clock. Rows of bottles of sweets filled the window – humbugs, silk cushions, liquorice sticks, bonbons, dolly mixture, sweet cigarettes, cough sweets, jelly babies, raspberry drops and chocolate buttons with hundreds and thousands on them. Toffees were always wrapped and we used to think it would be a nice job, wrapping toffee.

Tobacco and cigarettes were perhaps the best sellers for no one could make or grow them. Woodbines were sold five in a packet and would have a card, of a footballer perhaps, inside. If anyone came out of the shop with a packet we would ask for the card and if we had it, we swapped it with someone else.'

'In Ludlow there used to be a large grocery store called Gaius Smith's. Butter and cheese was cut from large blocks and weighed out. Sugar, tea and rice would also be weighed out in the quantity you asked for. The gentry would just drive to the shop door in their cars and sound the horn for attention. The assistant would run out with their grocery order and they were always called Sir or Madam in those days.'

'One of the shops in Hanwood was a newsagent from which it was possible to buy sweets, paraffin, aspirin and, above all, have your hair cut. The shopkeeper had regular customers in the miners from the Hanwood colliery who later, when the mine was closed, had to travel by bus to other parts of Shropshire. They often had their hair cut while the bus driver waited for them. In those days no-one ever seemed to be in a hurry and with every purchase made the shopkeeper would say, "Much obliged, I'm sure."

Over the road was a large shop where all the sweets were laid out in boxes in the window. During hot weather in the summer they were covered in newspaper to keep the sun off the sweets. The bacon was kept by the counter (uncovered), rashers being cut off by a great machine. There was no refrigerator in the shop – butter and cheese was kept on the shelf with the sugar and tea. How it ever kept in the summer I don't know.

It was quite common on a Saturday evening for a husband and wife to stand in the shop deciding what to have for Sunday tea, while other customers just stood and waited until they made up their minds.'

'In the early 1950s there was a post office in Ashford Carbonell but the only shop at that time was kept by an elderly lady who sold cigarettes and sweets. While she engaged one in conversation she sometimes had a finger lightly laid on the pan of the scales so that one's purchase was slightly underweight. This habit was rather a joke in the village.'

'The most important shop at Highley since 1912 has been the Co-op – always known as the "Co". Grocery orders, packed skilfully in brown paper parcels were always delivered to the customers, and as the Co had its own bakery, fresh bread and cakes were delivered daily, too. Your 2 lb bag of sugar was weighed from a large sack, and your butter cut from large wooden tubs. During the war it was said that you did rather better for rations if you knew someone on the "bacon side", and it was, in any case, a better source of gossip there.

Quarter ending at the Co was quite a ritual – members were allowed a quarter's credit, but accounts had to be settled at the end of each quarter, before you could start running up the bills again. So after stock-taking was done, accounts were paid and the "divi" handed out, one would see a long queue of customers outside the shop waiting to start all over again!

The "Co", run by a local committee, also involved itself in the social life of the village, by organising charabanc trips, sports days and children's parties.

At the time of the 13 week-long miner's strike in 1921, the Co gave out vouchers to the miners' families. Money was lent to the Co by the wealthier men in the community.

One is reminded that during this strike some local miners heard that the Madeley miners were strike-breaking, so they hired a pony and trap to visit the colliery – and then found the story untrue!'

THE POST OFFICE AND TELEPHONE EXCHANGE

'I was brought up in a small village with no church and no school but two pubs and a post office. The post office was also the local telephone exchange and I can remember someone phoning my mother to ask her to tea. She was out and a message was left. The voice of the postmistress interrupted. "No, Mrs B can't come to tea with you on Thursday, she is going to Mrs W." '

'The sending and receiving of telegrams took up a major part of the time in a post office in the 1930s. The kiosk at Beckbury was inside the post office. People came in and the message they wished to send was copied out onto a form. They often had to have it shortened as they found it too expensive. It was then phoned to Wellington post office, and we received telegrams from there too. There were quite a lot for Ryton Hall school which was a young ladies school. When delivering, the butler came to the door with a silver salver on which the telegram was placed and you always had to wait in case an answer was required for you to send back.'

'Church Stretton post office, which was a large main post office then, employed telegram boys, each of whom had a bicycle. When a telegram was received off went the boy with all haste to deliver it. He would wait for the answer, if any, then cycle back as quickly as possible with the reply.'

'The Ryton Exchange (our one claim to fame) was a small PBX board housed in a tiny room in an old cottage in the village and manned by Mrs Bentley, Mr Bentley helping when necessary. There were probably about 150 lines and it was a 24 hour job, 365 days a year with few holidays. It entailed logging each call to be billed as there were no modern methods of accounts recording. It was always heartening to hear a human voice answering, particularly when one was alone in the house, and as a means of communication of local news it was better than the newspaper. It was also a very useful service if one was delayed at all and needed to explain absence to another member of the family. When they returned home Mrs B would ring later to deliver the message, much more reliable than an answering machine. My husband often had to catch early flights or trains and would request an alarm call; it was several years before we discovered that Mrs B had to put her alarm clock on, or get a call from Wellington exchange, in order to ring us in time, so we bought a second alarm clock instead.'

OUR POSTMAN

'At the beginning of the century, our mail was brought by coach and two horses from Bridgnorth to Wellington. It usually passed the house here at Dawley at twenty to ten in the evening. And if we had been careless and had forgotten to post our letters in time, we would stand out on the pavement holding up the letters and the coach driver would halt his horses and take our letters and post them for us in Wellington; which of course was a great concession. I think really he was rather fond of my father, because in the bad winter weather, when he was driving his horses back, the roads were often very slippery and in those days they hadn't discovered about making stud holes in the horses' shoes, into which the driver himself could insert his studs and which acted as a safety device to prevent the horse slipping. My father was often called out by the driver of the mail coach to come and put frost nails into the horses' shoes, and then it was much safer for the driver to continue on his journey to Bridgnorth.

When I was young the letters were very often delivered at this house soon after six o'clock in the morning. We had rather a notorious postman, his name was Roger Latheham, and it was said there was no postcard ever delivered which he hadn't the knowledge of its contents.'

'He was small in stature was Bert "The Post", but he possessed an outsize heart and an indomitable spirit.

Part of one leg had been lost to him during the First World War and the ill-fitting false limb often left his, below the knee stump, chafed, raw and very uncomfortable.

Throughout many years he was our local postman in the Stiperstones area. With an ordinary pedal cycle he set out from his home at Pennerley, six days per week and in all weathers, to reach Minsterley post office by 6am, a distance of five or six miles over rough terrain, especially so in winter.

Here, local letters were sorted into bundles which were string strapped and, together with parcels, loaded into a large canvas bag which he carried slung over his back.

Then commenced the long haul back to the heights of Stiperstones, the first 1½ miles heavy pedalling, following by another mile of pushing up that weary incline – the Farm Lane. Making deliveries en route he would finally reach The Bog, but still had to deliver several miles beyond should it be necessary. At The Bog he had a small wooden hut for shelter and where he could take refreshment before making his return to Minsterley by 6pm, at which time the mail departed for Shrewsbury.

Bert carried a flash lamp, with bull's eye reflector and a small spring balance with which to weigh parcels and other mail picked up on the way down. Reaching Stiperstones at about 4.50, he announced his arrival by blowing a warning whistle as he approached. We had no post office then. At the post box (a Victorian model) set in the wall of the granary belonging to the Stiperstones Inn, a small crowd often awaited him. Letters to be stamped, parcels to be weighed and priced, registered packets to be received, etc.

It was quite common for "last minute" people to hail him from the roadside at any point of his journey for such services. He obligingly (often painfully) jumped from his cycle to perform the tasks.

31

In winter time his bag would be choc-a-bloc with parcels. Most cottagers kept an annual pig and parcels of pork etc were sent to distant relatives. I have seen Bert's bicycle handlebars and lamp bracket literally festooned with parcels with the carrier at the back piled high, as well as a bulging bag.

Apart from official duties, Bert was called upon to take messages, written or verbal, and to deliver packets of pills or bottles of medicine, sometimes even "samples".

Few people had telephones or private means of transport in those days Bert wrote a marvellous copperplate hand, so was frequently called upon to write letters, fill in forms or sign documents for others. He was never known to grumble or refuse such requests.

Passing our school at Stiperstones, invariably about playtime, Bert had always a cheery word for us children and a conundrum for us to solve. We all loved Bert The Post.

Reaching Minsterley in time for the 6pm mail train, mid-day on Saturdays, Bert had then to wend his weary way back home to Pennerley.

Deliveries were always made on the Sundays before Christmas and also on Christmas Day. It cost three halfpence for a sealed envelope in those days and one could be sure of it reaching its destination anywhere in the country by the next day.

Once asked why he gave so much himself to his job, Bert replied "When I was sworn in as a postman I was instructed to help the general public as much as possible." He certainly did.'

THE INN

'In 1933 my parents were granted the tenancy of an inn some three and a half miles from where we then resided and the last of our personal belongings, together with the family's two pet cats, were driven to Wall-under-Heywood in a pony and trap, my two brothers and I seated in the bottom.

As war approached in 1939 the countryside was being much enjoyed by people from the Midlands, who to my childish mind all owned cars. The road from Much Wenlock to Church Stretton on every summer Sunday was a constant stream of traffic, joined by as many as 30 coaches in an afternoon all bound for the Cardingmill Valley. My mother had by this time earned quite a name in the catering field and I was from the age of twelve roped in as waitress. On these Sundays we often served between 40 and 50 teas and on reflection I wonder how on earth Mother coped with only a black-leaded coal range. There was no electricity until 1950 although the public rooms did have calor gas lighting.

32

The guests were often given a choice of ham and egg, beans on toast, poached or boiled egg or fruit teas, each accompanied by bread and butter, fancy cakes and jam. Prices ranged from one shilling and threepence to two shillings and sixpence per head. The uncertainty of the numbers you were catering for caused problems during the war years as all meals had to be recorded and notified to the Ludlow Food Office every month; this way we were allocated quantities of food to use the following month.

As the war period lengthened we were inundated with enquiries from people wanting to holiday in the country away from the bombing in Birmingham, Coventry and the surrounding towns. To the delight of we children, from May to September for several years we were allowed to camp out and enable more guests to be accommodated in the house. Most of these families loved the country ways but you did get the odd request for the bus timetable and on being told they could go to Church Stretton on a Thursday and Shrewsbury on a Tuesday their faces would fall.

Living in the village pub was hard work but never dull. When I was about ten years old a young man from the village, Arthur Painter, did very well in boxing tournaments and went on to become "The Shropshire Lad" with an enormous local following. I remember creeping to the top of the stairs to try and get a glimpse of an

All kinds of social and sporting activities centred round the village inn, including shooting parties as shown here.

enormous cup which I gather was filled with "booze" and was passed round amidst much singing and jollification.'

'The Crown at Rodington was closed in 1972. Before the war many people bought fish and chips from Mr and Mrs Tom Gates – Rodington's first take-away before the mobile vans came round. The Yanks would come from Atcham Camp during the war to The Crown and drink all the bottled beer. As The Crown had no spirit licence they carried on to the Bull's Head for spirits. Then it was on their bicycles and crunch time! The Bull's Head is reputedly the second oldest licensed house in the county. My grandfather William Allen, the innkeeper, brewed beer there until just before the turn of the century. The post office was also run from the pub at one time, and shooting parties used to meet there. The bull ring is adjacent, though the actual ring to which bulls were tied was lost in the early 1900s.'

'My parents were proprietors of the Park Hotel, Wellington from 1937 to 1960. My father, Sidney Davies, was a well known larger than life character, being over 6ft tall and 21 stones in weight. Known locally as "Big Sid", he always believed in calling a spade a spade and could be somewhat outspoken!

Following the end of the war Scotch whisky was in very short supply and regular customers to The Park knew that Sidney could usually oblige them, but of course it was rationed to everyone. A local farmer who always enjoyed his drop of Scotch one day asked his wife to see if she could manage to purchase a bottle for home consumption. The good lady thought she might appeal to my father's compassion and related a sad story of a very sick ewe that they were nursing and that her husband thought might respond to a drop or two of whisky. Sidney listened to the sorry tale and said he would go along to his bottle store to see what could be found. As he was about to go through the door he turned to the farmer's wife and said "Any particular brand of Scotch?", to which she replied "Oh yes, Johnnie Walker if possible." She did receive the bottle for her cheek and ingenuity!'

'In 1955 we moved to Bishops Castle, where my parents took over The Black Lion public house, reputed to be one of the oldest public houses in Shropshire. The lounge bar was called a snug; the floor was large slate slabs and either side of the red brick fireplace were two settles with very high backs. The door into the snug had an old bell fastened above it, which rattled rather than rang when customers entered. There wasn't an actual bar in this room, drinks had to be carried from the public bar. All floors in the rooms upstairs were on a slope, in fact it was quite difficult to stand on one part of the land.

The beer was delivered in large wooden barrels. In the cellar there were wooden stands on which the barrels were placed. After delivery they had to be left undisturbed for a day or so, for the sediment to settle. They then had to be tapped; this involved knocking a tap into a hole that had a wooden bung in it, with a very large wooden mallet. A pipe was then connected to the tap, which led up through the floor, into the bar and again connected to the beer pumps. A pint of beer cost one shilling and two pence when we first went to The Black Lion. Four games regularly played in the public bar were darts, dominoes, crib and quoits.

There were some strange local sayings in Bishops Castle. One I particularly remember. A customer in the bar said to my mother, only two days after moving there, "Eh, Mrs, your drains is smellin'." This worried my mother who rushed off to find disinfectant and to try and locate the offending drain, only to be told, sometime later, that what was meant was – the dinner smelled good!'

THE PAWN SHOP

'On a Monday morning before the First World War a number of people from New Dale would make their way down to the pawn shop in Wellington. They would take a certain article out of the house, the pawnbroker would give them a certain amount of cash for it. Then on a Friday evening they would go back to the pawn shop and redeem the article they had deposited on the Monday morning. They would of course be charged interest on the money they had received. If they couldn't afford to redeem the article, the pawnbroker would eventually sell it. Times were hard then.'

SALES AND MARKET DAY

'For many years Craven Arms was famous for the ewe and ram sales held in the autumn. There were two firms of auctioneers, Jackson & McCartney and Morris, Barker & Poole, vying for custom.

As many as 16,000 ewes were advertised at one sale, mainly of the Clun Forest or Kerry Hill breed. These were two year old ewes being sold from the local hill farms to form the foundation of flocks in the Midlands and South.

The weeks before the ewe sale were busy on the farm as it was the fashion to trim the ewes' wool so that they were well turned out. In pre-war days it was fashioned to colour the sheep. The ewes were sold in pens of 20 or 40 and these had to be sorted so that the best ewes were in the first pen.

For those living within four or five miles the ewes were driven to the sale and it seemed that all roads leading into Craven Arms were a mass of heaving sheep – followed by collie dogs and men with sticks. The sales were held on fields where special pens had been made with hurdles and great was the competition to obtain the prize for the best pen of sheep. Farmers stood near their pens hoping to point out the best points of their sheep and when the sale began the ring was crowded with buyers and spectators.

The sale of the ewes was an important part of the farmers' incomes so a good sale lifted everyone's spirits and made the year's work seem worthwhile.'

'In the early years of the century at Gobowen, the roads would be full of cattle on a Wednesday being driven along to Oswestry market. On the first Wednesday in each month, a horse fair took place in Oswestry. The horses would go through the village all dressed up in ribbons etc, beautiful big cart horses.'

'Friday was market day in Bishops Castle. The horse was harnessed and the trap loaded with eggs, butter and dressed poultry. There were customers along the road for butter and eggs, the rest of the produce was unloaded at the market. Then the horse and trap were taken to the Castle Hotel where an ostler would take the horse from the trap and stable her until she was wanted again. The weekly shopping was done; sugar and tea weighed up as wanted. Flour was bought in large cloth bags, quite useful for making into roller towels for father when he came in from the garden. I can't remember any tinned stuff. There would be dried fruit for cakes. Friday was a favourite day for me. I got one penny to spend at the sweet shop and with that I could get six different kinds. The shopkeeper was so patient. The other treat was to get a ride home. It was many years later before a bus was to run along our road on market day. I must say that when this happened Dolly, the horse, disapproved very much. She could hear it long before we could and she would rear up when it passed.

Christmas was a very busy time – so many poultry to be dressed in only about three days, because of keeping them fresh. We did pray for cold weather, as, of course, refrigerators were not thought of then. Helpers would come in and work all night – some would be feathering into a big bath and then pass them over to be singed and gutted. Then Mother would perform marvellous acrobatics with the bird until it was showing off its well shaped breast. I am proud to recall the many prizes she came away with from the Christmas market.'

36

VILLAGE AMENITIES

'I have an aunt who is 95 who was born in Rodington and lived here until the Second World War. My aunt tells of the time when the 1914–1918 war ended. When the young boys returned from the war, and with some money they received from a "canteen fund" for boys who had been in the forces, they decided they needed a village hall to meet, instead of just on "Clayton's Corner". They bought an old army hut and put it on a piece of land given them by a local farmer. With the help of the other young people of the village they held whist drives and dances to finish paying for it and for the upkeep, taking it in turns to light the stove to heat the hall and generally keep it clean.'

'There were no dustmen in the 1920s at Hookagate. All rubbish was burned and vegetable peelings went in the pig swill. Piles of coal dust and ashes were to be found near the cottage gate. This was collected occasionally by a man with a flat cart drawn by a horse and was taken down the village and tipped on the side of the brook by the hump-backed bridge, where the winter flood water would wash it away.'

'Between the wars in Bayston Hill there was a library in the WI cottage. The library consisted of boxes of books provided by the County Library which were available to be borrowed and used to be changed from time to time, and a bookcase of books which were permanent. It was great fun when it was Mother's turn to be "librarian", which was done on a roster, as we were able to take the cards out of the books and put them in pockets in a box, and date stamp the books.'

THE VILLAGE POLICEMAN

'I think PC Davies' biggest job was going round the farms at Gobowen checking the record books or checking sheep dipping. There would be a feed of bread and cheese at the end of it.

All boys were afraid of policemen in those days. He came to the school one day, he got my brother out of class and asked if he'd been in an old mill. A lock had been broken and some other damage done. He frightened my brother that much he told him we had been in the mill. He got me out next and I had to say the same as my brother. We had not been near the mill!'

THE VILLAGE MILL

At the heart of the village, busy all year round, was the mill. At Vennington it was also the village inn, and at Baschurch the centuries-old practice of sheep dipping was carried out nearby.

THE MILL INN

'My father was born in 1910 in the village of Vennington and spent his early years at the Mill Inn. His father then ran the watermill, an occupation his family had carried out there from the middle of the 18th century, as far as we can trace.

The stream which ran through the village had a mill pool and mill race which worked an undershot water wheel. There was a Clayton and Shuttleworth stationary steam engine as a back up when the stream ran dry. Behind the engine shed was a sunken container for water for the steam engines. As a toddler my father went missing and was discovered head first in the water. He was saved in the nick of time.

The mill had mill stones for grinding the wheat. Local farmers brought their wheat in horse-drawn drays. After grinding, the wheat was placed in what my father recalls as a cloth drum, from which the flour dropped down and the bran was left behind. Many farmers' wives still baked all their own bread at that time.

Oats were brought for grinding or rolling into cattle feed. There was also a clover mill. Local farmers brought the clover cut in bundles. The seeds were rolled out for the farmers to reseed their pastures. Apparently the dust from this process was tremendous. The left over was called "pouse" and was waste, probably burnt.

The mill was also the village inn. Southerns Brewery in Shrewsbury supplied the beer, which was served in jugs from the cellar. The floor was flagstoned; after scrubbing the stones and when the floor was clean, the joints were chalked around. This was known as "scoring".

The maid employed at this time was perhaps not the brightest of girls. A local term for someone who wasn't very clever was "slick". Whilst she was serving beer it seems a local worker found the way to a cheap day's drinking, "going on a spree" as it was known.

After paying his sixpence for his beer he would wait for the girl's back to be turned and reach over the counter to the mantelpiece where she had put the coin, and continue to pay for his beers with the same coin. His activities were eventually spotted by my grandfather and his cheap day out was brought to an end.

It was the time of the Great War and local children were encouraged to go picking blackberries, needed to make jam for the troops.

In 1916, although aged 40, my grandfather was called to the Front. My grandmother tried to run the business as well as look after her family of four children. She received a Separation Allowance from the government to support wives and families left at home.

However, the mill and inn closed. Grandfather was hospitalised for some time after the war to recuperate from bronchial illness contracted in the trenches. The business did not reopen when he returned home.'

A WONDERFUL NOISE

'The mill at Baschurch was a hub of activity all year round. A Saxon mill was recorded on the site and up to the 1960s it was a fully working mill, grinding grain for animals. Horses and carts were always creaking down to the mill.

As children we loved to go inside and put our hands under the wooden shutes that the crushed grain rushed down. The grain was always warm and tactile and was collected in huge wooden hoppers. Sacks had chains attached and they were hauled upwards and wooden doors in the floor above would open as they hit them. There was a wonderful noise in the mill, the stones grinding, the grain falling and the lovely rhythmic splash of the water wheel turning. The water too had a distinctive earthy smell.

In summer flocks of sheep would be brought down to the mill race. They were put into pens and their bleating could be heard far away. Children hearing this noise would rush to the mill in excited anticipation. The water would be rushing through the mill and under a sandstone bridge. Two men, with large wooden rakes, would stand on walkways either side of the river. Two others would stand on the bridge, grab a sheep, haul it onto the wall and then throw it into the deep rushing water. As its head came up and it gasped for air, the men with the rakes would push it under. The speed of the water took it downstream, where eventually its feet would hit the bottom and it would clamber out. It would shake itself and water would fly in all directions, and then it would walk down the Mill Meadow and start eating grass. This practice must have gone on for hundreds of years. Later the sheep would be penned and the shepherd would sit in a shady spot and begin to shear the sheep.

One miller, Mr Ratcliffe, suffered a double tragedy. His son Bernard, serving in the Grenadier Guards, was killed in the First World

War. Then one day his daughter Hilda saw some swans landing on the river. She was in the garden and shouted "look at the swans", crossing the river on a plank behind the water wheel to get a better look. She missed her footing and fell into the river and was taken under the wheel.

The mill and waterfall during the summer acted as a magnet to local children and adults. It was a place to learn to swim and enjoy water games; it was a wonderful feeling to sit under the waterfall, with the water pouring over your head. An idyllic age, it seemed, when the sun always shone and fun and games were enjoyed by all.'

CHURCH AND CHAPEL

Sunday was a special day during the first half of the century, when Shropshire families attended church or chapel, sometimes three times a day, and the children went to Sunday School – and no work was done in the house or the garden. The church, particularly, was a yardstick of the social hierarchy, with the local gentry occupying the front, and most comfortable, pews. Sunday school is particularly remembered by generations of children because it provided one of the few outings they could expect in the year – the Sunday school treat. Seeing the sea for the first time was a wonderful experience!

SUNDAY WAS A SPECIAL DAY

'My grandparents were Methodists, and my grandmother was the caretaker at the little Wesleyan chapel in New Dale. She was paid sixpence a week for doing the job of caretaker; out of that sixpence she had to find all her cleaning materials. My grandmother was a very religious woman. For instance on a Sunday there was very little work done in the home; the eldest girl who was at home on the Saturday had to wash the quarried floor, and generally tidy up for the Sunday. Also the vegetables had to be got out of the garden on a Saturday for the Sunday dinner. There was no sewing, or knitting done, and no papers or books to be read.'

'The early Edwardian Sunday had an important influence on the upbringing of children, certainly Greenfields children.

I remember the great preparation that took place on the Saturday evening. Button boots or summer slippers were given that extra shine, clean underclothes were laid out and top clothes were brushed and pressed in readiness for Sunday. Then the enamel bath was placed in front of the fire and hot water was drawn from the shining brass tap of the range boiler. Soft rainwater from the water butts in the garden was added and the temperature tested. Then we youngsters had our dip in the warm soapy, scented mixture. We were rubbed down with a rough towel warm from the oven door and put into our warmed nightclothes ready for bed. No, not quite ready, for I had to have my fine straight hair coiled up in rags ready to compete with the other Sunday school girls the next day. And so to bed.

Sunday breakfasts were special. First we listened for the "Hot rolls, rolls all hot!" man. He came from the beetle-infested bakehouse in Caernarvon Lane but this was ignored as we waited for the man to produce the delights from under the doubtful hot blanket in his basket.

We then sat down to our Sunday breakfast, consisting of bacon accompanied by egg or any in turn of the following – kidneys, sausage, liver, sweetbreads or mushrooms. Satisfied, we then prepared for Sunday school, donning our Sunday best shoes, frock, coat and hat, according to the season. Easter Sunday was the highlight of the year, when we emerged in our new outfits, to be admired and to admire. Sunday school was held in St Julian's Mission Room or the "tin chapel", the latter quite soon replaced by the present building. Both were well attended and even overflowed into a nearby house.

We sang hymns, repeated collects or psalms, had a talk by the teacher of the group or, all together, by the superintendent.

After that we went for a walk along the lanes, through Berwick Woods, sometimes on our own, sometimes accompanied by our father. We picked flowers according to the season to arrange for our mothers later. We looked for birds' nests and were allowed to take one egg if we were making a collection, but finding the nest was the main accomplishment.

Back home we were ready for our Sunday dinner. Roast, with all the usual, sometimes special, vegetables, like new peas or new potatoes. A fruit pie of gooseberries, raspberries, whinberries etc, out of the garden if possible, followed, covered with custard. Not much good asking for "seconds", there was always tomorrow!

The teachers at the Sunday afternoon school were drawn from the lady living-in assistants at Grocott's high class shop in the Square. These were educated girls and were selected by the shop for their status, education, good speech and poise. I was very fond of my teacher and waited for the hiccups to start (as they always did after a big dinner), when she would hold my hand and press the pulse – it always worked.

Sunday tea saw the best china out and a best tablecloth, generally an embroidered afternoon cloth. For tea there was salad from the garden or greenhouse and an apple tart. The apples were from a tree in the garden. When a house was newly built someone, I suppose the builder, planted an apple tree.

Between the services and meals, and after the evening service, we read suitable books or sang round the piano. No one worked in the garden or house, sewed or knitted. Homework for school, if any, was already done on Saturday. So we were ready for work on Monday morning.'

GOING TO CHURCH

'Bill was brought up at Glascoed Farm, Llansilin, one of a family of ten whose mother died in childbirth. Bill recalls all the children going to church in the pony and trap, his father driving and putting the horse at the nearby Wynnstay Inn. His father always wore a top hat and morning coat, and having marshalled all the children into their pew, not making a sound, he sat down himself.'

'In our village there was the parish church and also a small Methodist chapel. Not such an ecumenical atmosphere prevailed in those times; it was rather a case of two factions – "us and them".

We were brought up to attend the church, as our parents and grandparents had before us. We usually went three times every Sunday – to morning service, Sunday school in the afternoon, and to evensong, as we grew old enough.

The vicar and his wife were people to be looked up to and respected – tho' it was rumoured that our parson who was excellent in church and as a preacher, and who spent a good chunk of his years in the same village, was not quite so "godly" in the home circle and could be quite a tyrant!

As children we always helped to decorate the church for festivals, and at Easter-time we would go out and pick primroses, and tie them in bunches to decorate the windows. At Harvest Festival we would help to tie bunches of wheat, barley etc for the same purpose. On Whit Sunday and East Sunday we always expected to have something new which would wear with pride when we went to church. At all times, however, and especially as we grew up, "going to church" was a good excuse to dress up and wear our very best clothes.'

'The church at Kynnersley was the centre of everything at the time of the First World War. I remember the smell of moth balls from Sunday clothes and camphorated oil used for bronchitis. If we had coughs we were given a "Peps" cough sweet to suck during the sermon. Everyone went to church and each family had their own pew. After evening service families visited each other during the dark evenings and had singing round the piano and supper.'

'It was always "Sunday best" when you went to church, complete with hat, gloves and well polished shoes (the polishing had to be done on Saturdays) and immediately you arrived home they were all taken off and hung up ready for the next time.

I well remember the sound of Rushbury church bells across the valley and it was quite a privilege to be allowed to sit up and listen to them as they rang in each New Year.

As in every walk of life in those days there was always a social ladder and we all knew our place on this. The rector commanded respect from all the children and it was woe betide anyone who stepped out of line.

The Sunday school treat was always looked forward to and this was usually held in a local farmer's field. I remember one day after tea on long trestles in the field, when we were running races, the farmer, who was the official "starter" suddenly looked round and said "Oh, Lord, the bull's out". At this point everyone dashed for the farmhouse which, fortunately, was enclosed by a strong wooden fence, to pleas from the farmer to "Be quiet – don't frighten him!" However, after investigating the tea tables the bull was quietly and uneventfully shepherded back to the farmyard.

Although times were not easy for the majority of the village folk they were happy ones with the church sharing our good times and bad and joining us all in one large family.'

'At Bicton the social order (we called it the pecking order) was very important. The seats at the front of the church were reserved for the gentry. In 1910 Miss Millbank at Bicton Hall gave a tea and presented books to children for good attendance at Sunday school. She used to arrive at church in a pony and trap. One day the village boys took the pony out of the trap, put it in the churchyard and then pushed the shafts of the trap through the railings of the gate and hitched the pony up again. Hence – pony in churchyard, trap out on road, questions asked! She was not amused.'

'My granny, in long black clothes, would never knit or sew on a Sunday. I remember going with her to church at Hanwood and having to be very well behaved. If she didn't attend Evensong, the vicar would be down the next day to ask why.'

'The church at Baschurch was full at festival times. Different members decorated the church and we knew where primroses and violets grew for Easter. The church had a mysticism about it, added to by the oil lamps and candles. At Christmas and Easter, Communion services began at six o'clock, hourly until Matins. At certain times it was Bread Sunday. After Matins on those days some of the congregation produced pillow cases and loaves of bread which had been stacked up by the door were put into them. There were six charities which gave money for the bread.'

'Weston Lullingfield's church, very much part of the school, was heated with a coal boiler, smelly but fairly efficient, and lit with beautiful paraffin lamps, a physical hazard to the Bishop in his head dress when conducting confirmations. The organ was pumped and it was difficult to get a pumper when you wanted to practice. It made a very peculiar wail when the pumper stopped for a rest. There was a little lead weight that went up and down to indicate the amount of wind in the bellows and it was a fine art knowing exactly the point at which you had to start pumping again.'

A FEW VICARS

'Grinshill was a very sociable village; everyone knew each other and Mr Dixon, our vicar for many years, was a friend to all. He was a very large man and loved to take part in the village cricket matches and hit many a boundary but always had a boy to run for him.

Church was well attended and my father was churchwarden. We sat beneath the pulpit. Sometimes Mr Dixon would get "carried away" with his sermon and forget the time whereupon my father would produce his large pocket watch and look at it, a hint usually taken, much to my embarrassment, but they had been to school together and always remained friends.'

'We had a church at Broome and two chapels, Baptist and Methodist, both now closed. A rector lived in the rectory next to the church. There were no cars then so he had to walk or cycle round his scattered parish. One rector about 1900 had a tricycle and while he marked the registers at school, the boys used to ride it round the playground. It was about 1930 before a rector had a car.'

'The Rev G.O. Brown was vicar at Gobowen during the 1920s and it was his wish to be buried the opposite way round to everyone else. It was customary in those days to bury everyone with their feet to the east, so if he was buried the opposite way round, on the day of resurrection he would arise to face his congregation!

We often hear about the good old days. In about 1920 there was very little money about but I don't think money was so important then. For instance, most of the vicars I knew were men of calling. Their pay was small but they had other compensations. I knew of a boy whose job was to go to the vicarage on a Saturday morning with a basket of food from one of the local farmers. This sort of thing was general practice.'

'When I went to live in Badger in the 1930s I got to know everyone there. Once when I was walking from Beckbury along the Badger road, I met the parson. We greeted each other, then he suddenly said: "Do you know, Mrs Broome, I've just been on holiday – and it was mixed bathing! I don't know what my aunt would have said." People were very proper in those days.'

AND THE CHOIRBOYS

'There is a story of the early 1900s in Bromfield of the choir boys and a very prudish and straight-laced vicar's wife, who wouldn't have a male bird in with her hens. The cockerel off the top of the church was in the church porch, waiting to be gilded, when some of these boys decided to paint it and put it into the vicarage hen run. I understand the culprits' mothers were told in no uncertain terms. One of those choirboys was an ace with a catapult and could hit anything. For a bet one day he shot the runner off the end poplar tree, one of a row that used to be a landmark by Bromfield bridge and were known as the Twelve Apostles – after that there were the twelve "spires" but only eleven trunks.'

GOING TO CHAPEL

'The chapel choir at Highley sang popular Methodist hymns round the village most Sunday evenings, and they also held an annual open-air service.

Once a year there was a Miners' Service at the chapel. Highley Brass Band led a long procession through the village and local miners were joined by others from Baggeridge and Hamstead. All carried proudly their colourful Union banners! At the service, mention would be made of any miner who had died during the year, and hymns such as "The Old Rugged Cross" and "Bread of Heaven" would be sung by the powerful male voices. In all, a very emotional occasion.

Sports and other social activities never took place on Sundays – that day was sacred.'

'We attended Wollerton Wood Primitive Methodist church in the Prees Green circuit. It was almost a family chapel as the families of the three men most active in its erection in 1868 were still members.

It was the centre of our social as well as our religious life, with Sunday school and morning and evening services every Sunday. Local preachers were the main occupants of the pulpit and I remember some colourful characters. One started most sentences with "Dear friends. . ." and we counted them to pass the time – our record was 49 in one sermon. Another old worthy always began his extempore prayer with the words "Father we come to Thy house with our hands hanging down and our knees knocking together"; what an abject picture. Another was annoyed by a bluebottle buzzing around and, to stress a point, swiped at it with the words: "As sure as I kill this 'ere fly, but I've missed it. . ." so we never knew what he meant to emphasise.

Yet another, on entering the pulpit hung a bundle in a red handkerchief on one of the knobs, and his emphasis was: "As sure as my dinner is in that red hanker. . .". He had probably walked some miles, but never had to bring his "hanker" again – a meal was always forthcoming.

We put on a concert every winter with the pulpit as dressing room etc, a wooden platform as stage and mother's pink summer curtains providing the decor. What fun we had practising (no one ever "rehearsed" in those days) and often we took our concert to other chapels. We went carol singing with hurricane lanterns and candles in jam jars round the scattered community.

The Sunday school Anniversary, with the obligatory new frock, was followed of course by the Sunday school treat, usually at a local farm with tea, games, races and a scramble for toffees and iced gem biscuits tossed in the air. Later we became more sophisticated and a "chara" was hired to take us to the sea at Rhyl or New Brighton. I recall one boy about six or seven who stared at the sea for a long moment and finally said: "What a big pit!". Ponds were always called pits in my neck of the woods, a term which my mother who came from Montgomeryshire hated.

All this excitement in a little chapel – we called it St Martins in the Fields – that was crowded with 60 people present.'

'There were never any services at the Anglican church at Edgton in my childhood because the vicar lived like a hermit in the vicarage on the outskirts of the village. He would go to the church every Sunday and ring the bell, after locking the door.

The Primitive Methodist chapel, therefore, was usually full on a Sunday for service. My sister or Auntie played the organ (Auntie taught my sister and she hated it), and Mum was caretaker, cleaner, fire lighter and everything else, including treasurer. We had to stand by the door handing out the books. The services were always taken by lay preachers from other villages; sometimes they got so carried away with their message they would thump the big Bible on the pulpit. Once a month the minister from Clun would come to give Holy Communion. Mum would lay everything out on a white linen cloth with another white cloth with lace to cover it. He would come on horseback, by pony and trap, on a bicycle, or even walking. He took both services, so he had to have dinner and tea somewhere, and one meal was often at our house. If it was dinner we certainly didn't have rabbit. It was roast hen or, if there was enough money, a joint of lamb. All the stops were pulled out for that meal, including the table – an extra leaf was put in.

It was the best dinner service or the best tea service, which had been wedding presents from the gentry where Mum and Dad had both worked in service before they married. The tea cups were so fine you could see the tea in them on the outside. I was not given one of these to drink from until I was quite grown up.

The white linen cloth and serviettes for adults, looked very posh after the oilcloth we usually had to save washing. Grace was said and Dad carved. We were all threatened if we misbehaved ourselves. Pudding was fruit tart and creamy rice pudding; we usually squabbled over cleaning the dish out but not on this day. But what I really enjoyed was the fact that we had a clean plate or dish for the pudding instead of having it on your meat dish regardless of whether all the veg had been eaten or not. If I complained I was told I was getting above my station in life, or that it all went down the same way anyway. It had been known for me to get any leftovers at the next meal to teach me a lesson and by then it looked even worse than the first time.

If it was tea the minster was coming to, bread and butter was cut thinly – butter was special, usually we only had margarine. Milk was brought in from Auntie's, as goats milk is like cream in tea and not everyone likes it. There would be a red jelly with fruit in it (tinned peaches or pears were an extra treat), a jam sponge but today with jam and buttercream in it, buttered scones and fruit cake. We were told it was high tea, so I suppose we had low tea every other day.'

MY FIRST CAMP MEETING

'My family had come to live at the Stiperstones Inn in 1928, an exciting change after our quiet life on the Long Mountain. I was so pleased to be invited to Perkins Beach camp meeting.

The meeting took place on a hot Sunday afternoon on a bank field, which I think belonged to Mr Ridge Morris. My cousin Phyllis and I found a clean piece of grass and made ourselves comfortable. Soon the field was covered with people and the service began.

The hymn singing was wonderful – all those voices singing together, everyone in tune – it was something I had never heard before. Mr J Corfield, complete with tuning fork, led that singing and although I knew neither the words nor the tune (there were too few hymn books to go round), everyone else seemed to know. I wished the hymns would go on for ever. It was something I will never forget.

But then, as we sat down and Mr Edwin Jones was just beginning to pray, it happened! A dreadful clatter of the banging of tins and iron buckets rent the air. A whisper swept through the assembled congregation: "It's Granny Chidley".

Granny Chidley kept bees and as luck would have it a swarm had settled in the lane. Beekeepers, past and present, know that if the queen bee can be induced to settle on a blackcurrant bush, there is a chance that the whole swarm will join her and so be trapped. One of the methods used to encourage a queen to settle was to make a sharp sound, any loud noise, such as banging a tin with a stick. Unfortunately, this method is not very effective on a hot sunny day, so the swarm took off, formed a column in the air and passed over the congregation. As this took place there was rather less interest in Mr Jones' prayer than there should have been (possibly a few individual prayers about bees and where they landed may have been said quietly).

Mr Jones finished his prayer, another great hymn was sung and the service concluded. We came down from the hillside, Phyllis and I, wondering if we dare call on Granny, everything was now so quiet. Going into the kitchen we found her old straw beekeeper's hat with its lace curtain hanging from the brim. Granny was laid out on the settee, too exhausted to get up, disappointed with her loss, as the swarm was just what she needed to fill an empty skep.

Even now I can recall her remarks. "If only they had sung a really good loud tune, something with a swing, there might have been a chance the queen would have settled. But no, he just kept on praying and everything was lost." '

SUNDAY SCHOOL TREATS

'I was taken to church on a seat on my father's bicycle when I was barely three. I sat with him in the choir and slept during the sermon. My sister and brother had to walk the two miles each way. Sunday school started an hour before the service, then the children were ushered into church for the whole of Matins.

One of the great events of Sunday school was the egg and flower service. All the children were dressed in their best outfits and took to church bunches of flowers and as many eggs as their parents could afford. Eight very good little girls were chosen to wear white, carry baskets of flowers and sit in the front choir stalls. At the end of the service, the flowers and eggs were collected up to be sent to the local hospital; there the eggs would be preserved in water-glass for use throughout the year.'

'The Dawley Sunday School Demonstration was a very popular event. Every Sunday school in the district marched behind banners held high with the name of the school and a religious picture embroidered on them. Brass bands led the parade and they marched through Dawley to the local park where a service was held in the open air. Afterwards, tea was provided at the local chapels.'

'We went to Sunday school at the mission rooms in Greenfields street. We belonged to St Julian's church. We had our Sunday school outing and went in a horse and brake to the Wrekin. Halfway up there were swing-boats which you had to pay to go on. The lady there used to watch to see who was going and when the Sunday School went they must have put a "squeak" on the swings so she could tell how many rides everyone was having. You were only supposed to have one go each. Then the Superintendant who was with us used to have a huge tin of toffees and when we were up at the top of the Wrekin he would throw the contents of wrapped sweets straight up into the air and then there was a scramble. Some people would have a pocket full and some wouldn't have any ... then we'd not be speaking to each other because they had two and we only had one!'

'At Pontesbury in the 1910s, Sunday school outings were usually to Happy Valley by the brook at the back of Pontesford Hill, a distance of about a mile, where we would have tea followed by games and races. One year we went to Corndon Hill seven or eight miles away and we travelled in an open Sentinel steam wagon – imagine the colour of us when we arrived.'

'Once a year at Edgton we had an Anniversary. A platform was erected in the chapel, which went up in seats, with the youngest in the front seats. It has been known for a young contender to fall asleep and fall off. All the children had to sing or recite or both, which was usually my lot. After this event we had an outing to Cardingmill Valley in pony traps, but one year there was enough money to go on a real outing. We went to Craven Arms and got on the train to Barry Island and we saw the sea for the very first time. I was about ten years old. We tucked our clothes into our knickers and paddled in the sea. We saw people in bathing costumes, with bare legs and arms – we were always told that everything should be covered.

One of the boys fell in the sea and finished up wearing all the spare girls' clothes the mothers had taken with them. It took a long time for him to live it down. We went wild on the return journey, playing ball with a tennis ball up and down the corridor. The mums just shut the doors and left us to it.

If an outing could not be arranged then a tea was organised. The squire was invited to attend. When we said we had had enough to eat, he would bump us up and down on our chairs until we took some more cake. After tea we played games.'

'Each summer the Sunday school children of Bomere Heath had an outing to a nearby hill or park. The boys travelled in cattle floats and the girls in haywagons. The first year we were taken to the seaside for the day was wonderful – a whole train was chartered for the occasion! Preparation for this began several weeks before when farmers and others donated cracked eggs and other ingredients to make rich fruit cakes. These were then cooked in the local bakery each Saturday afternoon after the bread ovens were empty.

The main event of the year was the Christmas party. On leaving for home every child received a "poke", a beautiful small bag which contained sweets, nuts, fruit etc.'

'Every year in the 1940s and 1950s the Sunday school at Meole Brace joined with the church choir for the seaside outing, which was usually to Rhyl or Llandudno. We went in a convoy of about six coaches and almost every year a bus broke down halfway up the Horseshoe Pass and had to back down again. We all found it quite exciting.'

'Times were hard between the wars and everyone saved a penny or two at school or Sunday school for an outing. There were two chapel outings. One was to the singing festival which was held in a different chapel to our own every other year. There would be a lovely tea between the two services. The other much looked forward to outing was to the seaside. All Oswestry Sunday schools joined together and had a special train which took us all to Rhyl. Later each Sunday school arranged their own bus, and of course we did go to Aberystwyth and Llandudno, but Rhyl was the favourite place with the Marine Lake and the fancy fair being the attractions.'

LOCAL CHARACTERS

Every town and village had its local characters, some permanent, some just passing through. The gipsies, with their brightly coloured caravans, were regular callers. Some events, such as elections, also seemed to bring out the eccentricity in people, and there were always practical jokes to pass the time – funny if they weren't happening to you!

REAL ROMANIES

'My father always allowed one tribe of gipsies to stay for a night in Tenches Meadow on our farm at East Wall in the 1920s. One night I went with him to see if the gates were closed, and there around a camp fire all the gipsies were kneeling and saying the Lord's Prayer. Although I was only about seven years old, I shall never forget the feeling of peace, as though in another world. These were real Romanies and respected my Dad for letting them stay and break their journey and did no damage.'

'Gipsies were regular callers at our farm in Mainstone. They brought a few wares to sell, such as pegs which they made themselves, linen buttons, bits of lace and tape and shoelaces. They really came to beg something to eat and they would go away with perhaps a loaf of bread, a piece of boiling bacon, a slab of cake, a bit of butter, or whatever they thought about. They always brought several children with them and a favourite saying was "Just a bite for the young'uns. You wouldn't like to think of 'em going to bed clemmed would you Mrs?" Clemmed was a south Shropshire word for hungry.'

'A fiddler regularly called at our farm near Buildwas, playing for a few coppers. An old lady in a long black coat and black felt hat came asking for any bits and pieces which she might sell, and always asked for skim milk. She would drink a large cup full nearly in one gulp and go off happily with a bottle full. She piled all her goods in an old pram and was quite a sight to see.

The real gipsies came with brightly painted caravans, horses and dogs, and stayed for about a week before moving on. They sold pegs which they made. They were never any trouble and when they moved on all they left was a pile of ash where their fire had been.'

'An old gipsy woman used to walk along the stream at Caynton in the 1930s, gathering wild watercress. She would stop at my mother's home near there and give her a bunch of watercress in return for being allowed to dry her feet and put on a pair of my mother's old stockings.'

'In the 1920s gipsies lived in an encampment in Ludlow called Dark Lane. They roamed the countryside selling pegs and collecting rabbit skins. Their names were Smith and Locke.

There were also raggedy tramps. They called at houses for boiling water to make tea in their billy cans. They could get a bed for the night at the local workhouse – in Ludlow it was called Ivy House. In return for the bed they chopped sticks for kindling or broke up stone for road building.'

'Our house at Mousecroft Lane was very lonely in the early 1930s. My mother (who was in fact a very strong character) was frightened of the tramps who used to pass down the lane on their way from the workhouse at Morda to the one at Cross Houses. She used to lock the doors and hide with my brother and myself if she saw one coming. One day when she was taking us for a walk we met a man and we passed him again on our way back. When we got home we had been burgled – he had broken a window with one of our toy bricks!'

OLD BILL AND OTHER CHARACTERS

'During the war I was a land girl working on a farm in Shropshire. One of the characters I met was Old Bill. Tall, gaunt, defeated by a hard life.

He left school when he was ten years old and went to work at a pub in Much Wenlock. A very hard life. One of his jobs was to clean out the stables. This was about 1883 when many people still travelled by horse-drawn vehicles, putting up at pubs on long journeys.

He had to make mats of woven gorse stems for outside the doors, and mats of plaited straws for indoor workplaces.

He told me how he used to herd cattle across country to market, or from one farm to another, before the days of cattle lorries. On long journeys the men had to sleep rough under a tree, against a hedge, or in a barn. The cattle fed on the grass verges when the men rested.

When I knew him he slept up in the attic at the farm. He owned a small cottage, but this, and some farms and land nearby, had been requisitioned by the War Office.

In late December 1946 his cottage was de-requisitioned, and he was looking forward to spending Christmas there. So one day he left the farm and walked across the fields to the village shop with a small bundle of clothes on his back and his oil can in one hand. He bought his bag of groceries and set off for his cottage which was about a mile away through a wood.

We had had quite a heavy snowfall all that day and it snowed for most of the next week. When the snow began to thaw, a farmer and his son going round their fields, found the dead body of Old Bill, half buried in a snowdrift.

Poor, gentle old man, had worked hard all his life, but at 74 years was not to be rewarded by ending his days peacefully in his own home.'

'I went one day to the Mill Farm down Gilbury Lane near Cardington to hear the old hedging words from Andrew Preece, who was then 78.

I had the good luck that day to find him down at the bottom of a small meadow below the house. Here he was tackling a job of considerable dimensions – a length of hedge, well grown out with alder and withy, all of 15ft tall.

His old arms reached and cut, bent and wove with slow, controlling, long familiar movements. It was April but warm in this sheltered hollow place and he took off his cap to brush his gnarled hand over his damp forehead and thin hair. He was a lean man and his body knew the work and went easily into it.

A great privilege to see because the next time I came down, in August, they told me on the bus that he was gone.'

'There were lots of interesting people living on the Rock at Telford and around the area. Some names I would not like to mention!

Blackie Shephard was a character. He was never clean, that's how he got his name, but he always wore a pocket watch. When people met him in the lane, they would say to him "What's the time

Blackie?''. He would always tell them but not another word would he say.

Mrs Sheldon lived in a cottage at the Rock. She always looked so old with her long black skirt, a shawl around her shoulders and wrinkled face, everyone called her Granny Sheldon.

Little Billy Lloyd lived at Lawley Bank. He was only about four feet tall, a real comic was Billy. He would get up on the stage anywhere and sing "The Little Shirt My Mother Made For Me". He would take the shirt on stage with him. Billy was known for miles around the area.

There were a few families in the area who did a bit of poaching. They took their catch to the pubs to sell, then came singing home afterwards. Also gipsy families came around the doors selling pegs, lucky charms and paper flowers.

Another man in the area called Matthew Henry Bailey had a very big head and feet. His feet were so big he was told to take his shoes off to turn the corner. One day he said to his wife, "Lena, where's my Panama?" She immediately replied "In the pantry with half a peck of taters in it."

Jacky Hadley with his muck cart was the man who came to empty the old earth toilets. One day he dropped his jacket in the druggon and Mr Lewis Price observed him trying to fish it out. Mr Price offered to give him a new jacket. He replied "It's not the jacket, governor, my sandwiches are in the pocket".'

'At Woolston the old blacksmith's shop was taken over by the Powell family who were chimney sweeps. The cottage is still known as Annie the Sweep's Cottage. Annie swept all through the war, dressed in men's baggy trousers and jacket and setting off for work on her bicycle with her brushes over her shoulder. She charged a shilling for the very poor, two shillings and sixpence if you could afford it and five shillings for the gentry. She covered a twelve mile radius including hills.'

UNITY AND DIVERSITY

'My grandparents were a living example of how to agree to differ. She was a lifelong convinced Conservative and he, perhaps because he was a railway porter in South Wales in the time of Keir Hardy, was an equally strong Labour supporter. Come election time, two cars came to take them to vote, as neither would ride in a car with the opposition's sticker.

My grandparents' unity and diversity was also very evident every Friday when they went to shop in Ironbridge together. They parted at the end of the famous bridge – he to go to the Co-op for bacon, butter, sugar, etc, while she went to a privately owned grocer to make identical purchases. Later they met again by the bridge and returned home amicably together.

My grandfather lived to be 90 and was the solid dependable rock of my childhood. His funeral was something I shall never forget. He was a well known and well loved figure in the village, and the people wished to show their respect. The bearers walked in front of the hearse, so for two miles we proceeded at walking pace to the church. As we passed, the curtains in all the houses and cottages were drawn as a mark of respect. The women peeped out from behind the curtains but the men silently joined in behind, all dressed in their Sunday best. By the time we reached the church we were a decidedly long cavalcade, and as more people streamed in to fill the church, I was very proud of my beloved "Grandad".'

ELECTION FEVER

'My granny used to tell a story of Robert More of Linley Hall, near her home, who was MP for the Ludlow Division during the latter half of the 19th century. He would return to Linley after the day's hustings with his horse-drawn carriage covered with eggs, tomatoes and everything else that could be thrown at it. Times change very little!'

'In the 1920s on the evening of polling day, an Annscroft man with a lorry would collect all the men who had been at work during the day at Hookagate and get them to the polling station at Bayston Hill.'

'There was no lord of the manor in Pant, as the village straddled two parishes – Morton and Llanymynech. Very few "knew their place" in Pant, which consisted up to the First World War of small cottages scattered on the hillside. A lot of poaching took place and this story is told. A landowner caught a labourer poaching. "What are you doing on my land?" he asked. "How is it that it's your land?" was the reply. "Well," said the landowner, "My grandfather fought for it". "Come on, then," said the labourer, "I'll fight you for it".

At elections there was much leg pulling and sometimes squabbling. The story is told of a red flannel petticoat hoisted in an apple tree by a staunch Liberal supporter, with threats by a staunch Tory supporter, that it would be shot down if not removed. This caused much amusement. But after the elections people were again the best of friends.'

PRACTICAL JOKES?

'The canal which runs at the edge of Whixall Moss had a bakery situated at a point on the bank near the bridge. A woman carrying a bag of coal she had collected from the coal merchant needed some bread. She placed her coal in the hedge and entered the bakehouse. Knowing she would be talking there for some time, local youths exchanged the coal for stones, hiding the coal in the hedge. The poor woman, having trudged home with the bread and the heavy sack, discovered the exchange and had to return to the canalside to rescue her coal.'

'After going to the fair one time I remember coming along a dark lane with my sister and we were aware of being followed by someone. We were a bit frightened and went to my aunt's house and told her. My uncle gave us a stick to defend ourselves and we carried on down the lane. We felt we were being followed again, in fact there seemed to be several people trying to surround us. Suddenly a horrible face with bright red eyes and grinning mouth appeared over the hedge and there was the sound of raucous laughter. It was only some village lads having a lark with a turnip lantern.'

PINK ELEPHANTS?

'If you came out of the Hart and Trumpet public house at Gobowen and saw some elephants walking past, you would think it was the result of having too much to drink. Oh no! Elephants used to walk from place to place as the circus moved.

Two men were washing the elephants in a brook by Pentre Wern blacksmith's. There were two old elephants and one young one. I don't know if one of the older elephants was the mother of the young one. As the men were encouraging them to wash themselves by putting their trunks in the water and squirting water over themselves, the one big elephant stepped back and put his trunk through the small elephant's legs and pulled him over onto the stile. They started to fight, the horses ran away and there was quite a commotion. The noise was frightening and we children all ran away for our lives. By the way, the stile has never been repaired and that was over 70 years ago.'

FLOODS AND HARD WINTERS

The river Severn has been a good friend to Shropshire, but it, and other rivers could also quickly become a life-threatening foe, swollen by flood water and spilling out over its banks. There have been times of particularly hard weather too, which have remained in people's memories over the intervening years.

CLOUDBURSTS AND WINTER FLOODS

'In 1902 there was a cloudburst and Gobowen was flooded in March, and again in May. The trains had to stop because the water was high enough to put out the fire in the engines. The railway porters put chairs on the railway trolleys and took some of the passengers over to the Hart and Trumpet Hotel, where they stayed until they were able to complete their journey.'

'We lived some miles downstream from Iron Bridge but still in the Gorge. The house stood on a slight rise so that it was never flooded. Our nearest neighbour was only some 200 yards away but as the river Severn flowed between and the nearest bridge was over a mile away, we always had a boat of some kind. Most floods washed our boat away but always left us another washed away upstream. For many years my father had a coracle that only too easily was holed by branches. To repair it, he needed a patch of finely woven material which was covered in molten tar. News that the coracle had sprung a leak was a signal for me to hide my school blouses, the material of which they were made being ideal for patches.'

'As our home was quite near the river Severn it was a common sight in winter to see the fields covered in water and looking like a huge lake. The rabbits would come out of their burrows and sit on any bit of land above the water. They were easily caught by Mr Harry Rogers, the coracle man from Ironbridge. Many times I have seen him, after he has come off the train, walking along the road with the coracle on his back and his legs sticking out below, looking like a big black beetle.'

'Living near to the river in Castlefields I can remember the floods very well. As soon as the river started rising my sister and I used to go to

Many will remember vividly the floods which followed the snowdrifts in March 1947 – as in this picture from Hayton and District W.I.

the weir to see how high it was. We could see it from our bedroom window coming up across the fields at the back of our house and one year it came into our cellar. I used to play on some steps leading down to the river and once when it was very low I walked across the weir, most dangerous as I could not swim. I can remember the river being so high it came up over the road in Coton Hill and under the railway bridge, and also into Frankwell and Abbey Foregate – that's when the planks were put up for people to walk on.'

'In January 1948 I was lodging at Buildwas vicarage and had to cycle to Dale End every morning. Heavy rain fell throughout the first fortnight of the year and by the 8th the fields bordering the Severn were flooded. On the 11th I walked out to Leighton Bank to see the lake which completely obliterated the famous meander, and on the 13th and 14th had to splash with some difficulty through the water on the Buildwas road. By this time Ironbridge and Dale End were both flooded, and people had been evacuated from the Wharfage.

Worse, however, was to follow for me. When I reached Marnwood on the 15th I found that the road was impassable as far as The Firs (roughly opposite the old power station). The only course of action I could adopt was to lift my cycle over the fence and hedge on the Marnwood side and push the machine up over the fields until it was possible to get over the hedge again and scramble down the bank to the road. Any cyclist with knowledge of this road will appreciate how difficult this whole operation was.

Two years later in February 1950 my wife and I were living on the Wharfage and at half past eight on the 11th received an official flood warning. The Severn rose all that day and we awoke the next morning to hear a strange and frightening roar. A dirty, muddy brown torrent carrying many kinds of flotsam was rushing by, incredibly rapid and awesome in its destructive power. The water reached our door, flooding the little garden. We made preparations for moving upstairs, but providentially the floods did not become worse and on the 13th began to recede. The Wharfage Steps, at the side of our house, proved a blessing, enabling us to move around Ironbridge while the Wharfage was flooded.'

FLOODING ON THE MOOR

'As Kynnersley was on the Moor, we used to have serious flooding when all the roads were impassable and the village was cut off for days. These were the times when the villagers looked after each other, as there was no shop. The old remedies were produced, bread was made with barm from the winemaking or as soda or tea bread, and potato cakes were cooked, both sweet and savoury. Sweeteners were honey and black treacle. There were always plenty of blocks of salt about on the farms.'

'The fields at Moss Farm at Harmer Hill used to flood regularly, before the drainage was improved, and sometimes they iced over. This was great fun for skating but a headache for the farm men. Sometimes it was too dangerous to bring the cattle in to milk so men took their milking stools and pails out to the field and milked the cows there – having tied them to the hedge.

At Black Birches Farm after a heavy storm, the kitchen flooded and the farmer's wife was surprised to find that her kitchen was full of frogs.'

THE CYCLONE OF 1889

'In 1889 a cyclone which began at Waterloo hit both Bostock Hall and Whixall Hall. At the latter a man was blown across a yard and hit on the head by a stone crest which fell with tiles. A dog in its kennel was lifted several yards. Over a wide area trees were uprooted and stripped of branches, haystacks were moved and roofs blown off, and barns and outbuildings demolished. Parts of a huge beech tree were carried 150 yards. The cyclone covered about three and a half miles in length and was 150 yards wide. It was described as "a great white mass of vapour which came on with a deafening roar as if it were the rush of a mighty body of water." People came from miles around to view the damage.'

THE COLDEST WINTERS

'1890–91 was one of the coldest winters recorded in England. The Severn froze from bank to bank. One afternoon my father was sent from the farm with a load of fodder for the haulage horses in Shrewsbury. It was nearly dark when he set off for home with the empty waggon, and he crouched down for a little protection from the bitter cold. The horses knew the way home to their stable and supper, and made good speed. The anxious household came with lanterns when they reached the stableyard, but my father was unable to move, being frozen stiff, and had to be lifted out and carried into the house to be thawed out, slowly.'

'In 1917 the Severn was frozen over. There was continuous frost during January, February and March and for two weekends there were hundreds of people skating and sliding on the river. T. Brown rode his motorbike and sidecar, carrying his son and daughter, from Dale End to Buildwas on the river. When the ice broke up it was like thunder; the water from the hills forced the ice to break up and it came down the river in great chunks like icebergs.'

'In the winter of 1947 snow drifts were well above the road signs, posts and hedges. We walked six miles on the top of drifts to fetch bread and groceries, not able to see a hedge anywhere; it was hard going. We came back with a sack on our backs carrying the food. There were thousands of dead sheep and hundreds of cattle lost under the snow drifts. The only means of getting a track out was by digging with shovels and there were gangs of men and women on the main roads for weeks. It was eight weeks before the snow cleared.'

'From January 1947 there were 49 consecutive nights of frost, ranging from 3° to 30° below freezing. Twelve inches of snow fell in 24 hours. Prisoners of war were used to clear roads around Whixall and also helped to put a bus back on the road after it ran into a ditch. It was the coldest February for 107 years.'

HOUSE & HOME

THE HOUSES WE LIVED IN

From tiny terraced town houses to picturesque old farms, Shropshire folk occupied a variety of dwelling places, many remembered with affection but also with a realisation that they were often cold and draughty, and overcrowded with the larger families common in the earlier part of the century.

A TERRACE IN SHREWSBURY

'In 1916 my family moved into a terraced house consisting of two bedrooms, a living room and kitchen, and an outside toilet. There was no bathroom or hot water, light was by gas mantle and cooking by a coal fire until gas stoves became available. Washday, with dolly and tub, mangle with wooden rollers and a rubbing board, was taken in turn with the other tenants, who shared a drying ground. There was no garden, only a small patch in front, so all vegetables had to be bought until allotments became available.

A similar cottage a few doors away had 15 in the family. One of the children slept in a cupboard at the side of the fireplace, frightening the chimney sweep nearly to death when he pushed his brush up the chimney and the cupboard door flew open and out fell Arty.'

NEW DALE

'Our cottage at New Dale had two bedrooms, a parlour, a kitchen, pantry and brewhouse; the pantry and brewhouse were lean-to onto the house. It had a big old fashioned cast-iron grate, which was always covered with various brasses; my mother was very fond of brass. On a Sunday morning she used to have a joint of meat hanging on a brass "jack" in front of the fire, and many a time I've asked her for a piece of bread to dip in the liquor that came out of the meat. It would be hard to beat that today.

In the parlour we had an organ, a piano, a violin, a melodion and a gramophone. We were a very musical family. We had various pictures on the wall, one of them of the Duke of Wellington in brass with a background of black velvet. On the piano stood three glass globes with artificial flowers done in wool, which were in small vases under these globes. Over the fireplace there was an overmantel on which there were three glass vases, and a little china basket in which mother used to keep her safety pins and other little pins.

Mother always kept the fire in at night. Before it got dark she would go out to the coal house and get a big lump of coal and a bucket of slack and before we went to bed she'd put this big lump of coal on and cover it with the slack, what we called a "raker". When we got up in the morning we would put the poker into this smouldering lump of coal and within a few minutes we would have a nice glowing fire. This was the custom in many of the houses because the men had to be up very early in the morning to either go to the pits or the furnaces.

The Long Row at New Dale were back to back houses. I remember best the two end houses in the Row. In the one end house there were ten daughters and two sons, and in the other end there were ten sons and two daughters. In these houses in the Row there was only one bedroom and a landing; many a time some of the children never went to bed – they would have to sleep on the old "squab" in the kitchen. This squab was made of wood and it had four legs and a wooden back and a wooden seat; they would put any old coats on these seats for the kids to sit on. In those days there were no such things as settees and easy chairs.

In New Dale there were no bathrooms. The old folks used to get these big beer barrels, cut about two foot off the top of the barrel and use that for a bath. We never even had a tin bath at home, we always used one of these cut down old barrels.'

One pound and five shillings was the quarterly rent for this Shropshire cottage in 1919.

A COTTAGE NEAR BRIDGNORTH

'The cottage near Bridgnorth in the 1940s had red quarry tiled floors downstairs. An old sack was used as a door mat, and the only carpet was a home-made rag rug in front of the fire.

The fireplace had an oven at one side and an iron tank at the other in which water was heated. There was a brass tap for running the water out. All the fireplace was blackleaded. The hearth was of flagstones which were whitened with a donkey stone. A steel fender was in front of the fire. A trivet hooked on to the bars of the fire on which the kettle or a pan could be heated. There was a mantel above the fireplace on which stood some ornaments. Underneath the mantel was a brass rail where clothes were aired after being pressed with a flat iron heated in front of the fire.

There were lace curtains at the window and pots of plants on the window ledge. At night thicker curtains were pulled across. An oak grandfather clock with a brass face stood opposite the door. There was no electricity. An oil lamp was lit at night and candles were used upstairs.

Water for drinking was from a pump at the back of the house and had to be brought indoors in a bucket. Rainwater was used for washing ourselves and clothes. This was caught in barrels placed under all the downspouts. We bathed in a hip bath in front of the fire.

The lavatory was at the far end of the garden, a stone building with a wooden seat over a pit. This pit was cleaned out twice a year and the contents were dug into the garden. There was an unglassed opening about a foot square on one side of this building through which one could view miles of unspoilt country, not a house in sight, but cold in winter with snow driving in.

Vegetables grown in the garden lasted most of the year. Apple, damson and plum trees grew in the hedge round the garden. Flowers grew in borders round the veg. A pig was kept in the sty, and a few hens scratching round the yard and in the adjoining field kept us supplied with fresh eggs and the occasional boiling fowl. The pig kept us in meat for many months. The pig and the hens were fed on all the scraps from the house and garden plus wheatings from a local farm. Each day we took a can to the farm for milk.

The old man who lived in this cottage used many Shropshire dialect words. "Fittle" for food; "cyack" – cake; "cyat" – cat; "suck" for toffees; "dyeth" – death; "yaffle" for the green woodpecker; "quice" for woodpigeon; and he ended most of his sentences with "surree". His wife would say to her child whose toys were strewn about, "Now move your tranklements." He and his wife believed the cattle knelt in their stalls on Christmas Eve, and the wife believed people could be "bewitched". They were unsophisticated, good, honest people, very happy and content in their little cottage. The old man was born in this cottage which he owned. He had a fund of stories about local farmers and their workmen.

One was about a farmer known for his meanness, and a man who came to do some hedge-brushing:

Farmer,   "I want you to make a good job on it, but I don't want me ear bit."

Hedger,   "Well gaffer, it's like this. I've a got two ackers; one'll do the job at 4d a perk (perch) an' t'other at 6d a perk. You can choose which you've a mind, an' I'll do the job to suit."

The same farmer had a young boy living in. One day at lunchtime the farmer said, "Would anyone like a second helping of pudding?" The boy said "Yes please, sir," "What did you say?" roared the farmer. "No, thank you," said the boy. "That's right", said the farmer, "Always speak your mind", and proceeded to finish the pudding himself.'

THE OLD FARMHOUSE

'Our house was a farmhouse near Morda. The living room was a large room with a black grate with two ovens each side of the fire. The oven doors had brass handles and the mantlepiece was about six foot high and had brass candlesticks and a pair of black and white dogs on it. There was a steel fender and steel poker, tongs and shovel, as well as a toasting fork.

There was a large dining table with oak chairs, and two armchairs and a very special one which was made of wicker. The floor was of black and red tiles and in front of the fireplace and around the room were rag rugs. There was a Welsh dresser with willow pattern plates, a corner cupboard and a housekeeper's cupboard.

The parlour had a seven piece suite of two leather armchairs, a sofa and four dining chairs to match. In here there was the piano, a sideboard and a tip-up table. Oil cloth covered the floor and a calfskin rug lay in front of the parlour grate and brass fender.

A passage from the front door led to these two rooms and the front stairs were opposite the front room. A dry pantry and the cellar led from this passage. In the dry pantry salt, sugar, flour, oatcakes and porridge oats were kept. In the cellar were the beer barrels and potatoes, onions, carrots and apples stored for the winter.

At this end of the passage was the back kitchen and the back door. Here was the well and the pump which supplied the house with water, and a pipe led outside to the farm yard for the animals. From this back kitchen you entered the kitchen, which was the living room of the farm workers.

This room had a table with a bench on either side. There were two wooden armchairs and a settle, a corner cupboard and a black grate with one oven. Also from here there was a chute which went to the pig barrel with waste such as potato peelings, cabbage leaves and buttermilk after the churning in the buttery.

The door to the buttery led from here. This held the separator – the cream was kept for butter making and the skim milk given to the older calves, poured onto scalded linseed meal. The young calves had full cream milk. The buttery was down three steps so was a yard into the ground and was very cool. Around the walls were shelves and cold slate slabs.

From the workers' living room, where they ate and spent their evenings in front of a log fire, led the back stairs which in turn led to another flight of stairs. In the bedrooms were iron bedsteads with straw mattresses, and on top of these feather beds. The room held a chest of drawers and a swing mirror. The maid slept on the first floor, as did the family.

Also in the workers' living room were two boilers, one for making beer and the other for boiling the clothes, making plum puddings and boiling water for feeding the animals and making warm drinks. The bread oven was not used after 1928 when the baker started coming round delivering with a horse and covered waggon.'

MOVING HOUSE

'When my grandparents came to Hawksmoor, Adderley in 1904 the cattle walked from their farm at Willington, near Chester, about 30 miles, resting en route at the farm of a friend. Grannie and Grandpa and the two youngest children, plus the remnants of their belongings, came by horse-drawn vehicle while the older members of the family came by bicycle. When the cattle arrived a friend who lived in the area had sent his sons to help milk the cows. Over the garden gate was a banner saying "Welcome to Adderley", put there by Mrs Bradbury, the village schoolmistress, who had also got the kettle boiling in the house.'

A FARMHOUSE KITCHEN

Life revolved around the kitchen, often the only warm room in the house. Here the cooking was done, baths were taken, meals eaten, children played and adults relaxed after a long day's work outside. One of the jobs done while sitting of an evening was the making of rag rugs, sometimes the only floor covering available – though at least one artistic alternative was discovered.

MY FAVOURITE ROOM

'My favourite room as a child was our kitchen – warm, friendly, full of life and welcoming. It was in a stone-built farmhouse, square with cream-washed walls and a grey flagstone floor and a beamed ceiling all white. It was essentially a living kitchen with a scrubbed deal table to seat the family of seven and squeeze in occasional callers, windsor chairs, a bench along the wall, two wooden armchairs, a nursing chair and a baby's high chair in oak. On one wall was an oak dresser with everyday dinner and tea services plus an assortment of mugs. Beside a door leading to the dining room was a flour bin three foot square, a solid job to take two bags of flour straight from Plowden or Bacheldre Mill all ready for baking day.

Against one wall stood a small table where the live-in cowman ate his meals in privacy whilst still able to join in the general conversation.

It was heated very efficiently with a large range with an open fire in the middle, an oven on one side and a boiler with a shiny brass tap which had to be filled, bucket by bucket, but gave a constant supply of hot water – a wonderful place for the family to sit around on winter evenings.

The day began with breakfast for the children, then the cutting and packing of lunches for each child, fitting them out with warm clothes, macs, wellies and umbrellas and sending them off on their two mile walk to school in all weathers. Peace at last – then Father came in for his breakfast, having been out and started all the farmwork for the day. As he breakfasted he was visited by the rector, a large and very gentlemanly bachelor who spent half an hour each morning conferring with my father, his warden – the only time he could be caught up with and kept still to talk to. While they talked Mother would bath the baby on the hearthrug, feed her and pack her into the cradle until next feeding time.

From then until night time the kitchen was a hive of industry according to the "job of the day" – plus ironing, mending and preparing meals. Baking day was the most wonderful. A large zinc bath full of dough was put to rise in front of the fire before breakfast and by the time that was done with and cleared away baking had begun, with cakes and pies to feed the family for a week. Then began the making of 40 loaves of assorted sizes. Meanwhile the bread oven was being heated in an outside bakehouse by a young maid who lived in and added one more to the family. When the oven was hot it was mopped out and all the loaves and cakes and buns carried to the bakehouse table. Then Mother, carefully balancing each tin onto a "peel", put it in the oven, the iron door was closed and it was back to the kitchen to a mammoth washing up session.

What a wonderful smell when everything came out of the oven – it lasted all day. A large loaf was set aside for the waggoner and his family in their cottage and a small loaf for each of the old people in the village.

After tea came the best time of all, when lamps were lit and work put away. From about 1930 we had a cat's whisker radio on which we heard anything but news. It had a wet battery which had to be carried to a man in Bishop's Castle to be recharged over two or three days.

First there was homework to be done and piano practice – then the time was our own and we spent it reading books and playing games. Too soon it was bedtime and we washed in a large bowl in the scullery sink or bathed in the only place we had, the icy-cold dairy. Then, wrapped in warm towels, we had a warm at the fire and a bite of supper before we took our candles and trailed through the cold dark rooms upstairs to our bedrooms.

Occasionally my father would play his concertina to us as we got ready for bed – a rare treat and enjoyed by adults and children alike.

Before we leave that kitchen I must not forget the bacon cratch suspended from the ceiling and holding four or five flitches of home-cured bacon, or the iron hooks around the walls on which hung home-cured hams in muslin bags. Or the wooden wall clock with a romantic history, a loud strike on the hour and a lovely leisurely tick.'

PODGED RUGS

'My first introduction to "craft" work was at a very early age. An annual event was to make a new "podge" or rag rug for the hearth in front of the kitchen range to be put down for Christmas. It was later put away and the old one returned until the better weather and spring cleaning had been done.

Throughout the year the best pieces of old clothes, etc were carefully gathered into a large "scran" or rag bag (this also made of pieces patch-worked together).

My paternal grandfather, who worked on a farm, got for us a large hurden or "gohanna" sack in good condition. This was carefully unpicked and washed. If sewn with coarse string, this was kept for tying up things; if fine cotton string, this was boiled in the copper and used for tying up puddings or joined together and crocheted into little mats.

On our Sunday afternoon walk with my father we searched for and found a hazel rod which he cut into suitable lengths, smoothed the top, bluntly pointed and smoothed the other end – all with a pocket-knife. (Incidentally he made marvellous whistles out of elder wood for us).

My father then marked the design on the hessian – always the same: a border all round, four or five inches deep; in the centre one large diamond with an intersected smaller one each side. This was a great source of wonderment to me and my two younger sisters. We thought he was very clever.

Work then began in earnest. The rags were cut into pieces and pegging commenced – jobs allocated according to age. My earliest recollection is of handing the pieces to my mother to be pegged in. My middle sister and I sorted out the colours, bright for the centre diamond, another colour for the flanking ones, dark for the border and as they came, all mixed up, for the rest. The result was a warm, gay rug. While this went on (we usually did so much each evening before going to bed) my father used to nurse my youngest sister and sing to us. He had a fine voice. There was no radio for entertainment, still less television!

Times were extremely hard then, but looking back I think there was a greater feeling of togetherness in families, gathered together in the warm kitchen with the soft light of the oil lamp.

In case you are wondering what happened to the old rug, it did another stint of duty in the wash or brew – house under the dolly tub to take the strain of the violent "possing" mother used to give the clothes, (marvellous for frustrations) and then finally the bonfire, the ashes going on the garden. Not a thing was wasted in those days!'

'We used to make rugs in the wintertime at Longville out of old clothes, tweeds etc. They would be washed, then cut into strips about three quarters of an inch wide by four inches long. The backing was usually a maize sack because the weave in them was fairly open. They would be cut open and washed, then with a rug tool the pieces of material were threaded through in rows. When finished it would be turned over and glued and after this had dried it was lined with another sack.'

AN ALTERNATIVE

'At my grandparents' farm at Upper Botville the huge kitchen had a floor of square stone flags. Every spring my cousin gathered a bath full of young dock leaves and with the strong green juice she outlined the flags and drew a circle in the middle. The shiny dark green pattern lasted a year and was as pretty as any carpet.'

MONDAY TO SUNDAY

Every week and every home had its own routine, certain days when the washing, the ironing, the baking, the marketing etc would be done. The day which nearly everyone disliked was washday, when for hours the drudgery of soaking, boiling, washing, blueing, starching, mangling and drying filled the house with steam and frayed tempers.

EACH DAY HAD ITS APPOINTED TASK

'A week's work in my farmhouse home in the Clun Valley in the 1930s followed a regular pattern.

Monday was washday. It began on Sunday night when the whites and coloureds were separately put to soak. Next morning the fire was lit early under the large boiler, which had been filled with water. When it was hot we began the work. All garments were washed by hand or dollied in a large tub. We also used a washing board and scrub brush. The whites were then put in to boil and we cut soap into small pieces to go in with them. After this, all had to be rinsed twice and blued, starched where necessary, put through the mangle and taken out to the orchard to the line between the apple trees and left to dry. Later the ironing took place with the old flat iron heated in front of the open kitchen range.

Tuesday was churning day. This was a messy job and at times very time consuming. The milk was brought in twice a day and separated. This was done by a very intricate machine and it was my job to wash, scald and put it together – one tiny mistake and you had the milk coming out where the cream should have been! The cream was collected in large steins in which there was a long wooden paddle to stir the cream daily, this helped it to ripen as it needed to be very sour to make good butter.

On the given day the large end-over-end churn was brought outside into the yard, though if it was very cold or wet we were allowed to churn in the back kitchen. The actual churning could take a long time depending on the temperature and time of the year. When it had "come", the butter was washed several times, salted and made into half pound pats. Some of this would be sold at market and it was customary to use a special pattern (always the same) on the pats so that the buyer would know which farm had produced it. This could make a difference to the flavour, as the herbage which the cows had eaten varied from farm to farm.

Wednesday was baking day; another early start to light the wood fire in the large baking oven. The sticks could be several feet long as they were poked in (the best heater was gorse, but this was agony to use). In the meantime half a sack of our own milled flour was tipped into a large wooden mitt. We had masses of skim milk so the bread was mixed with this and a quarter pound of yeast. After much kneading the dough was always indented on the top or it may never rise!

By early afternoon the oven would be white hot. The bread was kneaded again and made up into large loaves. The ashes were taken from the oven and the loaves put in with the peel (a long-handled tool with a flat "tray" on which to put the bread). While this was baking we would be busy making lots of cakes and fruit pies (in season) and usually several rabbit pies. These were quite delicious as the meat would be previously boiled with pieces of home-cured ham, making a tasty jelly, and hard boiled eggs were put under the crust. All this was put in the oven after the bread was removed, as it ws still quite hot. This would usually last a large family most of the week.

Thursday was market day, when several of us would drive a pony and "covered car" into Knighton over the border into Wales, about six miles away. The butter, eggs, poultry or rabbits were taken in and sold to a local dealer, who would have a room in one of the pubs. The pony and cart would be put up at a local hostelry and the horse stabled until it was time to come home. The week's groceries were purchased and shoes or clothing if required. We never carried away shopping but it was sent by an errand boy to the market room where the horse and cart were "parked". We paid the hostler sixpence for looking after the turnout.

Friday could be threshing, pig-killing, sheep shearing, cider-making or bear brewing day! All these busy days had to be fitted in. This made us in the farmhouse very busy preparing lots of meals for the extra labourers, who were often borrowed from neighbouring farms and ours went back to them when wanted. Several of the workmen were given rooms in the farmhouses, their meals, beds and washing were provided and they were also given a room or kitchen to sit in of an evening. In those days their only mode of travel was on foot or bicycle. These "live-in" men were usually hired at the local May Fairs. The farmer would seal the deal by giving the hired man one shilling, then he would start work the following week and hopefully stay until the following May.

Saturday was a day for sport or any pastime we were involved in. I had a horse and hunted with my father with the United pack of foxhounds. I also walked a couple of puppies for the Hunt. A puppy show would be held in June and I have many trophies won over the years. Summertime was for tennis at the local club.

About this time we were involved in a terrible slump and farming was badly hit in the recession. There was no real cash, but we were well dressed and fed on good wholesome food. Then the war came and nothing was quite the same again.'

'Each day at our farmhouse at Bitterley had its appointed task, beginning with washday on Monday – a marathon when it entailed washing for a family of nine. In summertime drying was no problem but in winter it was a different story and wet clothes draped on clothes horses were very dreary companions.

Tuesday was ironing day. Flat irons were heated on the open fire and consequently often left dirty marks on the clothes. Wednesday was baking day, which entailed making a bathful of dough and while it was rising, heating the baking oven. Gorse was often used for this. When the bricks in the oven were hot and the fire had burned away, the ashes had to be scraped out and the loaves put in with a "peel". Cakes and tarts were also inserted and left for the required time. As this was the baking for the week it was a minor tragedy if anything went wrong.

The rest of the week could be spent on cleaning – bedrooms on Thursday, kitchen and blackleading the grate on Friday, back kitchen and outhouses on Saturday. Everything had to be clean for Sunday, which was a day of rest. Everyone rose late and no field work was done, but Sunday school and attending a service at church or chapel was important. Sunday dinner was special and a family tea provided for anyone who arrived during the afternoon.'

A HAPPY WOMAN!

'Grandmother, in all her married life, never once cleaned the huge kitchen range. After she had gone to bed each night, grandfather cleaned all the steel fire-irons, trivet and fender; he would be up early next morning to blacklead the grate, light the fire and take grandmother a cup of tea before going to work. Each night he would clean any shoes which were put under the old horsehair sofa. We children discovered this early in life and it was a real holiday when we did not have to clean our own shoes.'

WASHDAY

'Washing actually started on Sunday evening. We four children always walked to Sunday school three miles away – we rarely missed, we loved the songs, the stories, the attendance stamps and the anniversaries. After Sunday school we started off for home. We walked the footpaths and lanes as had we gone by the roads our journey would have been even longer. Along these lanes were spotted and collected "morning sticks", the broken twigs from the trees and the hedgerows that were the kindling for the boiler fire. We were not supposed to gather sticks in our Sunday school clothes, but if we dropped our heap of sticks by the bottom gate and brushed each other with grubby hands to remove tell tale dirty marks from our clothes, then we could return and gather our sticks later after Sunday tea.

Sunday tea was a treat, usually some home boiled ham or pressed tongue with salads (but not often tomatoes), bread and real butter, followed by tinned fruit and cream and maybe a rather rubbery jelly, which had been made on Saturday so that it would set. This was followed by homemade slab cake which mother made in a large square meat tin. It went into the oven after the Sunday roast had been taken out. There was no lingering after tea. We had jobs to do. My brother had to saw logs and he balanced the long branches and trunks of trees on the old sawing horse and worked hard until he had a fair heap of logs, not short and chunky for the sitting room fire but much longer to be pushed under the boiler and into the greedy fire that burned all day on washing days. We girls had to go down the fields, along the ditch banks and down the brooks in search of more of the thinner "morning sticks". If we couldn't find enough then we would get the brummock, a lethal wooden-handled, long-bladed chopper favoured by the hedge-layers, and chop logs into splinter-thin kindling. I still have a scar on the first finger of my left hand from holding on too long and missing the wood. It was quite skilled to cut and hold the thin sticks and let go at the crucial time or risk cutting your hands. You never got sympathy if you went in crying or dripping blood. The cut was washed, wrapped up in a piece of old, clean sheet and off you went to fetch more of the wretched sticks. If I forgot to take a sack with me then I would lift up my skirt and, holding it up in front of me, fill it up with sticks and return home to empty it by the washhouse door. The boiler fire had an insatiable appetite and needed vast quantities to keep it going; precious coal was not used.

After the sticks were gathered, then water had to be carried. We had no water in the house, it was at the bottom of the "well-patch". We would each take two buckets and make our way down a zig-zag path to the old well, fill our buckets and make our way back up the zig-zag path. The first two buckets were no problem, but as we got tired, so the buckets got heavier and we would slop cold water down our legs and into our shoes – not too bad in the summer, but not much fun on cold winter days.

The boiler which stood in the corner of the washhouse was brick, built with a fireplace at floor level. The boiler, which had a wooden lid on it, had to be filled and it was this first filling that was the start of the day-long washing. Clothes were sorted on the floor into the piles, the white sheets and towels, the children's clothes, and so on until the last heap of dirty farm clothes and socks. The fire was lit before we went to school.

The first water was used to hand wash and rinse the sheets and the whites, which were then put into the boiler with shavings of a hard green, smelly soap. Then the fire was really stoked up until the washing was boiling and it was important to keep the washing moving in the boiler. The soap formed scum and wasn't very effective at holding the dirt that had been washed out, so constant movement kept the scum at bay. The pride of the washday, the white sheets and towels, were rinsed and put out to dry, down the garden on a good day or under the empty bays of the dutch barn on a wet day, or if the barns were full, hung steaming on lines around the kitchen. The rest of the wash was done using the water from the boiler, but using the deep white sink and an old zinc bath, with various pieces of equipment as aids. There was a gadget like a three-legged stool with a long handle, called a dolly, which was pushed up and down on the wet clothes, and there was a metal contraption with holes in it and a wooden handle, a posher, which was used in the same way, forcing water through the clothes and hopefully forcing the dirt out. The zinc scrubbing board was used in conjunction with soap, again the hard green evil-smelling stuff, a scrubbing brush and lots of elbow grease. Dirt-encrusted farm trousers were scrubbed outside with the yard broom before they were taken into the washhouse. If we were lucky Mother had only the socks left to do when we got home from school, otherwise we would have to give a hand to finish off.

The water that was left was used to scrub down the kitchen floor and swamp out the washhouse. Some of the old chairs had been "cut down" and this was because the floor was washed with copious amounts of the hot washday water and the wooden legs standing on the stone floor would eventually rot. Father would solve the problem by sawing off the leg at the next turned part.

Was I glad to see the last drops of water being swept to the drain in the corner of the washhouse, the fireplace empty, the boiler lid on and the washhouse door closed until the next week.

At the time I wasn't really aware of the amazing step forward when Mother had a calor-gas boiler but, oh, what progress when we had water laid on from our own well and electricity came in 1959. Dad bought Mother a Servis washing machine with a paddle in the middle and an electric wringer on the top. The old mangle was outside and for years was hung with pot plants as its wooden rollers gradually rotted away; a cast iron relic to the hard old days.'

'My father had a clean white stiff collar to wear each morning, the bane of my mother's life. She hated laundering and polishing them to the state of perfection he required. Ten years later she discovered a mail order firm from which my father bought two dozen stiff collars. Each fortnight the soiled collars were posted back to the firm and freshly laundered ones sent to replace them. Mother felt the extra expense was well worth while.'

'Washday was a marathon for all the family – in one household at Oswestry five different fires had to be set and lit before anything else was done, and the one under the built-in copper had to be watched so that no water overflowed and put it out. Because we lived in a hard water area, rainwater was collected in butts and then transferred in buckets into the copper, or else no lather could be obtained. Rinso or Oxydol were the soap powders most often used. In one family there were four boys who all slept in one room and two girls in another, as well as Mum and Dad and the farmworker who lived in, so washing was done for all these people. In winter or bad weather it was a nightmare drying it all, because there was only the old wooden roller mangle to squeeze out as much water as possible.'

NO MOD CONS!

All the things that most of us now take for granted – running water, indoor plumbing, light at the flick of a switch and electrical appliances – were dreams beyond the reach of most of our families in even the recent past. Instead there was the long walk to the privy at the bottom of the garden, the well or pump to provide water, and candles and oil lamps to shed a soft light at night.

DOWN THE GARDEN PATH

'Our privy at Welshampton in the 1930s was outdoors down a rather long garden. It had a longish scrubbed wooden seat with a hole in the centre (some had two, or even three seats) and a red brick floor. There was no lock on the door. On occasions when we were ill or had to obey the call of nature in the night time, we used a chamber pot; these important utensils had a place in every household, though they were usually kept well out of sight! At the back of the privy was a square dug-out about four feet deep into which the sewage collected, and it had to be emptied three or four times a year. A long handled scoop

Whixhall. A small cottage like this with no electricity or indoor sanitation, was often home for large families with eight or ten children.

76

known as a skippet was used. Needless to say, neighbours were in no doubt as to what was happening on these occasions.'

'The toilets at school in Baschurch in the 1920s were earth dugouts, which smelled terrible in hot weather. Our "petty" at home was some 50 yards up the garden and attached to the pigsty. It also had a loft where straw was stored and it wasn't unusual for tramps to spend the night there – a bit disconcerting for the householder making the trip late at night in the wind and the rain to find the loft occupied.'

'One day we had a visitor from the town to our farm at Rodington, and just at dusk she went to use the lavatory which was quite a few yards down the garden. She returned very quickly, white and trembling. We had forgotten to tell her that like most country lavatories there was a pigsty attached. The pig was in residence at the time.'

'In the early years of the century at Coalbrookdale, the majority of people living at the Forge had to share the toilets; there were at least three or four houses to each toilet. When we moved into the Fountain Villa there were two families using that toilet. We had heard of water toilets, but of course we had never known what they were like. All the toilets in the Forge were connected to the brook and eventually all the effluent went into the river at the Dale End.'

'At Weston Lullingfield our toilet was a double-holed piece of wood over a well – we used to say for twins or newly weds – and it could be quite a sociable occasion! We children had a box with a hole in it and a chamber pot inside. Newspaper made very interesting toilet paper. The lavatory was a long cold run along the back of the house.'

'At Wem, just after we moved into Noble Street in the 1940s, I was awakened by very peculiar noises in the Street – a horse clop-clopping along, then it would stop, then much clanking and sloshing and then the horse moved on again. I looked out of the window and saw a horse and cart with lanterns swinging at the rear. I expected to hear a cry of "Bring out your dead!" On enquiring next day I was told that most of the houses in the street had bucket lavatories. On certain nights the buckets were put outside the front door, along came the cart and two men and they had the horrible job of emptying the buckets into the cart.'

'The mains sewer was laid through Pontesbury in 1913. There were no drills or automatic tools and by our house was a seam of rock, so dynamite had to be used to blast the stone out. Before lighting the fuse, bundles of sticks were put on top to stop the rock from flying.'

77

A PRECIOUS COMMODITY

'In the 1920s we lived two miles from Bishops Castle, in lovely open countryside. It was a smallholding called the Seven Wells. My home lacked the basic comforts which today are taken for granted, but we were compensated in other ways. Water was the most precious commodity. We saved every drop we could. A brook running through the fields was dammed to provide water for animals, and for washing. Our drinking water had to be carried a few hundred yards from a well in the lane. This came from a spring and never dried up as did the other supply. We saved every drop of rainwater, and I have even melted snow when the brook was frozen.'

'Our drinking water, a few miles from Ironbridge but still in the Gorge, came from a spring about 100 yards from the house. To me it meant more pocket money as I received a halfpenny a bucket to carry water for special purposes. One such time was when my father made wine – nine gallons at a time. Our other source of water was three large butts which collected rainwater. This was used for washing hair, clothes and ourselves. No modern shampoo can produce the shine and softness of hair washed in this water.'

'There was a piped water supply to our house at Lydbury North in the 1920s, but it was often in danger of running dry in the winter months because the cattle yards were supplied first and when these were full during the winter the cattle drank a great deal of water. However, there was still a board in the house with the following inscription, obviously a relic of days before water was piped to the house:
"A place for everything and everything in its place. No person to take water out of the kitchen boiler without putting more in."'

'I lived in Great Bolas as a child and my father dug his own well with only the aid of a hammer, chisel and shovel. A cover was placed over to keep out debris but the method of drawing water was primitive. A bucket was lowered down by rope and hauled out when full by the same method.'

CANDLES AND OIL LAMPS

'Candles were made by one Ludlow family until the early part of the 20th century. Tallow candles were made by rendering animal fat. Younger members of the family would dip the candles repeatedly in tallow to build up a good thickness. It was a unpopular job because of the acrid smell. High quality beeswax candles were also made.'

'Our lighting wasn't needed much in the summer months when work was from dawn to dusk, but when darkness came early we had oil lamps, or I suppose it was paraffin. One big glass lamp stood on the middle of the table to do my homework by, with Mother knitting her never-ending socks on four needles. I never could turn a heel! There was a hurricane lamp for outdoors, for tending the animals and of course, for going to the loo, which was in the back garden. There was a big tree overhead and often an owl would hoot, but I never worried about it. Candles were used at bedtime so I was never allowed to read in bed.'

'Care of the hurricane lamps was a weekly household chore in the 1930s on our farm at Hodnet. Some eight had to be checked, glasses washed, wicks levelled, and filled with paraffin. In addition there were some eight lamps in the house, two with double wicks which were used in the dining/drawing room and were the ones by which sewing and reading were done; two for carrying around; two which hung on the wall in the kitchen and bathroom; and one very small one which lived on the landing and was left lit all evening.'

THE COMING OF ELECTRICITY

'The river Cynllaith flows through the meadows below Llansilin and at one spot there is an attractive small waterfall. The flow of water is somewhat seasonal, but with the age of the dynamo around the early 1920s some enterprising men, led by Mr Petters who kept the post office and Mr Dick Hughes who ran a bus service, harnessed the power of the waterful, wired the houses for electricity and fixed up a local supply for lighting. What a blessing it was compared with the trouble of trimming and filling oil lamps. One disadvantage though – on a Sunday when the church lights were in use, lights in homes went very dim. In 1933 North Wales Power Company brought mains electricity to the village.

'At Highley electricity came in about 1930 – one lady has a bill showing that two houses were wired for £13 at that time. Paraffin lamps had been used until that time, in homes, shops and the church.'

'Electricity came to Uppington in about 1932 and made a great difference to our lives – electric light instead of paraffin lamps and candles to go to bed with. It seemed miraculous to be able to just switch on and there was light! Mother was able to have an electric sweeper instead of the old wooden Ewbank and we acquired a new radio instead of the old bakelite wireless which ran on batteries. We still didn't have a washing machine and even when I married and came to Meole in 1947 I still had only a gas boiler at first.'

'After the war in the 1940s we had electricity connected to our house at Acton Burnell. It was a great day for us. I remember my mother remarking on the fact that all corners of the room were now visible. For a while we didn't realise why the house was so cold. The oil lamps had given out warmth as well as light.'

'Our lighting system in the 1950s in our house on the Long Mountain was Tilley lamps, candles and torches – lamps in the main downstairs rooms, candles upstairs and lamps for the hens (yes, this was important when you were selling eggs because if they had longer hours of daylight they produced more eggs). I don't remember any accidents with the candles but this is very surprising because I used to read books under the bedclothes with the aid of a candle! Then that wonderful thing electricity arrived – not mains but a generator driven by a petrol engine and we really thought we were in heaven. The first light to be switched on started up the generator and the last one off stopped it. My husband often laughs about having to light candles when he took me home from a dance because if you put a light on, you woke everyone else up with the noise of the engine. It was well into the 1960s before we had mains electricity.'

BATHS AND BEDTIME

With bathrooms a rarity, the weekly bath was often taken in front of the fire, the water laboriously poured in bucket by bucket. If you were one of a large family, you probably hoped you would not be the last in line, as the water was merely topped up and not changed between each dip. Then it was off to bed, a flickering candle the only light to guide you through the dark, cold rooms upstairs.

KEEPING THE FIRE BURNING

'I think we had gas in some of the rooms, but in our kitchen we always had a coal fire. Coal, of course, was very cheap and the kitchen fire was never allowed to go out. At the end of the day, before my father and mother retired to bed, the fire was raked, that is, there was a very big lump of coal placed in the middle of the fire grate and then round that was placed what was called slack, which was a very small kind of coal, sometimes not more than a dust. That kept the large lump of coal smouldering all through the night. Then, when my father got up in the morning, between half past five and six o'clock, he always came down into the kitchen, poked up the fire, breaking the lump which would then burst into the most beautiful flames, place on this fire the kettle with the water in it and after that he would make a pot of tea. And then it was our great joy to have a cup of tea in bed, brought up by my father.'

'At Whixall we used peat on our fires. The brown peat burned quickly and was known as "esse". The black peat was slow burning and gave out more heat. The best coal came from Stoke to Fenns Bank station, on the line from Whitchurch to Oswestry.'

'Fuel for heating we had in abundance at Bishops Castle. If I went down the fields, I came back with an armful of sticks – I never needed asking. Old trees were felled and sawn into logs. A good supply for needed for the cooking range in the kitchen, which was always kept burning.'

'As we had a coal fire the chimney had to be swept about twice during the winter. A local man from Cressage came with his rods and brush; he pushed the brush up the chimney, screwing rods onto it as it went up and came out through the chimney pot. The soot fell into the grate and was carried out on to the garden. Dust sheets covered the furniture, for the fine soot got everywhere. Curtains had to be washed and pictures cleaned – it was quite a task when the chimney was swept but better than smoke billowing everywhere.'

BATH NIGHT

'Our bathroom at Betton Abbotts was the washhouse. Hessian sacks were put on the floor and the long tin bath put on these to keep the water warm. The water was then taken from the brick boiler which had a fire underneath to heat the water. As a special treat we sometimes had a bath by the fire, a black lead grate in the front room. This was in a smaller tin bath.'

'Saturday night was bath night, when a large tin bath in front of the kitchen fire was filled with water boiled in large saucepans It was hair-wash night as well, hair put into curlers with strips of cotton material and twisted around the head and left to dry.'

'In 1940 we were living in a hamlet of eight houses in the country. Bath night was once a week. After carrying twelve buckets of water in six journeys, we filled the copper, lit a fire underneath and boiled it up, having an extra bucket of cold water handy. The galvanised bath was pulled out of a cupboard in the corner in front of a lovely glowing fire in the blackleaded grate. We ladled the water from the copper to the bath. A lot of work, but the joy of stepping out in front of a lovely fire with warm towels was wonderful.'

'Our first home in June 1948 was a cottage in Willey. There was no electricity and no running water, just a pump outside which was shared with our next door neighbour. Bath nights involved a tin bath in front of the fire. One night when I was heavily pregnant my husband had a job to get me out! A few months later I had made friends with Kay who lived in half the rectory just across a field from us. She would hang a towel out of her bathroom window to signal that I could come and have a bath if I wanted, so I hung a towel out of our bedroom window and pushed the pram with small daughter over the field to enjoy a full length soak. Heaven.'

'Bathing was usually once a week, in a large zinc bath in front of the fire. Water had to be heated in the copper or the small boiler at the side of the blackleaded grate. All the family used the same water, no happy experience when there were six children (average family size). Menfolk came home from the pit covered in coal-dust, so they needed plenty of water for cleansing purposes. It was not until 1951 that pit-head baths were installed, so we saw no more black faces after that time. We were told about empty oil containers which had been used for the mine and were sold for one shilling and sixpence each to the miners. they were set on fire to burn the oil residue and then sawn in half – one half for a dolly tub and the other half for a bath.

To warm the beds at night a metal plate was taken from the oven and wrapped in a piece of blanket. Fire bricks were also heated in the oven and they too were put in the beds.'

'In the Wistanstow hall was the only bath in the village and you booked it. It cost you sixpence with plenty of hot water.'

OFF TO BED

'In the early years of the century there were usually six or seven children in the houses at St Martins. There were six in ours, three girls and three boys. We slept "top and tail".'

'The bedrooms in our house at Edgton in the 1920s were quite large. Mum and Dad slept in one and two double beds in the other room were for my sister and I and my two brothers. A long curtain divided the room, but my sister and I had the small window on our side. Our bedsteads were black metal, with diamond mesh under the horsehair mattress – very hard. The sheets bought from J.D. Williams, Manchester, were unbleached and came on a roll. They were the colour of sand, but after many washes they became white. These sheets were always turned top to bottom once before being put in the wash. Blankets were grey or brown and Mum would blanket stitch them all round the edges in coloured wool to stop them fraying. Bolsters and pillows were filled with feathers from the geese, ducks, chickens and turkeys, all plucked at Christmas in one of the farm barns. These feathers were dried in the baker's oven to kill any bugs in them. Mum and Dad had a feather bed and eventually we would get one too.

In the very cold weather a hot log from the fire would be put in the warming pan and this was run up and down the bed. As the pan came out we would jump in and wrap our feet up in our flannel nightdress. The boys wore nightshirts. We all wore knitted woolly hats in bed. The oak floors were covered with patterned lino, with rag rugs or coconut matting to get out onto. A chamber pot was under the bed and it had been known to freeze solid in the night – no water was kept in the jug and basin on the washing stand in the winter months.'

'When we moved into Bostock Hall Farm at Whixall in the early 1950s, there was no electric lighting. I was always apprehensive when going up the open wooden stairs to bed, as the flickering light of the candle cast eerie shadows on the walls and on up the attic stairs, which were just outside my bedroom door. No chance of darting to the bathroom at night, just use the chamber pot, then there was no need to leave the room and face the eerie corridor. The timbers had sagged and moved, so that none of the floors in the rooms were level. My parents' room was large and there was a big dip in the middle, and my own room sloped from the window to the door.'

SHOPPING AND CALLERS
TO THE DOOR

Unless you lived very close to the village shops, it was more than likely that your shopping would be an occasional outing to town or village, with most everyday needs being met by tradesmen who delivered to your door. There were other regular callers too, including the gipsies with their pegs and lace.

GOING TO TOWN

'At Longden, the first Monday in every month, Mrs Swire from the Manor would walk down to the village hall. If wet, the chauffeur would drive her down. She was like the bank manager of a clothing club. Practically all the women would go to the hall to pay in a precious half crown which was then banked. At the end of the year they would have the proud sum of £1 12s 6d. Then the next time they went to Shrewsbury, what a great shopping spree was had. Usually they would take the older children with them to help carry home all the goods, mainly consisting of bedding in huge bales. Perhaps if there was half a crown to spare, Mother would buy herself a new hat. The five mile journey to Shrewsbury and back was a rare event on Beattie Hughes' bus, called "This Is It", all for tenpence return.'

'When my mother went to Shrewsbury in the 1920s, she always went to Morris's, the High Class Grocer, for a few extra items of provisions. First to the bacon counter where the slices of ham or bacon would be cut to the thickness she required. At the cheese and butter counter the butter would be weighed on the scales and then shaped with butter pats. If she wanted cheese, she would be given a little taster from whichever large round cheese she asked for. Tea, sugar and dried goods would be served from the provisions counter – each item weighed on the brass scales and packed into bags. The various brands of tea were stored in large tins from which the customer made her choice. While Mother gave her order, she sat on a chair always provided for customers. The bill would be added up, the money put into a container then screwed into a holder on a wire. A handle was pulled and the container with the money whizzed across the shop to the cash desk. In a minute or so the container whizzed back to the counter with the change. All the assistants wore white aprons. Mother would be asked by what train she was going home to Cressage, and lo and behold a boy with the parcel of groceries would be waiting on the platform when she arrived there.'

CALLERS TO YOUR DOOR

'In the early years of the century, the nailers came to Kynnersley from Staffordshire in their caravans, selling nails, buckets, milk pans, bowl dishes and many other wares that they had made. They would also repair goods bought earlier. Gipsies arrived selling lace and pegs and flowers they had made and dyed from thin strips of wood. The bread was delivered round the village in vans drawn by horses, one baker from Newport and one from Wellington. An old man came once a week in a covered cart selling paraffin, dollies and dolly tubs, soaps and Hudson dry soap, wire clothes lines, Robin starch, Monkey brand soap and tins of soft green soap.'

'Every day at Broseley the milkman called morning and night and measured the milk from a churn in the back of his cart. He tipped it into your jug, nearly always giving a "little blessing" – similar to the baker's dozen. Each week the butcher called with a selection of meat in his huge basket and took orders for the weekend joint. Also the grocer called for his order and sent the errand boy on his bicycle with the groceries wrapped in a brown paper parcel. He had already weighed the tea, sugar, dried fruit, flour etc from bins in the shop, and made lovely little blue sugar bags, turned in at the top. None ever filtered out.'

'At Hookagate in the 1920s bread was delivered three times a week by a baker from Annscroft. Nothing was wrapped so Auntie always put a clean cloth on the doorstep with the bread money. She liked cottage loaves and if there was any change the baker put it in the depression on the top of the upper piece of the loaf. Auntie thought this was most unhygienic and scraped the bread well before it was cut.

A pikelet man came on a bicycle and a horse-drawn cart brought fish on a Friday from Mardol Quay. One day our cat stole some fish from the cart. Ice cream also came by horse and cart and coal, at half a crown a bag, was delivered to the cottage gates – the occupants bucketed it to the coal shed. Miners had "home coal" – five hundredweight every ten working days. A man, pushing a barrow, sharpened knives and scissors.'

THE BARTER SYSTEM

'The barter system in country districts was accepted and expected! On a Sunday morning it was our job as children to deliver a half pint of cream to the head gardener on the estate and in exchange we had a fresh cabbage and other vegetables and sometimes a peach – a real treat! A couple of rabbits was a weekly exchange for some wheat for the head gamekeeper's hens – and often a brace of pheasants in the shooting season or a couple of wild duck. You see, my father was the farm bailiff.'

PRICES PAST

'In 1937 when I got married, I had £170 in the bank plus my bottom drawer, which had three of everything. My dining room suite cost £25, my bedroom suite £30 including the bed and we were given a wedding present of glass dishes from the furniture shop. My wedding ring cost 30 shillings and we had a gift of six teaspoons from the jeweller – this seems to have been the custom then.

At the ironmonger's £25 bought a dolly tub, a mangle, three washing bowls, three zinc baths, three enamelled iron cooking saucepans, a jug for drinking water, a bucket, dolly pegs, basins, cups and saucers, a teapot, a broom, an Aladdin lamp with a shade (very posh) and a coal shovel. I wanted one with a wooden handle but Bert Slin, the shop manager, pointed out that the one he advised me to have would last forever, and sure enough he was right!'

'A few prices – bread was fourpence ha'penny a loaf; cheese sixpence per pound; bacon and butter a shilling a pound; dripping sixpence a pound; sugar twopence ha'penny a pound; Sharpe's Creamy Toffees were five for a penny ha'penny) sherbet with a liquorice sucker or a lollipop a penny each; gob-stoppers were five for a penny and aniseed balls twopence per ounce. A grocer was known to break a biscuit in half or split a raisin to get the exact weight.'

THE CLOTHES WE WORE

Only the better off could hope to follow fashion to any extent, most families happy just to have sufficient warm clothing to get them through the year. Clothes were fewer and expected to last, as every child who lived in hand-me-downs could testify.

CLEAN AND TIDY

'We had far fewer clothes than people have nowadays nor were they changed as frequently. It was much easier to tell the status of a child's family by the quality of the clothes than the type, since being clean and tidy was much more important then being pretty or smart.'

'Most shirts were made without collars. Loose collars were starched when washed and ironed when slightly damp and must have been quite a trial to wear. Farm workers didn't wear collars to work but put collars on their (probably grimy) shirts when they dressed up.'

'When I was young there were no "wellies" – I remember that men wore leather boots with gaiters or puttees which were wound round and round the legs, starting at the top of the boot. The puttees had to be dried if they became wet.'

'In the 1940s sheep wool was gathered from barbed wire, washed and dried, then stitched onto cardboard soles for shoes and wellingtons, so our feet were always lovely and warm. All flour came in linen bags and when these were washed and boiled they became pure white. These were made up into babies' frocks and they looked very nice when starched.'

PRETTY DRESSES AND SAILOR SUITS

'I remember women wearing long skirts, leg o'mutton sleeves, blouses with high necks or black velvet ribbon round their necks. My grandmother wore a black bonnet and black shawl out of doors and a white lace cap indoors.'

'All our dresses were made by a dressmaker. We children had very pretty dresses in crepe de chine, voile, satin and other fine fabrics.

Earlier this century, most children were dressed more for warmth than fashion. But here six year old Alice Rickus poses in her best outfit, including muff and button boots.

Our gay little hats were trimmed with artificial daisies, buttercups and violets. We always had new outfits for Easter and the autumn. Sailor suits (complete with whistle) were very popular Sunday wear for boys.'

'In winter my hands were snug inside gloves and a muff. If it was very cold I had a tiny hot water bottle inside the muff. Our boots were buttoned with about twelve small round buttons and had to be fastened with a button hook. But, oh, my knees were often chapped with the cold – no luxury of long stockings. When shoes needed repairing they were taken to a private house but the great disadvantage was that it took a long time to get them back. In the meantime the cobbler's children had been wearing them!'

THE NEW LOOK

'After the war in the 1940s I was demobbed and, back in civvy street, I lashed out and bought the New Look suit, in grey suiting with a short jacket and long, flared skirt. I felt more conspicuous in this than in the ATS uniform. A pretty blue hat with small veil, and handbag, shoes and gloves in black, with a string of pearls and a white blouse, completed the ensemble.'

OUR DAILY FOOD

Even where there was hardship, women provided their large families, and often the farmworkers as well, with rabbit pies and stews, fresh baked bread and cakes, home churned butter and matured cheeses, and fruit and vegetables fresh from the garden or allotment. There are some dishes which we would perhaps not be so ready to try though – such as sparrow pie!

RABBIT FOR DINNER

'We had four weeks holiday in August and I well remember how we used to go in the fields when the grain was cut and run the rabbits. If we were successful and caught some we would take them home very proudly and our mothers would make lovely rabbit stew with them. My mother used to split the head open somehow and cook the brains in the stew and we children would take it in turns to eat them. We also used to have a rota system to have the crust off a lovely brown loaf on Sunday tea times.'

'Mr Bill Wainwright was the rabbit catcher in the surrounding districts of Ash in the 1930s. You would see him off on his rounds on the cold and wintry mornings, well equipped for the job. Most people would know where their next dinner was coming from and sure enough, knock, knock at the door, rabbits a shilling each.'

'Summer holidays from school were never boring in Badger. My cousins came to stay and when we were old enough we would "pick" potatoes for the local farmer for threepence per hour. But what we liked best was the corn harvest, watching the binder going slowly round the field throwing out the sheaves which we stood up in stooks. Eight sheaves to a stook if I remember correctly. The sheaves of corn were later put into stacks to await threshing. Some men stood around the field with shotguns at the ready and as the standing corn got less and less towards the middle the unwary rabbits hiding there ran out and were promptly dispatched. As the sun went down and the stubble became damp with dew we walked home tired but happy; as we were only very young we sometimes had a lift home on the broad backs of the carthorses.

In the 1930s, when money was short, my mother would give me sixpence and tell me to fetch a rabbit from Mr Botley, the local rabbit catcher who lived at Stableford Lodge, Badger. We used to have roast rabbit, stewed rabbit with lots of onions, rabbit pie and even fried rabbit if it was young and tender enough. This was the equivalent of chicken today but we had chicken only at Christmas when we feasted on a cockerel specially fed for the occasion, or sometimes we had boiled fowl – an old boiler – when one of our laying hens became too old to produce eggs. All these dishes tasted delicious as my mother was a very good cook.'

GRANNY'S PANTRY

'To me, part of my granny was her pantry – it was a world all of its own, clean, cold and whitewashed. Before her marriage granny had been an assistant cook in a country gentleman's house, and she knew all the tricks of her trade. She had brandy snaps, fig biscuits and other delicacies, and there was a distinctive smell about her pantry. It was a smell impossible to describe, of old wood and spices, intermingled with a cold, damp smell of seasoning cheese and impregnated with a thousand home-cooked dinners. My granny had a butter churn and made her own farm butter, sometimes cheese as well. She knew how to deal with anything her sons might bring home from a shooting expedition – pheasant, partridge, hare or rabbit, and she had the gift of making them into the most delicious dishes. I used to love to look at the cooking utensils arrayed on the lower shelves of the pantry – great big earthenware mixing bowls, jugs of all shapes and sizes, a great big black jam pot (happy recollections of sickly damson jam scraping sessions), and all sorts of oddly shaped pots, pans and womanly tools. There were meat plates – enormous ones – with unusual patterns. I particularly remember a beautifully proud peacock design which used to intrigue me. I also remember my granny's treasured best china rose-patterned tea-set, kept for special occasions, which I was scared to death of breaking.'

EVERYDAY FARE

'I remember eating something called Browis for supper when I was small in the 1910s. It was a mixture of bread, salt, pepper and dripping, mixed with hot water.'

'A sheep's head simmered till the meat fell from the bones; this was a cheap meal in the 1920s, often as little as fourpence.'

'In the 1920s at Kynnersley we ate rook pie and also sparrow pie. At night with a torch we used to run a riddle down a stack and get about a dozen sparrows each time. Only the breasts and legs were used. Lovely.

I would be sent to my dad in the field with bacon and egg and bread for his breakfast. We made a fire and cooked the bacon on a stick and the eggs in a shovel.'

'We did not have much meat. Mum and Dad had what little they could afford and we children had plenty of vegetables and gravy. Potatoes and buttermilk made a regular meal for us. Most people had good sized gardens of vegetables and fruit trees. The fruit was picked but few people had enough money to buy enough sugar to make jam, so they would stew the fruit and seal it down in earthenware jars and cover it with mutton fat. It would last well into the next year and there was always something for puddings.'

'I have seen my father coming home with a bucket of broth from the farm where he worked. Probably the farmer's wife had been boiling a lump of beef. A man with a hungry family would be very grateful for it. Those who had, gave to those who had not.'

'Farmhouse days were long and busy, threshing days especially. The huge steam engines came and at least twelve men had to be fed. They had bait at eleven o'clock, cold boiled bacon and cheese, cider or beer. Then lunch, which could be a piece of boiled beef, swede or parsnip mashed with cream and pepper (that was my job) and onion sauce, followed by jam roll boiled in a cloth – these were all boiled in the same pot, the onions in a net; or it might be two fowls and fat bacon, parsley sauce and lashings of potatoes, followed by apple pie.

In the afternoon tea was taken to the men in the stackyard, and in the evening they came for a cold meal of boiled bacon, cheese and jam tart.

There would be three men with the machine and thrashing box, several from neighbouring farms, and the usual gang who followed the machine from farm to farm, some of them sleeping rough.'

'My mother was excellent at making a small amount of meat go a long way, hence a shoulder of lamb would provide Sunday and Monday lunch and a shepherd's pie on Tuesday, similarly a large joint of brisket. We could never afford the best joints, except when we killed our own animals. My mother was also the chief gardener. She did not buy any vegetables at all because she always had something in the garden or salted beans (ugh!) to fall back on. Damsons, plums, gooseberries, rhubarb and raspberries were all bottled or made into jam, as were blackcurrants, blackberries and even pumpkins. Nothing was wasted. After all, where else would you bury the waste from the little house at the bottom of the garden but in the compost heap.'

MUSHROOMS AND DAMSONS

'The gathering of mushrooms was an event. If we wanted to get any we had to be up at crack of dawn or else there would be someone else there before us. We always tried to get them on market day at Market Drayton, ie Wednesday, so that they could be sold to people who would then take them either to the Potteries or Manchester. We must have eaten a lot of mushrooms when they were in season and I particularly remember them being cooked in milk with a little butter and seasoning and then thickened. Another great event was damson picking time. These also used to be taken to the market at Market Drayton, and were sold by the measure, ie 90 lbs.'

'In September every year at Bomere Heath we were all madly picking damsons. We had 22 trees in our garden in those days and we were paid £1 a pot, which was 90 lbs. I remember being at the top of a ladder in 1940 and seeing a wing fall off a Spitfire plane which crashed on the outskirts of the village. I came down my ladder very hurriedly!'

BUTTER AND CHEESE

'We used to milk by hand, morning and night, at our farm in the All Stretton area. In the summer when the milk was plentiful we made cheese but in the winter when there was less milk we made butter. In the early days the milk was put into large wide pans and left for the cream to set; this was skimmed off the next day, put into a stein and churned once or twice a week. Later we had a separator, a very complicated but efficient affair. Cream that was separated made much nicer butter. Our cheese was bought by a cheese factor from the North who came about once a month. On the day of departure the cheese was weighed then loaded onto the float, taken to the local station, put onto the train and transported to Manchester. During the depression after the First World War, we had difficulty selling the cheese and the lowest price we got was fourpence a pound.'

'Butter making was a regular chore, usually once a week. Cream was removed from milk by a hand-operated separator each day, and collected in a large shallow container. When "ripe", which meant soured, the cream was churned in a large "end over end" or barrel churn until the curds of butter formed. Cold water was then added and the churn turned slowly until the curds "gathered" and separated from the butter milk, which was drained away and most fed to the pigs. A little was retained as a healthy drink excellent for clearing milk in mixing scones and pancakes. The butter was washed very thoroughly by the addition of several bowls of cold water before being lifted from the churn and "worked" with a pair of Scots hands on either the upturned lid of the churn (if the quantity was small), otherwise on the wooden tabletop, scrubbed scrupulously beforehand. Salt was added, to taste, the butter "worked" again and then weighed into suitable quantities, usually half pound or one pound and made up into brick-like shapes. These were decorated either with the hands or wooden butter prints which were pressed onto the surface of the block – or on a basin if the butter had been packed into one.'

'The cheese instructor came to Harmer Hill from Shrewsbury to teach a small class of girls cheesemaking; they had to be there for 7.30am and they stayed until the cheese was made – about midday.

The milk from the previous night and the morning was placed in a large vat, beneath which was a bath of hot water. The water had previously been heated in the copper and was bailed out by bucket into the bath.

The vat contained 200 gallons of milk, which was stirred until it reached the right temperature – about blood heat – when the "starter" was added. (The starter consisted of about half a pint of curdled milk and rennet.) When the mixture had thickened the water was drained off from the bath and returned to the copper for further use, ie washing dairy utensils.

When the milk was set like a jelly, it was cut with a special tenblade knife to release the whey, which floated up to the top, while the curds sank to the bottom of the vat. A sieve was then placed in front of the tap at the bottom of the vat and the whey drained out. The curds were gathered up into a cheese cloth about a yard and a half square and then placed on a wooden rack inside the vat for further drainage. An instrument was inserted into the curd to test the acidity (it had to turn green); then it was processed through a curd mill, having been weighed and salted. The curds were then placed in circular moulds, which were lined with cheesecloth and left to drain overnight.

Next day, they were removed from the moulds, wrapped in a clean cloth and placed under a cheese press, where they remained for two or three days. Afterwards, the cheeses were removed from the press, bound with a special calico and stored for several weeks in the cheese room, being turned regularly on alternate days.

The cheeses were sold at the monthly local cheese fair at Wem or Whitchurch. Cheese factors visited the markets and sampled the cheeses. In 1933 the price of cheese had dropped to fourpence ha'penny per lb and it was impossible to make a living from cheese-making. Fortunately a milk retailer from Wolverhampton bought the entire milk production of several farmers, paying them one shilling and sixpence per gallon on condition that they transported it to Yorton station.'

ICE CREAM

'In 1921 my father opened a greengrocer's shop at Pontesbury. I remember Canary bananas came in tall crates, they were wrapped in something like cottonwool to keep them warm and we had to be very careful how we opened them in case there were any foreign spiders or other creatures in hiding.

When in business mother made ice cream. Ice was bought by the hundredweight from the ice factory at Meole Brace; to stop it from melting it was covered with lots of sacks until we were ready to use it. The custard was made using fresh milk and a special custard powder, cooled then put into the ice cream container. The container was then placed into a special ice cream bucket which had a lid with beaters attached and a handle at the side. When the lid was closed, ice and salt was packed between container and bucket. The handle was then turned very, very quickly for about ten minutes which activated the beaters. After ten minutes, when the ice cream began to thicken (and how our arms ached), the handle became harder to turn. The whole process took about half an hour and this would produce about a gallon of ice cream. It sold very quickly, we just could not make enough of it.'

KILLING THE PIG

The pig was the mainstay of many a cottager's diet and the keeping of a pig was commonplace in country areas till after the Second World War. Everything could be used but the squeal, it was said, but the actual killing of the pig was dreaded by many who had grown fond of the animal over the preceding months. Yet, as one woman remembers, "I couldna' bear the squealing but I didna' mind the pork pies and the scratchings."

A GREAT DAY

'When I was a girl in the 1910s at New Dale, my mother and dad always kept a couple of pigs in the sty. I can remember it was always a great occasion when they went to the auction at Wellington (which was always held on a Monday) to buy these pigs. They always used to dress in their best clothes for this event. They would drive these pigs home from Wellington back to New Dale; they would come across the Mill Fields, turn by the Bucks Head and up the lane through Arleston, and sometimes it would be seven or eight o'clock before they got back. They always enjoyed auction day because that meant that they could have a pint in the pub at Wellington before they returned.

We always kept one of the pigs for meat for the house and the other we sent to the butcher. The butcher would collect his pig and the following day my mother would go down to the slaughterhouse at Wellington to see the pig after it had been killed. I always remember my mother going down to the slaughterhouse to see the pig which she had sent to the butcher. The butcher took her to see her pig hanging up and she right away said "That's not my pig". He said it was, and there was quite a conflab about it. She said "I will show you my pig, and I'll fetch the police if you don't pay me the money for the right one." She knew which was hers because she had put a small pin in the pig's tail.

Pig killing day was a great day. My mother had to be up early and get the water heated up in the boiler in the washhouse. There was only one man in the village who had a cooler, and if somebody else wanted it we could not have the pig killed that day. Everywhere had to be spotlessly clean around the house and washhouse, and then so many bottles of beer would be put out for the helpers. As soon as the pig was killed the liver and the lights were taken out and these were put on plates, and it was my job to take these plates with the liver on to some of the near neighbours. On no account must they wash the plates before sending them back as it was considered bad luck to do so: this was the custom in New Dale and all the neighbours who had

Up to and beyond the Second World War most cottages kept a pig which provided them with meat all year round. Everything was used except the squeak!

a pig killed carried out this custom. Of course a big block of salt was always kept handy so that they could salt the bacon and hams. I remember that when we used to go to bed at night we had to squeeze past the pig hanging up in the kitchen.'

'Until just after the Second World War many people in Ashford Carbonell kept a pig. This was fed on scraps from the house and garden; these being boiled had some barley meal added and were made into a sloppy mash which the pig found very palatable, judging by the noise it made and the speed with which it lapped it up. When the pig grew to the desired weight, George, the pig-sticker, was sent for. A handsome man with rosy cheeks, white hair and moustache, he arrived on a motorbike. The pig had to be killed, its squeals were piteous but the deed had to be done and George did it quickly and skilfully.

When the pig was dead the bristles had to be singed off. It was then hung up and cut open. The entrails were cleansed in several changes of water and later used as the skins of sausages and white and black puddings. Surplus fat was rendered down and sometimes flavoured with rosemary to make rosemary lard, delicious on toast. Before the war there was a lady butcher in Bridgnorth who sold this lard. The legs were severed to become joints of pork, or salted down in brine, saltpetre and brown sugar to make hams. The sides were cured to become bacon. The flitches of bacon were laid on cratches suspended from the ceilings of larder or kitchen. Slices of bacon were cut off as needed, delicious to taste and smell, unlike the insipid modern bacon which quickly becomes rancid.

The timing of the killing of the pigs in the village was staggered (no refrigeration then) and as each pig was killed the owners sent presents of sausages or joints of meat to friends, so for several months there was a supply of fresh meat going round the village.'

'Pork was diced for pork pies and scraps of pork meat were diced for the sausages. Fat, groats and blood was stirred together for the black puddings. The tongue was pickled and pressed. The lower jaw and cheek meat was salted and cooked, making the "chawl" and the "chaps", as lovely sweet if fatty meat, delicious when boiled and eaten cold with pickles.

Liver and pork meat together with herbs and spices and fat was mixed together and rolled into tennis ball sized rounds and individually wrapped in the lacy veil of fat. These we called "savoury ducks" or faggots and every housewife had her own variation on these recipes. The feet were boiled and became the trotters, leaving the clear gelatine broth that was later to be poured into the chunky meat pies with their hand-raised hot water crust pastry. Brawn was made from meat from the head and was seasoned well with pepper and pressed into basins and covered with a layer of fat. The hams were salted and rubbed with brown sugar to give a delicious sweet-cure. After the arduous salting was completed, the hams and sides of bacon were well wrapped in fly-proof material sacks and hung up on the many hooks around the kitchen. Sometimes an odd fly would get in, the maggots being seen dropping out of the covering onto the kitchen floor. The bacon or ham wasn't discarded. The affected piece was cut out and thrown away. But the rest was eaten. Sometimes the hams and bacon were stored in a wooden box which was filled with sawdust.'

'One day the local pigkiller was just about to sit down to a meal when a man came to his door. "Come quick," he said, "the pig is dying." If the pig had died of some illness it would be a heavy loss to the family. When he came back later and his wife put his meal in front of him, she asked him what had happened. "I arrived in time to save his life," he said, winking at his wife.

Another old lady was quite fond of her pig, who she called Percy. When the time came to fetch him out of the sty she said to the butcher, "You wunna hurt him, wun you?" That was what I call being optimistic.'

'In the early years of the century around Bettys-y-Crwyn, when the farmworkers killed a pig they would throw the pig's eye to stick to the ceiling so as to have good luck through the year.'

CIDER AND HOME BREW

Home-made wines, home-brewed beer and home-pressed cider were welcome additions to the diet and offerings to visitors and workers. Most of the ingredients were to hand in the hedgerows and gardens, free of charge.

CIDER MAKING

'At one of the pubs in Alveley it was common for the publican to take the equipment round to farms or bigger cottages with orchards, and make the apples and pears into cider on the premises.'

'Cider making in the 1930s and 1940 was an exciting time for us on the farm at Willey. The cider apples which were shaken from the trees about mid October after corn harvest had been finished, were picked off the ground into sacks and stacked together ready for the coming of the cidermill, which was brought by horses. The cidermill was an odd looking contraption about two yards square which was placed on level ground close to the apples.

The apples were then placed on squares of coconut matting, about four hundredweight on each, which were layered up to about five layers. Water waas added and then the cider press was screwed down to squash the apples and cider began to run. Everyone had to taste the first pressing!

The juice was taken to the cellar in buckets, put in big 50 gallon barrels then left to mature until May or June the following year. Most of the cider was drunk in the harvest field, taken out to the workers in lovely old stone gallon bottles. Sometimes the cider tasted like vinegar; it seemed every barrel was different, but on a hot day working in the fields it was pure nectar.'

HOME BREWED BEER AND WINE

'As a child in the 1920s I lived at the bottom of the wood from Lyth Hill. Mum brewed some very good beer, made in the traditional way with malt, hops and sugar. The strongest beer was saved for the grown-ups and, I might say, we had quite a few visitors when we had beer! We children were allowed to have a small beer, which we used to drink with bread and cheese. Very good too!'

'My mother's hobby, in our home at the Wrens Nest, Bishops Castle, was wine making and she made varieties – mangold, parsnip, blackcurrant, beetroot, orange, elderberry and elderflower, wheat, gooseberry, blackberry and dandelion, to name but a few. She also made herb beer with nettles and dandelion flowers. She held an exemption from the local police allowing her to brew beer. At Christmas time the carol singers always called and some left as drunk as a fiddle.'

'Dad used to brew his own beer in an outside boiler at our farm opposite the then Buildwas station. The grain was thrown out to the poultry who found it a treat, but staggered about after eating it looking very comical. The beer was taken to the hayfield in a large stone bottle with basketwork all round it; believe me, it was quite a feat to drink from one of these.

Wine was made from damsons and cowslips. The heads of the cowslips were picked and then the blossoms were picked off one by one and measured by the pint. It takes an awful lot to make one pint. Each year cowslips seemed to grow more widely in the fields.'

'Gallons of home-made wine was made around Morda, also herb beer which was sold at the door of many cottages. I remember seeing a notice on the gate at one cottage which read: "Herb beer sold here 2d a bottle 1d a glass."

There were two old men who walked to the Drill Inn every evening for a pint of beer, the one fastened a lamp to the front of his coat to see his way home, and the other on a wet and windy evening stayed at home by the fire and sent his wife to fetch his beer in a tin can.'

'One year my mother made some apple wine which would not be ready till the following summer.

On a hot day early in July my father was cutting hay with two horses drawing the mower. At midday my mother walked up with his lunch in a basket and a quart bottle of the wine, which she thought to be equivalent to home-made cider.

My father, sitting on the fresh-mown grass, drank the whole bottle with his lunch. He dozed off and woke with a splitting headache to hear Broseley church clock strike four and to see the horses, which had wandered to the top of the field with the mower still attached, munching the freshly cut grass.'

'We used to brew our own beer at home in New Dale and I remember when my Dad came home from the forge there was always a little barrel of beer on a stool in the kitchen with a mug by the side of it for him to have a drink. When our home-brewed ran out at home my mother used to send me down to the outdoor licence by the chapel in New Street Wellington for a pint and a half of beer in a quart bottle. On this bottle they used to place a red seal of wax on the cork so that we children could not take a swig out of the bottle on the way home.'

'Our wine was mostly drunk when very new and had little alcohol content, but a few bottles of the better vintage were sometimes laid aside for keeping. One of the stronger brews was mangold and after two or three years was as strong as whisky but the drinker did not realise this immediately. One summer's night, the farmer John, his farmer friend Charlie and my father ended a busy evening by

100

enjoying some bottles of matured mangold wine. At dusk my father took his pals across the river in the boat. On the other side John got out, and both he and Charlie were commenting – you can imagine it – "Grand evening, Harry"; "Drop of good wine that, Harry"; "Thanks, Harry" as John climbed the bank for home. Unfortunately, Charlie had got out on the wrong side of the boat and was walking steadily, up to his knees, towards the centre of the river, and it was with some difficulty that he was persuaded of his error.'

WHISKY AND BEER

'I remember lambing time when our shepherd at Condover would have a fire in the saddle room where he spent many hours. Some evenings he would sit in the kitchen with Lucy, the maid and we loved to go and listen to his tales which were often frightening, he had a firm belief in ghosts! Then we were sent to bed and upstairs in the candlelight; it looked very creepy.

His remedy for a starved lamb was warm milk flavoured with whisky and many a little lamb wobbled about in a drunken daze, but they survived! My father had to keep a firm control on the amount of whisky allowed.

Tractors had not yet arrived and two waggoners had three shire horses each and there were two more for use for odd jobs. They took great pride in the horses and when harvest was over and the barley thrashed they took it on drays to Wem Brewery for malting to produce the famous Wem Ale. The day before, after work they spent a lot of time grooming the horses and polishing the brasses which they attached to the harness, each trying to have the best turned out and they looked very smart as they set out in the morning. After delivering their loads, it seemed only right that they should sample the famous ale and sometimes it took them a long time to return home, but as long as they returned safely my father did not object.'

FROM THE CRADLE
TO THE GRAVE

At one time you would more than likely be born in your own home, endure illness and even minor operations there, and finally die there and lie in state before leaving on that final journey to the churchyard – perhaps with the local community paying their last respects and the church bell tolling mournfully as the procession wended its way through the town or village. The funeral was saved for over several years to ensure that the dead did not have to suffer a pauper's lonely fate.

GETTING WED

'Marriages were not such grand affairs as they are today. They walked to the church and afterwards had a family celebration at home. Plenty of beer would be drunk – they would have had a special brewing, and there would be a sing-song. It was very rare they went on a honeymoon, they just went to their new home.'

'My marriage in All Stretton in 1936 was a quiet but happy affair in our local church, where I had been christened. A little old lady from the village made tiny posies of primroses and violets to strew down the church path instead of confetti. The church had only been licensed for marriages shortly before we were married; it was done for the wedding of our local doctor's daughter. As was the fashion, we had a party at home and our dairy was large enough to put up trestle tables to accommodate us all.'

INTO THE WORLD

'There were few if any babies born in hospital in the early 1900s. Every village had a woman who would come to the delivery, though she had to be booked in advance. With plenty of hot water, and more than a little experience, they would give support and encouragement to bring about a safe delivery. These women were the salt of the earth, because doctors had to be paid for and families were poor in those days. The District Nurse would look to mother and baby after the birth, but it was the "women" who were important in every district.

102

Giving birth seems to have been the only time women could rest in bed, usually for ten days. They believed the more rest they had, the better the milk supply for the child. It was unheard of for a mother to go out after a birth until she had been churched. This practice still went on in the 1950s.

When babies were born they were dressed in long clothes, with long petticoats and gowns, as well as matinee coats. It was usual too, for them to be bound around the middle with a binder to ensure that their tummies wouldn't stick out where the umbilical cord had been cut.

The eldest child would be kept from school to housekeep while mother was in bed, and was expected to do the housework, cook the meals and look after the other children. Sometimes, if grandmother lived locally, she would come in each day; it was unusual for farm-workers to have people to stay, since with big families there simply wasn't room, the children often sleeping top and bottom of the bed.'

'We had a midwife at Rushbury who used to cycle to her mothers-to-be on a three wheel tricycle with her little black bag tied at the back – with the new baby in, we were told.'

'In the 1910s my mother went round on her bicycle to collect subscriptions for the Adderley & Norton in Hales Nursing Association. Two shillings twice a year entitled the subscribers to have the nurse when they had a baby.'

'My brother was premature. He was born at home arriving at about the same time as the midwife. Fully clothed in a long thick night-gown, nappie etc he weighed exactly one and a half pounds. He had no nails and parts of his skin were like raw beef. Mum could not feed him. The doctor's comment when he saw him was that he would not live. Nothing would stay down. They kept saying water the milk down because it was too strong, until he was just about surviving on boiled water.

One day, an old gipsy came to the door and told Mam she would lose him if she did not do something. Mam said she did not know what to do. The gipsy said "Give him some linseed". Being desperate, Mam tried it, putting a spoonful of the jelly-like stuff in his bottle. He never looked back. He slept and thrived. Nowadays, an incubator would have been essential.'

'A lady who lived in the neighbourhood acted as midwife. After the baby was born she acted as housekeeper, looking after mother and baby and the rest of the family and living in for about a fortnight.'

'I trained as a nurse and midwife from 1948. Pre-war conditions were still prevalent but were slowly beginning to improve. Most babies pre 1950 had been home deliveries, but now things began to change. Mothers were encouraged to have their first babies in hospital. Second, third and fourth babies, barring abnormalities, to be delivered at home, and subsequent babies again to be delivered in hospital.

Working as a pupil midwife at a time when cars were still a rarity, I cycled to all my cases, night and day, with my bag on the carrier of my bike.

One of my patients lived in a very small cottage, one of a row of farm labourers' cottages. A very small room was the main living room downstairs, the height, length and breadth miniscule and dominated by a large kitchen range. Through a small doorway into a small scullery and up eight steps were two even smaller bedrooms, with a curtain in place of a door. The only water supply was a tap and water butt in the yard. The toilet was the inevitable privy midden at the bottom of the very large garden. It was in these conditions that I delivered this woman's sixth child. She was a very happy woman with five very happy and well adjusted children. She demanded little of life, only that her family would be happy. She had the support of a loving husband who, when not working as a farm labourer, spend his time growing vegetables and looking after two pigs and a few chickens.

Whilst not recommending these conditions, she did teach me one salutary lesson in humility. She was one of the happiest people I ever met and of all the patients I subsequently encountered, I remember her with great affection.'

DOCTORS AND NURSES

'If one needed to go to the doctor in the 1920s, well it was a mile walk from East Wall to catch the 8.15 train at Longville station to Much Wenlock, then a walk down to the doctor's surgery. Then there was the return trip, getting home about midday and by then you either felt better or a lot worse. When I was small the doctor did have a car, but when my mother lived at Oakwood Farm the doctor came from Much Wenlock on horseback, about seven miles.'

'We rarely saw a doctor except when accidents happened. Both a sister and a brother had fingers cut in the chaffcutter but they healed amazingly well. I often heard the story of how my brother, then aged about two years, had his leg gashed by a spade wielded by another brother. He was carried across several fields to a farm where the doctor was attending someone, was laid on the settee and had his little leg stitched up with horsehair because there was nothing else available.'

'Alf Hughes was sexton of St Barnabus church, Hengoed in the 1920s and he lost an eye. He ran a bag needle into it whilst mending a sack. He was rushed to the doctor; when I say "rushed", he was probably taken in a horse and cart travelling at about ten or twelve mph. He was strapped in a chair, the doctor heated a silver hammer over a flame and put it on his eye. Alf said, "I prayed to die there and then". The doctor said, "What's the matter with you? You'd cry to have your hair cut next." No medical science. No anaesthetic. No nothing!'

'Coming as a doctor to a village in the country in 1947, I found life so interesting after living in a city. The community was self sufficient and there was always time to chat and someone to chat to when shopping or collecting water at the village pump.

Farmers and farmworkers related the survival of their infants to their knowledge of animals and often spoke with relief when the child was more than a year, saying "We've reared him (or her)". A common saying when patients were feeling better was: "I'm a king to what I was last week."

Medicine bottles were graduated and patients would put their thumb on the mark and take a good dose before leaving the surgery. Babies were delivered at home and the doctor would give chloroform from a dropper bottle and use forceps for a difficult birth.

A country doctor was often asked to extract teeth and also to pierce ears – men could not always be bothered to make them level. Patients were not afraid to phone the doctor. On one occasion I was called out at two o'clock in the morning and had to walk over two fields, to be met at the door by the patient's daughter who said, "Please don't tell Dad we sent for you, just say you were passing and looked in to see how he was doing."

Doctors held surgery Saturday evening and Sunday morning.'

'My father was an ambulance man in the early years of the century at Annscroft. Anyone who hurt themselves in any way came to him to be bandaged up. He went with the St John Ambulance party from Shropshire for duty at the British Empire Exhibition in London in 1924.

During the First World War there was a serious accident at the Moat Hall pit. A fall of coal buried a Hookagate miner and he was killed. My father had to go and break the sad news to his wife in Hookagate. As he arrived at her cottage gate she came out and said,

"You needn't tell me, Ern, he's dead. After he went through the gate this morning he came back and kissed me again. He put his arms around me and said, "Ta ta chuck" and he never done that before." '

'My aunt was a District Nurse on Clee Hill and had many horrific tales to tell of walking at night in the middle of winter over the common to isolated houses, usually to deliver a baby.

Most of her visits entailed walking for long distances, but she used a bicycle whenever possible. The Nursing Association decided she should have a quicker form of transport and bought a "Ner-a-Car" for her; this was a glorified motor cycle with huge leg guards. She did manage to use it sometimes, but it was so heavy that she could scarcely hold it up.'

'Few people could afford a doctor but the village District Nurse attended births, illness and laid out the dead. Before the days of the National Health Service she would have a Lady Superintendent, unpaid, who would check her records and expenditure and be responsible for raising funds for the nurse's support. Dances and concerts etc would be held. The village nurses were very highly thought of and all fund-raising activities were well supported. In the event of heavy snow everyone turned out with shovels to get the nurse through to her patient.'

'If one works as a nurse in a very rural area as I did, superstitions are part of the everyday life of every family, and affect the work of parson, doctor and nurse.

Perhaps the funniest was during the Foot and Mouth epidemic, very severe in this part of Shropshire, and farmers were terrified of the infection being brought on to their land. A large bath of disinfectant stood by every gate and gumbooted feet were well washed in it before passing through. One farm had no such bath, it was isolated too, and when asking why no precaution, the doctor was told: "Well, we're not worried, you and the vet are sterilized"!

More mundane superstitions were that one must not put the left shoe on before the right (the devil's, perhaps). And the new baby must go up before it goes down (stairs) so the nurse must stand on a chair, baby in arms, before descending to the kitchen.

The most bizarre was almost biblical in its idea and though it wasn't talked about I was surprised at its widespread secrecy. It was that a pig must not be killed if the farmer's wife was menstruating. This was not about consideration for the farm-wife *but* that if she as much as touched the pig whilst in that condition the meat would immediately turn bad. So this lent a new meaning to Farmer Giles asking his wife if it would be suitable for the butcher to come to do the job a week come Wednesday. But the mind boggled at the ancient lady who showed me a rather sick-and-sorry pork pie, the morning after the WI demonstration. "It was the demonstrator's fault," she said. "She turned it bad for it was her monthly". I've heard some excuses but this one rendered me speechless.'

GOING TO HOSPITAL

'When I was about eight years old at Rodington in the 1920s my tonsils were removed at the Ear, Nose and Throat Hospital in Shrewsbury. Was it a dream or did the porter (with a rubber mac over his shoulders) really carry me from the theatre to my bed on his back? It was certainly true that Mr John Morris took me home in the sidecar of his bicycle.'

'The first orthopaedic hospital in the world was begun in Baschurch. Dame Agnes Hunt, from Boreatton, started it in 1900 as a home for cripples. She devoted her whole life to this cause.

At first, any operations were performed in Liverpool; patients were taken on the morning train and returned to Baschurch at night. My aunt had toes amputated and returned on a spinal carriage in the guard's van. She began to get cold and Dame Agnes took off her fur coat and wrapped my aunt in it.

Patients used to sleep in huts which had three sides and with the front open, whatever the weather. The patients had waterproof covers over the beds and a stone hot water bottle to help keep them warm. The villagers of Baschurch helped support the hospital and lots of fund raising went on. The home moved to Gobowen in 1920 as the Robert Jones and Agnes Hunt Hospital.'

'My father broke his leg very badly in 1941 and he spent two and a half years getting it put right, most of that time at Park Hall. It was the coldest place on earth to visit. All the sides of the wards were open. Fresh air and good food were the main treatment. There were shutters, but only in very bad weather were they used. The patients had large metal heaters in the bed to keep warm.

Having my own tonsils out in 1941 was an experience. In the children's ward at the Eye, Ear and Throat Hospital, we were all dressed in gowns, thick woolly socks and a rubber hat and were taken up in the lift to the room next to the theatre to wait.

We sat on a wooden bench (three of us). The door opened and out came a man with a bloodstained gown. He washed his hands, changed his gown and back he went together with the next child. Inside, we were given a leg up onto the table and our face covered with a mask. Thankfully, the next thing we knew was waking up in the ward.

We were sent home the next day. After a long wait for a train to Wem and a four mile ride on a bike home, I was glad to get into bed.'

MUTUAL HELP

'The Ancient Order of the Foresters was the working man's bit of security in Longden in the 1920s. If you fell ill at the mines there were no wages, but the Foresters did give a few shillings to help feed the

Longden & Pulverbatch Friendly Societies.

THE TWENTY-THIRD

ANNUAL PARADE

FOR HOSPITALS,

WILL TAKE PLACE AT

PULVERBATCH,

On Sunday, 3rd August, 1941

The Procession will be formed at 5-30 p.m. at the WOODCOCK INN.

LONGDEN BAND

Will be in attendance.

OPEN AIR SERVICE

On the Historic Mound, "The Round Nap," at 6-30 p.m., conducted by the

Rev. OLIVER G. CROCKETT

(RECTOR)

ADDRESSES will be given by

Admiral SIR JAMES STARTIN, K.C.B., A.M., J.P.

and

Mr. FRYER (of the Royal Salop Infirmary).

(If Wet, in Church).

HOUSE TO HOUSE COLLECTIONS

Will be made by the Members in the Societies' Area.

The Hospitals need your kind assistance!

GOD SAVE THE KING.

LIVESEY, LTD., PRINTERS.

Before the introduction of the National Health Service in 1947, local hospitals were supported by fund raising events like this one at Castle Pulverbatch.

children. During the 1926 strike the miners' children were given a free dinner every school day in the parish hall. And they call them the good old days.'

'There were two charity concerts at different times in the village hall at Morda, both to help men go to London hospitals for treatment. Both men recovered and lived for many years. We paid threepence a week to cover the family if any one of us had to go to hospital in Oswestry or Shrewsbury, and another threepence was paid so that the District Nurse would visit us. To be ill was terrible as the doctor's bill was a dreaded thing. The farmworkers belonged to clubs and paid threepence a week in case of illness. The sick benefit was 18 shillings per week for the first year, eleven shillings for the following year. There was £3 allowed for funeral expenses. It was a hard, hard world. Thank God for the National Health Service.'

'Hospital Sunday was a special Sunday held annually in August up to 1945, concerned with fund raising for the Shrewsbury hospitals. A service was held at Castle Pulverbatch on The Knapp, the site of an 11th century motte and bailey castle. The Knapp is 750ft above sea level; the gathering took place on the west side of the site where there is a plateau.

Hospital Sunday was organised by the Friendly Societies of Pulverbatch and Longden: the Oddfellows of Pulverbatch and the Ancient Order of Foresters of Longden. The first service was held in August 1919. Every year Hospital Sunday was preceeded by house-to-house collections in both parishes, with the final collection at the service on The Knapp.

Until 1948, when the NHS came into being, the Highley and District Nursing Association existed to serve the community in time of sickness. It was run by a voluntary committee, whose members collected weekly subscriptions from those households who wished to contribute. People paid what they could afford, sometimes as little as threepence, but usually sixpence or a shilling. The money raised would pay for the services of the District Nurse who would attend nearly all confinements and do general nursing. She worked closely with the local GP.

Fund raising for the Association was held regularly; for instance a local publican gave a silver cup to be competed for annually for football teams in the district.

The GP dispensed his own medicines for private patients (until 1948) while the local chemist dealt with prescriptions for the panel patients. He is best remembered for always being short of supplies which "would be coming tomorrow". The poor of the parish were entitled to parish relief – again until 1948 – this qualified them for free visits and free medicines from the doctor, who himself was paid five shillings a year for each "Relief" patient, by the authorities.

Miners contributed cash to Bridgnorth Infirmary and also organised raffles, dances and whilst drives in aid of Kidderminster Hospital. In return, vouchers were given to patients who would then be able to have free treatment should the need arise.

A committee of local women ran the Child Welfare Committee, and sessions were held in the old Assembly Rooms to hand out the Ostermilk, the Farley's rusks, orange juice and rosehip syrup. A doctor appointed by the County Council dealt with inoculations and vaccinations against smallpox, which was then compulsory.'

FEARFUL DISEASES

'During the spring of 1919 there was a series epidemic of diphtheria and scarlet fever. About ten children died from it, three in one family, and the school at Cruckmeole was closed for several weeks. This was followed by the flu and about 20 adults died from this. My father was very ill with it but fortunately got over it.'

'In 1938 we had an epidemic of diphtheria in Acton Burnell. My mother caught it, but because she had four children the doctor decided to let her stay at home. Our home was officially isolated, meaning no-one could visit and we had to stay put. No relatives or friends were allowed in and we children nursed my mother as best we could.

The local squire's wife from the Hall brought a basket of food every day, soup for the patient and good food for us. I remember one day, we lifted up a whole rabbit from the pot. It was no doubt boiled to perfection but we couldn't eat it. We had never before seen a rabbit cooked like that, only disjointed and roasted in lovely gravy. I can see that rabbit even now.

The basket was in the early days left on the wall by the gate but later was brought into the house. This good lady was a friend to my mother and started to paint the patient's throat with iodine. For this she used a long paintbrush. We children watched in wonder as the paintbrush went into Mother's mouth and down her throat. It must have been dreadful for her.

We did not get diphtheria, but were away from school for five months. We could not go until Mother was clear of the disease. In the end she resorted to smoking Craven A cigarettes and swallowing the smoke, as directed by someone! This caused lots of fun for us as she puffed and choked away. And it did kill off the germs, for after a few weeks she was pronounced free to leave the house.'

'The fear of disease is another memory. My mother talked about scarlet fever. Grandma hung sheets dipped in disinfectant over the bedroom doors and a double sheet over the door between the house and their shop. She was the only person who saw to the children who were ill. They were kept in one room isolated from the others. In this way, they kept the business going. Otherwise, it would have had to close, or the children go to the fever hospital.

At the peace celebration for the 1914–18 war, my mother's cousin, an eleven year old boy, picked up diphtheria. Another child the same age had had it and he went to the party before he was clear. Being friends, they spent the day together. Jack died.

On arriving at the church for his funeral, his mother and father were heart-broken because the vicar refused to let the coffin come into church and conducted the ceremony a distance away from it in the churchyard. He said the risk of infection was too great, especially as he had a young family at home.

GROWING OLDER

'When Lloyd George introduced the retirement benefit of ten shillings a week for men of 65 we heard of a tragic case. A strong and healthy man who had recently married a younger woman, and had a young son, was automatically retired because of this, and they were faced with greatly reduced circumstances. How they managed I never knew, perhaps he had a good garden, grew his own vegetables and kept poultry and a pig. Perhaps she took in sewing and other part time jobs.

This incident caused much deep thought in the area and no doubt those who could afford it took out insurance against their unknown future. Previously men had worked until 70, if strong and able, my own grandfather retired from the railways at 70, but hating to be idle took a small job at Horsehay, cycling to work every day on the formidable Jiggers Bank as he was unable to get off his bike once on it. When my grandmother died he came to live with us and was a familiar sight at 4.30pm when, unable to swing his leg to dismount due to increasing stiffness, he fell off as best he could, to the great amusement of passers by, who exclaimed "Old Mr Read, has come off his bike again".

As the years passed and he became 80 he suffered several strokes and spent his remaining years in a comfortable armchair beside the Coalbrookdale grate in our kitchen. There was never any question of his going into a home or the workhouse. My mother nursed him until his death.'

A DEATH IN THE FAMILY

'Deaths were "celebrated" with a sitdown meal and plenty of drink after the funeral. When there was a death in our family mother made my sister and I mauve dresses; she already had her black but with us girls growing all the time it meant her making at least two mauve dresses each, which we wore for several months and were not allowed to wear anything else.

A tale my mother-in-law told, which she said was true, regarded the funeral meal. The very ill old man upstairs in bed could smell the home-cured ham boiling in the kitchen and fancied some. When he asked if he could have some his wife replied, "No, you canna, that's your funeral ham, you canna have any o' that else there wunna be enough for all the folk."

Another tale related by my father-in-law was of an elderly man expecting to die soon, living in an isolated spot in the hills and receiving a visit from the vicar. The vicar assured the man he had lived a good life and Jesus had died to save us all. "Good gracious," said the man, "Is Jesus dead then? That's the trouble living here in the hills, you never get to hear anything."

Diphtheria was a killer in my parents' childhood. My mother's three cousins, aged two, three and five, died within a few days of each other and the undertaker wouldn't go to the house so the father had to make their coffins and take them to the churchyard himself.'

'In the 1920s the Rock village was a small friendly place where everyone knew and helped each other, such as acting as midwife or nursing the sick. Mrs Bailey used to lay out the dead. One man laid out suddenly awoke and asked her what she was doing, in a very pleasant way as you can imagine.'

THE LAST JOURNEY

'My father often told us stories of his childhood in the early 1900s. He and his quite large family lived in appalling conditions at Longden Coleham. Coleham was then an extremely busy industrial area. There were many poky little houses in passages, resulting in squalor, malnutrition and disease. His cousin, aged nine, being left an orphan, was admitted into Besford House in Coleham, then an orphanage. It had apparently a very harsh regime at that time. After a few months the boy died. None of the extended family had money for a funeral, so it was arranged that he should have a pauper's burial. The body, wrapped in sheets, was taken to Shrewsbury cemetery on a handcart. My father, then also aged nine, followed this cortege and watched while a hole was dug and the body buried beneath a tree. The spot was not marked in any way. It must have had a profound affect on my father because he visited the spot regularly for a long time to, as he put it, talk to his cousin.'

'In the 1930s I left school at 14 to work for a neighbouring farmer at Burlton, but I was allowed time off to help my father with funerals – he was the village carpenter, wheelwright and undertaker. He dispelled any initial squeamishness with the advice: "Never be afraid of the dead, lad, it's the live 'uns you need to be wary of."

Most houses had a corner cupboard in which was kept the money to cover the cost of the coffin and the burial fee. This money had probably been scraped together over many years to ensure that "everything was done right" when a member of the family died; having enough "put by" was a matter of great importance. The three great estates in the area – Burlton, Loppington and Sansaw, provided the timber necessary for local needs: oak for coffins, elm for wheelbarrows and ash for cartshafts.'

'When I was a girl in the 1920s most of the mothers in New Dale had their babies at home, and there were a couple of women from the village who attended at the birth. My grandmother was one of them, she would also go to people when they were ill. When anyone died she would be called on to 'lay' the dead person out, because in those days a dead person lay at home until the time of the funeral, there were no such things as chapels of rest. It must have been very difficult where there was a large family when a body had to lie in the house for a few days; in the houses in what we called the Long Row, as you walked through the front door you went into their living room, and there was one bedroom, and a landing at the top of the stairs where some of the family had to sleep. How they managed I don't know.

Funerals in the village were always great occasions. On the day of the funeral the family and friends would gather at the house. The coffin would be in the living room or, as most people called it at that time, the kitchen. If people were lucky enough to have a parlour the coffin would be on two chairs in there. Before the coffin lid was screwed down the mourners would file round the coffin to what they called "pay their last respects". They would then place two chairs outside the front door, on which they would place the coffin. Someone would say a prayer or two, and then they would sing a hymn before setting off for the church. The undertaker was Jabus Barrat who had a hearse pulled by two black horses with black plumes on their heads. The bearers, usually six, would walk in front of these black horses all the way to Lawley church. When they got to Lawley village the church bell would toll just once, this would be about halfway up the village, then at the crossroads it would toll again. It would then toll for the last time as the funeral procession entered the churchyard. The family had to pay a half a crown on top of the funeral expenses for the bell to be tolled.

From what my mother and grandmother have told me, many of the families in their day remained in mourning for the rest of their lives. They always dressed in very dark colours, and for funerals they always dressed in deepest black. My grandmother was made a widow in 1898 and I never remember her wearing any other colour than black. In those days it was the recognised thing for a widow to remain in dark clothes for the rest of her life.'

'Coffins were made of oak and took roughly two days to make. One gentleman in the Churchstoke area remembers holding a candle for his Dad so he could work at night and would often be told off for lighting himself and not his father's work. In 1911 a funeral cost between £3 10s 0d and £5.

Many years ago a coffin would be lined with white material for unmarried women and coloured for married women. A returned undertaker remembers his grandmother telling a tale of two old spinsters asking for "all white, with a little bit of mauve in each corner." '

'A receipt for my great-grandmother's funeral at Stottesden in the 1930s included:

1 best oak coffin with solid brass fittings	£11 7s 6d
Hearse and pair of black horses and plumes	2 18s 6d
Gloves and hat bands	15s
Clerk	10s
Tolling bell	2s 6d
Vicar	4s
Total	£15 17s 6d

Quite a smart funeral!'

'Funerals at Whixall were arranged with the hearse coach and horses. The coach was kept in the hearse house alongside the village school. Fruit cake was always served to the mourners, with special funeral biscuits. The mourners walked behind the hearse to the churchyard.'

114

HOME REMEDIES

Most minor illnesses and physical problems were treated by tried and trusted home remedies, handed down within the family or community. Many of them sound dreadful, and are remembered with a shudder of distaste, but nevertheless generations of children lived to tell the tale – perhaps there was something in them after all?

RED SPIDERS AND CATERPILLARS

'For pneumonia we had linseed poultices back and front and hot wet packs. For bronchitis the chest was rubbed with goose fat or camphorated oil and covered with brown paper. For earache a small onion was heated in the oven and put in the ear, and for sore throat a woollen stocking wrapped round the throat. When I had whooping cough I had a tin of tar to sniff and a locket with holes in it and filled with camphor. Two gipsy remedies I had were a red spider inside a nut shell and a frog held in front of my mouth. The nut shell was hung around my neck. We had brimstone and treacle and syrup of figs on Saturday mornings.'

'A cure for whooping cough in the Acton Burnell area was to get a hairy caterpillar, put it in a bag and hang it round a child's neck. By the time the caterpillar was dead, the whooping cough would be cured. When, as children, we had whooping cough, Mother took us to the gas works at the nearby small town and the smell of gas cured us (or did it?).

Comfrey, chopped up and made into a poultice, was supposed to cure boils and sprains. House leek made into a poultice was considered good for earache, and it was also considered lucky to grow it on the roofs of cowsheds and pigsties. A bat clinging to the outside of a window pane was a sure sign of a death coming to that house.

My aunt died when she was 19 years old of pernicious anaemia. My mother used to tell us of the trauma of that time, and how for lengthy periods the invalid was prescribed raw liver sandwiches, in the hope of a cure.'

'For boils and carbuncles, a bread poultice on which had been sprinkled a few crystals of epsom salts was applied as hot as you could bear it. It would make you dance. As a blood purifier a spoonful of sulphur and treacle was considered good, but after this no one would want to stand behind you as it gave you the wind a bit. We made our own liniment and embrocation for sprains and chilblains, mixing together vinegar, turpentine, camphor and an egg.'

'One remedy from an old soldier at Gobowen who had boils after being in the trenches in France, was to get a small portion of warm cow dung, put it on the boils and they would be gone in a day or two. The best I was told was to get an egg, boil it hard and eat the shell and all. That was an old gipsy remedy, but the end result was they were lanced by the doctor.'

'In severe weather farmworkers' hands were often painfully chapped and split. A local woman at Caynham made a soothing and healing ointment called Hopewells Salve. This would be warmed and applied to the affected hands, which were then bound with rags in order to enable the men to continue their work.'

'When my grandmother was a child in the 1800s she cut her thumb quite badly. An old woman told her to put a spider's web on the cut to stop the bleeding; thankfully it stopped, as poor Gran had lost a lot of blood.

'When my grandmother at Ketley had a sprain, she used comfrey and marshmallow. Hot water was poured over the leaves and the affected part bathed with this lotion. When babies had teething problems, mothers made cinder tea. They dropped hot cinders into water, then gave the strained water to the babies to drink. Scalds and burns were treated with tea leaf poultices.'

'At Morda, fat bacon was secured with a piece of flannel under your chin for a sore throat. Vinegar and sugar was useful for curing a cold, also blackcurrant tea. Rheumatism was cured by drinking broom tea.'

'One treatment of which I heartily disapproved was the weekly purge. Most families did this. Every Friday at our home in Shrewsbury would see the senna pods infusing in a jug by the fire, the liquid of which we were obliged to consume in the evening regardless of whether we needed it or not. We were told it was essential to clean out our insides in order to keep us healthy. Far from that, it must have done a fair amount of harm. I know I spent many miserable Saturdays.

My mother was a great believer in nasturtium leaves. These were chopped up and used in salads, quite delicious. She also used them to make an infusion which she said would enrich the blood.'

CHILDHOOD
& SCHOOLDAYS

THE FREEDOM TO WANDER

Perhaps the most evocative memory of childhood is the freedom children had to wander and to explore their surroundings. Helping with the haymaking, fishing and paddling in the brook, searching out wild flowers, going on picnics – life seems to have been spent in the open air, without a care and without any fear. They were kept an eye on, however, and misbehaviour could result in a visit from the local bobby.

MAGICAL DAYS

'My earliest memories date back to 1925. I was born in a tall house in Abbey Foregate, nearly opposite "Monks Mill" where my father and his brother lived and worked the ground and the mill. This farm and mill occupied all my early years. My father milked Jersey cows and the joy of calling them in for the twice daily milking was the highlight of the holidays and weekends. I remember the big apples red and juicy in the orchard adjoining the cow houses. We would wait for our favourite cow and give her a juicy apple. Mine was named Rosie. The milk was strained and put into oval cans which had a metal bar inside the top, just under the lid. This held the pint measure, but if anyone wanted a half pint they could, but always there was the "blessing", that little drop extra to the measure. Folks waited for us with jugs in hand, and when all was sold the little pony was led back, given a feed of oats and left to graze until the second milking took place and the milk round started all over again in the evening.

All through the long summer holidays we wandered the fields and we fished with jam jars and long string and stale bread. We paddled in the brook and when we grew older we ventured into the deepest part and learned to swim. I do not ever remember a wet day. I do recall the wonderful haymaking days of July/August. There were no tractors or balers but the men all rallied around, the hay was cut with a type of large scythe, horse-drawn. When it was dry it was turned with a two-pronged fork, and later piled into "cocks". Often when the men were busy loading at the far end of the field we would taste the cider which had been left in the shade of a huge oak tree. There were several large stone jars with a narrow neck, and the maker's name on the side.

Saturday was our penny day. What a treat. Long before I reached our little shop I had changed my mind a dozen times. I could have four different bars for my penny, but the brightly coloured sweets in the glass jars were often the choice, a halfpennyworth of this and that. I would stand, deciding in that little flyridden shop, watching the insects fighting for their life on the sticky orange papers suspended from the ceiling. I loved to watch the owner take the bones out of a flitch of bacon and put it under the knife of the machine, then set the blade depending on the thickness you wanted, and turn the handle by hand.

When it was my turn and I indicated my choice, the lady would take a pre-cut piece of newspaper, all ready in a pile, and proceed to make a cone which just held a halfpennyworth of sweets. For the other halfpenny I could have a "dab and sucker", this being a packet of sherbet with licorice. The till was a flat drawer with compartments containing half crowns, shillings, sixpences, tiny silver threepenny bits, halfpennys and farthings with an occasional one pound note.

Sunday was different. We were not allowed in the fields. We went twice to St Giles' Sunday school and into church. Our yearly treat was a walk to the top of Lord Hill's column. After ascending and descending all 175 steps we were ready for the lovely tea party. This was on the lawn of a large house in Abbey Foregate, I think it is now the ambulance station. I can still see the large picture window in this beautiful house, and behind the glass was a heaped pile of toys, books, games etc. After a tea of sandwiches, iced cakes and jellies we were given our toy.'

'When I was four years old I spent most of my time outside with my father and grandfather doing jobs which are not done these days, thistle bodging and stone picking. I spent weeks with my grandfather down some lovely fields with a brook running through; it was a marvellous place for exploring, and enjoying our bread, cheese and cider – always accompanied by a beautiful blue cat.

There were magical days going with my father in the horse and cart taking corn to be ground into flour at Wrickton Mill about four miles away, or riding the cart horses to the blacksmith at Farlow; especially when I ws old enough to go alone, but I really think the horses took me.

Christmas Eve and the bellringers' older children were allowed to sit in the belfry to listen to the ringing in of Christmas Day: always a great time. We went to my other Grandad and Gran Yardley at the Woodhouse Farm for the day with masses of food and fun. If we stayed the night my cousins and I all slept in one room with two huge beds. Boxing Day at home was a big day for shooting and rabbiting; everyone wrapped up well and plied with home-made wine and sandwiches. Then another huge meal at night with a card party in the parlour afterwards, we children on the alert for any money dropped under the table.

Not everyone was so lucky. We had the usual village characters-Nipper Cook who lived in a hut by the rickyard and George Hodnett who lived in the old stables at the pub; they did odd jobs around the village. A travelling man used to sleep in the "bing" in front of the horses; he always gave my father his tobacco and matches at night and we used to peep through the boards and listen to him saying his prayers.

Summertime always seemed to be sunny; there was sheep washing at Prescott or Hinton in the river Rea, harvesting and taking hot meals on the cart to all the men and women working in the far fields; corn harvest and running rabbits, which on reflection was very cruel. A few days afterwards the "Rabbit Skin Man" called for the skins and mole skins. Threshing was another great day, with the old steam engine, and all the local farmers helping each other; a meal at midday with roly poly puddings boiled in the washing boiler and us children providing gallons of cider, it was such a dusty job.'

'We moved to Brockton when I was just two years old and my first memories there were playing with my brothers and sisters (lots of them) in the huge garden; all the fruit picking, jam making, father milking by hand, ploughing with horses and hay-harvest. Haymak-

Tong Norton in 1926, when streets and lanes were safe for children to play in – cats also.

ing was a lovely time for us as children with lots of picnics in the fields. Mother would pack pies, salads and cakes, large bottles of tea wrapped well in newspaper to keep them hot, and of course plenty of home-made wine towards evening. Many's the time when the load of loose hay would slide off the waggon as the day was coming to a close.

Madeley was a big mining community, with lots of public houses and chapels around. I remember the miners would walk out in the country with their little whippet dogs, catching rabbits etc. Often they would call to buy fruit and eggs from the farm. At Christmas we had the usual parties of carol singers, it was always "While shepherds watched" and after Christmas would come the wassaillers, black faces and cap in hand.

Sometimes when we came out of school the rag and bone man would be on the street giving a goldfish in a bag in exchange for a bag of rags. How I wished my house had been near enough to go and fetch a bag of rags! We did get a bit of excitement on the way home, like the day we encountered the beagles hare-coursing and my brother and I decided to follow. A few miles on and no idea of time, plastered with mud we arrived home to be met by a very irrate mother. Then there was the time we encountered a shooting party. As they wanted to shoot across our path, they told us to wait at the stile. Instead we took a short cut down the hedgerow, only to be showered with bullets and acorns, as the guns took aim at the oak tree.'

'Did the sun really shine every day when we were children, or did it just seem so? I have a host of really happy memories of picnics spent at Preston Boats in the early 1950s. I then lived in Cherry Orchard, Shrewsbury, and nearly every Sunday the entire family including aunts, uncles and cousins all made the trek to the "boats". Everyone was expected to carry some piece of picnic equipment as of course we went on foot. This was in the days before the Highfield Estate was built, so we were practically in the country as soon as we left home. It was a wonderful adventure all the way, with Uncle Jim making up stories about going through the jungle, and was that really just a newt in the pond or was there some dreadful creature lurking in the murky depths? These stories were mainly told to keep us children from getting tired, but we didn't know that then. We were all as quiet as mice going through the "bull" field for obvious reasons, and none of us ever wore red.

Not for us were there soggy sandwiches, and tea from a flask. We took bread, butter, kettle, tea-pot, and all the niceties that make up a proper picnic. When we arrived at the hallowed ground it was our job to find sticks to make a fire, and then to go up to the farm for a container of water, not forgetting our please and thank you's. While the grown-ups got the food ready, we children played, and climbed trees, and caught minnows in jam jars, and there were always wild flowers to be gathered and presented to Mum. These were the halcyon days when children could play without fear of menacing strangers. Sometimes we went across to Uffington on the ferry, and that short river trip was the best adventure of all.

All too soon it was time to pack up and make the homeward journey. Why did it always seem further home? Tired feet and wilting flowers, oh were we glad to see our house, but as soon as we got in we were already making plans for the next week's "picnic". Happy days.'

'It was good to be young in Wem and the surrounding countryside. We could wander for miles and be safe. We always knew where to find the first primroses and wild raspberries. Father knew where to find mushrooms but we never told anyone.

I remember collecting water hen's eggs with spoons tied to sticks. We paddled in the streams and caught Jack Sharps. we were always busy on the farm and after school; we put the mangolds into the "booseys" before the cows were brought in for milking.

There wasn't much money but we were easily pleased. Children pushed little carts or prams to collect wood from the timber yard. Bark chips were given away free. Coal was fetched from the coal yard and cattle feed from the mill. We helped on the farms with haymaking and harvesting and the arrival of the threshing machine was one of the highlights of the year.

The Sunday school treat was another important day. We would be taken to Soulton Hall in carts provided by Wem Mills and later their motor lorry. We had a wonderful day, picnics in the grounds, playing games and having races for sweets.'

'After school, or during school holidays at Highley, children would go to the woods along the Borle brook, climbing trees there, or fixing up a swing. They might also indulge in a little trout tickling. In the springtime, they would collect wild daffodils which abounded in the fields near the stream, and then bunch them up and tie them to a long pole, later selling them for a penny a bunch. Sadly, during the war, the fields had to be cultivated and very few wild daffodils remain. Children also picked primroses and "bunched" them on a stick too.'

'During school holidays at Howle in the 1920s we wandered the village. I loved to find wild flowers and birds' nests and to pick blackberries. Really, I suppose, we were watched over by everyone, for they all knew us and were ready to tell us off it we were doing wrong. We often visited the old people, especialy those who lived alone. We were welcomed, petted and fed too, particularly when we sang carols before Christmas. But we had to behave at home and at school.'

'We had very loving parents but we had to toe the line and punishment would be meted out for any transgression. One day my brother had committed some misdemeanour, probably stealing apples from the orchard. The local bobby, one Dick Chidley, well known to all of us in our part of Shrewsbury, came to report this incident to my father. The following conversation took place:
"Well, Jack, you will agree that the boy needs to be punished?" Dick began.
"Indeed I do, Dick."
"Will you punish him or shall I?"
"Leave it to me, Dick. It's my job to correct him if he misbehaves."
"Very good, Jack. I know I can rely on you to do the job well."
"That you can, Dick."
Whereupon my brother was given two strokes of the strap across the backside. The strap was a leather belt which hung in the hall as a constant reminder not to stray from accepted behaviour. I only remember it being used on two occasions, both times on my brother, but the threat was enough.'

GAMES, TREATS AND SWEETS

With little or no motorised traffic about, the roads were safe playing areas for yesterday's children and they took full advantage of them. Games had to be played with the minimum of equipment and the maximum of inventiveness and cooperation. Treats were occasional and eagerly anticipated, any trip out of the immediate area being a rare event. Sweets, too, were to be planned for and carefully chosen.

GAMES WE PLAYED

'In the early years of the century, my mother had a large wax doll. She put her in a little chair in the garden on a hot summer's day and went in for her dinner. When she came back all that was left of her doll's face was two large blue eyes and the wax which was running down the front of her dress. She also had a large wooden horse with a lovely grey mane and tail. It was on wheels and she was able to sit on his back and her father would push it along.

In an oak tree at the back of the house her father made them a swing on one of the boughs. They were able to swing over the low roadside hedge and many children who were walking past would ask for a swing.'

'As a child at Annscroft I joined in a nuisance game called Pin and Button. A large-eyed darning needle was threaded with cotton and a bone button was threaded on. The thread was halved and knotted at the end. The point of the needle was pushed into the putty on the outside of a cottage window and the knotted end of the thread was hooked round a nearby branch. The boys would then tap the thread with a stick and the button would go down and strike the window!

The lads played football all the year round in the fields and on the roads. I remember playing football in the moonlight.'

'The way I wore my shoes out was a continual worry to my Mum, so after school I was put in a pair of boy's boots, lace-ups with rows of hob-nails knocked in and steel toe and heel caps. These were ideal for playing football with the boys and they soon learned to respect my flying feet with these boots on the end. I was asked to keep goal, between two bundles of clothing – I thought I had been promoted at the time. Perhaps it was because I played with the boys more than the girls that my hair was short like a boy's, but at least I didn't have to have a silly bow on top of my head. My hand-knitted stockings were always round my boots and the wide black elastic garters were where the stockings should have been.

For the football we had an old leather case from somewhere and when we had patched the inner case till we couldn't patch it any more we used a pig's bladder. The bladder took weeks to dry and the problem was to get it inside the leather case without splitting it – it crackled but when blown up inside and then laced up it was all right. At about this time my brother had to have his leg amputated above the knee and when he came home from hospital he was given an iron leg to walk on. He was happier on crutches and could soon swing over a five-bar gate and play football. The game was getting tough

124

with my boots and his crutches – we felled many a player.

Other games were hopscotch and tippet. The latter was played with two sticks, one small and double pointed and the other about a yard long – a striking stick. Rings of chalk were drawn on the road; the inner circle was the bull and worth 50 points, the next ring was 25 and the outer ring was 10 points. The aim was to strike the tippet, the small stick, on its point. It would then fly into the air and hopefully it would land inside the rings and earn points for you. We also skipped with a short rope, but more often with a long one held by two people, for two others to run in and skip while rhymes were sung.

Dolls were scarce in Edgton in the 1920s. One girl in the village had one but we were not allowed to play with it often because it had a china face which would break if we dropped it. But we had a gollywog which Mum had knitted clothes for and my sister had a teddy bear from somewhere, also with knitted clothes. We played house in our pig sty – cleaned and whitewashed – down the garden. We would play being Mum and we would have had a Dad to if we could have got the boys there but they wouldn't come near. We often fell out about who should play Mother – no-one wanted to play the granny because they were too old and had wrinkles.'

'At Morda the games fell into seasons. There was hopscotch. A diagram of six squares was drawn on the ground. You had a piece of wood called a taw and you hopped on one leg pushing this piece of wood along; in square four you were allowed to rest. If your taw landed on a line you were out. Then a new game of hopscotch was invented with seven squares, called aeroplane hopscotch. Other games played were marbles and spinning the top. Then there were bowlers, not to be confused with cricket – this bowler was an old bicycle wheel which we hit with a piece of wood and kept it up and going along the yard or path. We also played conkers, using baked horse chestnuts. We skipped to "Who are you going to marry? Rich man, poor man, beggar man, thief." If you tripped on one of these, this was your man. It went on "What will you marry in? Silk, satin, muslin, calico, rags. How would you go to the church? In a coach, carriage, wheelbarrow, dustcart. Where would you live? Kitchen, parlour, pigsty, closet." '

'Many games were played in the round, such as "The wind, the wind blows high", "Oats and beans and barley grow" and "What's the time, Mr Wolf?". Others left the playground to follow the hills playing Fox and Hounds.'

'The recreation ground – The Rec – at Wem wasn't so smart in the

125

1920s. The grass was cut only once a year, in June, and harvested. We had such happy times playing in the drying grass, building houses and castles etc and generally having fun. In the summer months on Sundays, the local brass band would play and half the people of the town came to listen and would bring their families too.

In the winter we had great fun sliding on the frozen pond, which was quite a long one but not very deep. It was situated where the playground is now. Some lucky children had skates but most of us just wore out the soles of our shoes and sometimes our navy blue knickers too.'

'In the 1910s at Lower Frankton we used to play marbles on the way to school and we also had tops called Jack Jumpers. Other games we played were football with a heavy leather ball, cricket and Fox and Hounds. Bowlers were a piece of iron hurdle which the blacksmith, Joe Strange, would make into a circle for us. Then he would make an 18 inch piece of iron with a hook on the end of it, so that when you hooked it round the bowler, you could run along with it and make it jump.'

TREATS

'During the 1920s, children from the Broseley area came to Acton Burnell for their annual summer outing. They travelled by horse and brake, arriving at the village shop, where the horses were stabled, fed and watered.

The children proceeded to the park to walk to the lake to see the swans and other waterfowl, after which they played games and ran races before returning to the village shop for tea, which had been prepared for them in the clubroom.

A visit to the village shop concluded their outing, where they spent their coppers, getting eight sweets for a penny.'

'One of the highlights of the year in the 1920s at St Martins was the Sunday school trip. Very few children had a holiday in those days. The first trip I remember was by canal boat from the Moors to Llangollen. The boat was drawn by a horse. It took about three hours. We just had time for a paddle in the river and a climb to Crow Castle. Then, another great day, we went to Chester by charabanc. Another highlight was the Co-op Sports Day. We all assembled in the "Old Hut" – a relic of the First World War which stood where the children's playground now is. We had a tea party, to which we all had to take our own cups and spoons, with sandwiches, slab cake, fruit, plain and seed cake, and jellies made in large enamel bowls. Afterwards we

126

marched behind the Ifton Band to a field for the sports. Then the band played on for dancing on the field. It really was a great day.'

'As children in the 1930s we were never bored. During the winter nights we played board games, cards, knitted, sewed and painted. The summer sent all the village children playing together in the fields with hoops, skipping ropes, balls etc. We did not get a lot of toys, but Captain Maddox, who lived at the Woodlands, Northwood, used to walk his Great Dane dogs across the fields and past our houses on a Saturday morning.

He was a really kind man and used to always give the children a few sweets, or, on rare occasions, tennis balls which had hardly been used. All the village children soon started to look out for him coming and as soon as he was sighted, they would all be sitting in a row on the fence waiting for him, ready to say "Good Morning" and always hopeful. He never let them down.'

SWEETS AND ICE CREAM

'I remember aniseed balls being 16 for a penny. At the Toll House in Tilstock lived an old lady. Every Saturday me and the schoolmaster's daughter used to visit her. She was one of the few in the village to have a radio, the old cat's whisker type. She also used to cook chips. We would take a penny, knock on her door and ask for "a ha'p'orth of wireless and a ha'p'orth of chips".'

'At Wroxeter we looked forward to the day when members of the Sidoli family would come round the country villages selling ice cream. It was in a little square float with a canopy over the top and was pulled by a lovely little pony. They used to arrive at our school at about a quarter to four as we were leaving and those children who had a penny would buy a cornet, but those who hadn't (the majority) had to run behind the float to get home (in my case a mile and a half) to see if Mum could spare a penny for us to buy one. In fact, the smallest cornet was only a halfpenny. It was absolutely delicious and I've never tasted any as good since. The ice cream was in deep canisters in the float and must have been packed round with ice to keep it cold.'

'We had two whole pennies pocket money a week and walked to a sweet shop half a mile away at Hookagate to buy four different items each costing a halfpenny – like aniseed balls, liquorice braid, everlasting toffee and black and white humbugs which all got stuck together in your pocket.'

127

'Children received little or no pocket money at that time. To have more than a penny to spend per week was luxury indeed, and great was the deliberating at the shop counter before parting with one's wealth! Gob-stoppers or bulls eyes were popular; they were large, round, marble-like sweets, white in appearance, but as one sucked the diminishing layers the surfaces changed colour, and so did our tongues! We also bought "bootlaces" which were strings of liquorice about 24 inches long, sold knotted together just like the real thing. We also loved "Kay li" – a delicious white powder which effervesced in the mouth. It was sold either in a yellow tubelike container with a liquorice "straw" up which we sucked or in a triangular paper bag with a liquorice straw issuing from the apex of the bag. We also bought toffee sticks – a disc of toffee mounted on a thin wooden stick.

During summer months we would buy tiny bags of lemon flavoured crystals which would make a drink of lemonade. Also, once a week when the weather was hot, the ice-cream man would call at the playground and we could buy a tiny cornet for a penny. The really wealthy children could even afford a wafer of ice cream which cost twopence.'

CHORES AND POCKET MONEY

One lady recalled that in her childhood in the early 1900s, 'pocket money was unheard of. If we wanted money we asked Father for it and if we were lucky we got a penny, but more likely a halfpenny.' Money for sweets and toys had to be earned in many cases and most children had their chores to do before or after school, unpaid and simply expected of them.

MOLE CATCHING

'After starting school one tends to grow quickly and get more independent, wanting to do things on your own. One of the things we used to do at Plealey in the 1930s to get a few pence was mole catching.

On our way back from Lea Cross school through Shorthill and by Sibbersott, the place was littered with moles through the winter months. We used to catch them in traps, skin them and open them up into squares. We'd get fourpence each for a skin from Neville's in London. We'd go round the traps each night and keep them until the weekend – they were a bit high by Saturday, you know! We'd hang the skins out to dry – they were chiefly used for coats. We spent some of our money at Mrs Bromley's shop, where I would buy Sharpe's toffees, ten for a penny.'

LEARNING TO MILK

'I was born in 1927. Everywhere there seemed to be fields, sunshine, animals and poultry. We had a very mixed farm. My earliest memory is of the cowshed. I would be about two or three years old and to keep me occupied during the afternoon milking, when everyone was required to help, I was placed on a stool by the side of Foxy (a blue and white roan shorthorn cow of great age) with a bucket and asked to see if I could get some milk like everyone else was doing. While Foxy was having her corn she would turn her head around, pause in her chewing and look to see what I was doing. I was very determined to get the milk and how long it was before I achieved the first squirt, I couldn't say, but success did eventually come. Whether Foxy decided that she had had enough or I got the knack it would be a job to decide, she could have hoped the disturbance would go away if she co-operated. The swish swish of all the milkers and the peaceful munching of the cows I can conjure up today.

The milk was then transferred to a large pail called a carrier and carried to the dairy to a large cheese vat. Next morning would come the cheese making. When the stage came for the salt to be added to the curds I was given a saucer with some of the saltless curds and I sat on a wide window sill watching the cheese makers line the moulds with muslin and then fill them ready for the pressing.'

STICKING AND OTHER CHORES

'One of my Saturday morning jobs in the summer was to take a sack and gather the fallen sticks. The Squire allowed us to go sticking as long as we didn't pull branches off the trees.'

'My early memories are of a crowded farmhouse kitchen as we were never less than ten people – Mum and Dad, Grandad, seven children and one or two farm "boys" living in as family. I was the sixth child and I think very privileged as the older children worked hard on the farm, having to suckle calves, feed pigs and hens etc before going to school, which was a two mile walk away.

Fires did not stay in all night but had to be lit every morning. One child was allotted the task of gathering morning sticks every day and putting them in the side oven to dry. This job eventually passed on to me and I in turn passed it on to my younger sister. Older children also had to help with the wash, as well as looking after the younger ones.'

'Drinking water had to be fetched night and morning in buckets from the well at Lydham Mill, behind the church, some 400 to 500 yards from the house. Eggs had to be collected – what a wonderful life those hens had, roaming freely in the fields and stackyard among the plentiful grains to be found there. There amid happy scratchings and clucking we hunted to find the nests as they lay their eggs where they chose, in hedges, on stacks, on a farm implement, in a manger. It was great fun.

In spring and early summer the kitchen would resound to the clip clop of lambs' hooves on the stone floor. There were always one or two orphan lambs (cade lambs to us) to be mothered in the warm kitchen and fed from a baby's bottle through the day and night until they could crop grass for themselves. These lambs were a great joy and even when fully grown would immediately come to us when we went into the field.

There were rabbits, ferrets and a pony to be fed and cleaned out daily. I don't know whether these tasks were work or recreation – a bit of both I think.'

'Summertime we would help to make the hay and cock the corn. There were always lots of jobs to do with pigs, horses and other animals to feed, chicks in a box on the hearth to keep warm, lambs to bottle feed, sticks and coal to get in for the fires. We had our jobs to do and if they were not done or not done properly, many's the time I have been run around the garden with the buckle end of a strap.'

'As a boy I was paid sixpence twice a year to collect 20 to 30 Irish cattle from Wellington station and bring them back to Kynnersley. I would bring them down Town Walls, along the Whitchurch Road and down the Dukes Drive, a journey of five miles which became five times further as the cattle strayed all over the place. The local farmer was keen to use cheap child labour and the children were happy enough to let him. Another boy had to take the cow to the bull at Kents.'

MAKING MONEY IN WARTIME

'Rabbits were quite a staple diet in the war years and having eaten them, the boys were allowed to take the skins to the Skin Yard, in

130

Barker Street, and the reward for each was three pennies. At ten years old that was quite a fortune.

Children gathered empty jam jars from the neighbourhood and by taking them to Morris's shop in Shrewsbury they were given two pennies for a two pound jar and a penny for a one pound jar.

Newspapers were collected by children in the neighbourhood and taken to the home of Gavin Gibbons, who later became a well known author and astrologer. All the comics and magazines were extracted by the children before being delivered to Gavin Gibbons, to pass around as such things were too expensive for the children's pocket money.'

THE HAPPIEST DAYS
OF OUR LIVES?

For some people perhaps they were, but in the early years of the century schooldays were short and often not very educational.

THROUGH THE GENERATIONS

'My family lived in Loppington and Common Wood from the mid 1800s. My grandmother lived in Nottingham and trained as a teacher at Derby Training College. After pupil teaching in Staffordshire, she travelled to Loppington to become the head teacher – in fact, the only teacher at Loppington school, around 1870. She lodged at the alms-houses at Noneley and met and married my grandfather.

Collecting the pennies of each child on a Monday morning was one important job, each child having to pay one penny to come to school. When she first started, registers were very important and a mistake in these was unforgivable.

The Dickins family and the vicar had a great say in how the school was run. Feeling very ill with a type of "flu one day, she wished to go home, but the only way she could do this was to have permission from Captain Dickin. A walk to Loppington House was nearly a mile and the kiddies could not be left so she soldiered on. On marriage, teaching had to be given up. Still, with 18 children of her own, it would have been impossible.

My mother talked of starting school on Ash Wednesday, 1899. It was a part holiday. They went to school and then marched, two by two, from school to church, all wearing hats, of course. If they met any of the gentry, the girls all had to curtsey and boys doffed their hats.

Most of them left school at the age of twelve, but all were fluent readers. My cousin, who was about the same age as my mother, lived at Common Wood. She had to walk to Loppington school, starting at the age of four years. She had suffered from rickets and was not strong enough to walk the two and a half miles to and from school, so eventually she had to stay for the week with her grandma in Loppington, only doing the journey on a Monday morning and Friday evening. Still a long walk for a four year old.

Another memory of my mother's was being taken out of school to line the road to watch a traction engine trundle past.

Attending Newtown school during the 1930s and 1940s, my memories of school were different. Bad winters always stick in my memory. The school never closed. An iron stove was the only means of heating. One of the two teachers lived in the village, so was always there and we village children walked through drifts, sometimes hedge high, to school. Since those on remote farms did not make it on the first snowy days, the rest were allowed to sit round the stove – a luxury.

In the afternoon, we were allowed to have the puzzles and building blocks out – something hardly ever allowed. Sitting on top of the stove during the winter months was the urn. By dinner time, this would have boiled and the head made a large jug of Horlicks. Each child who had paid their halfpence a week had a cup.

In summer, each child had a cup of lemonade made from very yellow lemonade powder. If you had not paid your halfpence, you could have a drink of water from the pump in the yard, using the communal cup.

In 1939, war was declared and a large number of children appeared from Liverpool. The school was so crowded. They brought their own two teachers. These were nuns. None of the village children had ever seen a nun so we were very curious.

Gas masks had to be taken to school. Sewing classes were used to make gas mask cases. Each Scripture lesson in the morning had to be sat through wearing the gas mask. I could not bear the smell, especially after the green end piece was put on. We soon discovered that queer noises could be made in them and the culprit go undetected.

So crowded was the school that half day schooling was introduced. We went mornings one week and afternoons the next for quite some time.

The scholarship was taken and I passed it. I greeted the news with mixed feelings. Of course I wanted to go the High School at Whitchurch, but I also wanted a bike. All the children who failed went to Wem Secondary Modern School and they each had a bike supplied, together with a new yellow cape and leggings. The scholarship children had to supply their own transport to school, so mine was an old second, or third hand bike.

My new bike came towards the end of the war. It was nice, but all black. There was no chrome then and I did so want a bright one.'

IN THE EARLY YEARS OF THE CENTURY

'My father could read but he couldn't write so when he had to sign anything he had to put his cross, like a good many more people in my younger days at New Dale. Many of them had very little schooling.'

'The school at Linley was not opened until 1874 and education was not compulsory in England until the 1880s so Granny and her brothers and sisters attended a dame school in the village, which was so called because an educated lady would teach the children in her own home for a charge of one penny per child per day. They were taught to write on slates and also to read. Granny's writing, with perfect spelling, was in a beautiful copperplate style right up to the time of her death in her 96th year.'

'I was born in 1906 in St Martins and went to school when I was five, till I was 13. There were two schools in the parish, Ifton Heath council school and St Martins Church of England school. Both headmasters lived in houses attached to the schools. In those days there was great rivalry between the two schools and very frequent fights. Lord and Lady Trevor used to visit the schools in their carriage with the coachman driving. Everyone had to curtsey or touch their caps to them. If they didn't they got the cane.'

'At Broome the roads were very bad with deep ruts from the waggons and timber carriages and traction engines. In winter these ruts were filled with mud and in summer, dust. The roadmen scraped this onto the sides of the road in heaps, which was dreadful if you happened to fall into it. Some children lived about a mile from the school and some much farther. No dinners were provided then so they had to take sandwiches and a cold drink. We used to toast bread and butter in front of a tortoise stove on a pen and call it French toast. We had about a month's holiday in summer, a week at Easter and one day at Whitsun. The Craven Arms May Fair was on 24th May and we had a day's holiday then, not because of the fair but because it was Queen Victoria's birthday.

School began at nine o'clock with a bell in a little turret, rung by a chain which fastened onto a peg in the boys porch. This was once struck by lightning which ran down the chain and into the pantry of the school house, giving the master's wife a big shock as she was in there at the time. The children assembled in the porch and marched into school singing "Down in the Canebreak". The toilets were across a small yard, three or four for girls and the same for boys, divided by a wall back to back. They were a bit smelly.

We had slates and slate pencils when we first started. Later it was steel nibbed pens dipped in ink, contained in an inkwell in the front of the desk. Most things were written on the blackboard by the teacher with chalk. Music was written on the blackboard and that was how the choir learned the hymns and psalms for church.

The rector or one of the school managers came in regularly to check the registers. An inspector came to check our work and the attendance officer was often there. A lady from the village, a Miss Lucy Marston, came to inspect our sewing.'

'At the beginning of the century, and before, boys and girls wore boots. Girls usually had long dresses covered by a white apron. They took sandwiches for dinner, often of bread and cheese – no butter. Sometimes it was bread and jam and the jam soaked through the bread, but they were hungry and ate it just the same. The sandwiches were wrapped in newspaper.

Punishment was in the form of a number of strokes of the cane across the hand, according to the severity of the crime. Children had to raise their hands for attention and were not allowed to shout out. When visitors arrived at school, pupils were instructed to stand when they came into the classroom, and to open and close doors for them. There was never any noise when lessons were going on.'

FROM PUPIL TO TEACHER

One of the careers open to young women in the early part of the century was the teaching profession. Hardly out of childhood themselves, they stayed on in the classroom as pupil teachers. Church and school were closely intertwined, especially in the villages, and teachers could face problems if they were not of the "right" religion.

A PUPIL TEACHER AT 15

'Some of the children from poor homes at Dawley were always anxious to leave school and help their parents. If they'd made a certain number of years at school and had good attendance during these years, I think they could leave with what they called the "Labour certificate" at about the age of eleven. I wasn't one of these. I remained a scholar with Miss Breeze until I was 15, because then I became a pupil teacher, a post which I had to fill for four years. This was a good thing because then you knew at the end of four years whether you loved the work and whether you would like to go on with it.

When the girls and boys left Langley school there was not much in the way of work in Dawley itself that they could do. The boys chiefly went into the mines and the girls either went to work on the pit banks or into domestic service. The wages for domestic service in Dawley were very low and the girls found out that by going into Lancashire they could earn very much better wages, because of course the Lancashire women and girls could go into the cotton factories and earn good wages, and they were very glad to get domestic help. And our girls knew of that and many, many of them left Dawley and went to work permanently in domestic service in Lancashire. They often met their husbands there and never came back to their own town of Dawley.

The Langley school had three separate departments, with three different heads. There were not many schools in the district which had separate girls and boys. So many people, from some distance round, sent their children to Langley because they preferred girls and boys being taught in different schools. I also think that was a very good arrangement in those days.

We drew all the children from Dark Lane. These children brought their lunch to school as it was impossible for them to walk home in the hour and a half which was allowed us for our dinner break. Sometimes the girls' dinners got lost. We always kept a cupboard especially for these dinners, but somehow or other, dinners sometimes disappeared. If this happened, I always brought the poor one who had nothing to eat a little bit of dinner.

The school holidays were not as long as they are now. We had just the four weeks in summer, the month of August. Unfortunately that was not the time when fruit picking and hop picking provided good work. Many of the children from Langley school went with their parents in the fruit season and in the hop season, to pick. That was their mode of having a holiday. The parents and the whole family would go away. I think they always got excused from school as even in those days we had an attendance officer, who used to have a list every Friday of the children who had been away from school more than half a day. He had to visit the homes, find out the reason for their absence, write down by their names why they had been absent and produce that to the head teacher at the end of the week.

Our attendance officer, whom I remember very well, was Mr Joe Cabman, and he was the brother of Doctor Parks Cabman, the noted preacher who went out to America. But he often came back to his native town of Dawley and preached in our local chapels.

I became a pupil teacher at Langley girls school when I was 15 and after I had qualified, which was in 1904, I became an assistant mistress. While I was in this office the Stirchley Forges, at Forge, closed and many of my scholars were children of the men who were thus thrown out of work. They were very, very poor, as of course there was no out of work pay in those days. The teachers organised a plan to feed the children; some days these poor children only received bread and jam. But we had many friends, including my mother, who made fresh stew and such meals as that and sent this food in buckets to the schools.'

FROM SHREWSBURY TO THE COUNTRY

'My childhood days were spent in Shrewsbury where I lived with my parents, two brothers and two sisters. We lived in Abbey Foregate and attended the Abbey School or, as I recall, it was sometimes referred to as the Brown school. Here most of the pupils stayed until the age of leaving which was 14 years of age, but in some cases at 13 years. This was when it could be proved that the child was needed at home or that an extra wage was needed to supplement the family income.

After the Infant classes the boys were then taught by Mr Toman in a separate part of the building. Girls were taught by Mrs Toman who was called "governess". She always wore black – long black skirt and blouse and apron and white oversleeves from wrist to elbow. She screwed back her hair into a tight bun on top of her head and to us children was an awesome sight and certainly one to be obeyed. I liked going to school and had a medal from Salop Education Authority for regular attendance, which was probably about 1912.

Apart from the usual subjects we were taught how to sew and to knit. I remember when learning to knit we were told to say "in over out off" as we inserted the needle.

We wore dark dresses and white pinafores. Some of these were quite elaborate. We had several layers of underclothes with flannel petticoats and always a white one with lace trimming. We had black woollen stockings held in place with garters and buttoned boots. In winter we sometimes wore buttoned gaiters but best of all were the muffs. Mother used to make these from odd pieces of material which she lined with flannel – usually red – and threaded with a cord which was hung round the neck. Great joy when she decided her fur was past its best and we girls had fur muffs.

On summer Sunday evenings we generally went for a walk with our parents. This was usually along the riverside to the Quarry where we listened to the band.

Indoors we played board games, snakes and ladders, ludo and draughts and one called Halma. There were card games which have stood the test of time such as snap, strip Jack naked. Old Maid and many others. Outdoor games for boys were football, marbles and conkers. We girls played hopscotch and had skipping ropes. With a long length of rope and a girl turning it at either end, we would skip to a ditty which we sang. It began

"All in together girls, this cold weather girls,
I saw Peter girls peeping through his window girls."

We attended Sunday school and sometimes we saw a magic lantern show but this was never very exciting as we were shown rather indistinct pictures of foreign countries of which we knew very little and usually the lantern gave off paraffin fumes which made everyone cough. We looked forward to the school summer outing when we were taken by horse-drawn brake into the country where we played games and had a picnic. The brake was a long vehicle with benches down the centre and where we sat facing each other.

In 1914 Mrs Toman came into the classroom and told us that we were at war with Germany. This didn't mean a great deal to us at the time but we were soon to realise that brothers and fathers were soon to leave home. Although I was only nine years old I felt the sadness when my brother enlisted and, like many others, said he was older than he was, but he was lucky and came home safely from France.

I left the primary school and went to the Priory which was then near the swimming baths with boys at one end of the building and girls at the other. Miss Ellison was the headmistress and Mr Florian was headmaster.

Our history mistress was very keen on amateur dramatics, something which I very much enjoyed and we put on many school plays including Shakespeare for which we had a good report. Yes "Happy Days".

At the age of 20 I took up a teaching post at Hopton Wafers. Then I really knew what it was like to live in the country. There was very little transport and of course no school buses. One bus ran to Ludlow once a week and one to Cleobury Mortimer. When I went to Hopton I went by train to Ludlow, caught a bus to Clee Hill and was met by the vicar's son with a pony and trap.

Lodgings had been arranged for me at a farmhouse which to me seemed so cold and bare after living at home in a small town house.

When I was shown the lavatory I had my first surprise. It was the little house at the end of the garden and on entering, there it was in all its glory, a three seater. One of the spaces was smaller, which I presumed was for a child. I thought it must have been built for Father, Mother and Baby Bear. I never tarried there in case someone decided to join me.

The children walked a long way to school with no school dinners or milk. Sometimes they were caught in storms and arrived in very wet clothes. We had large fires in the classroom so the coats were draped around them but it was a very steamy atmosphere. If there came a sudden fall of snow the fathers would come to school to take them home, often having to carry the little ones. We had some bad winters when the water in the jugs in the bedroom would freeze. No electric blanket, not even a hot water bottle so when I undressed I would get into bed and put my feet in my fleecy lined knickers – so much for hygiene!

The children seemed to get on well at school. One or two managed to pass the exam to the grammar school but most of them left school at the age of 14, the boys to work on farms and the girls having to move further afield to find domestic work in the town houses where they "lived in" and did not get home very often. Whilst Drives and dances were held in the village hall and if there was one at another village several of us would walk there together.

There was a good attendance at church, I think people looked forward to meeting friends there after the service. It was the place to hear and pass on any news.

It was at Hopton Wafers that I heard my first wireless. The vicar's son made a little box affair called a crystal set, we wore head phones and by moving a small wire called a cat's whisker we could faintly hear music or someone reading the news but it wasn't very clear.

I met my husband to be at the village hall and in 1931 gave up my job and we were married at the Abbey Church in Shrewsbury. It cost an extra half a crown to Have the Great West door opened for the ceremony.'

THE WRONG PLACE AND THE WRONG RELIGION

'In Shrewsbury only persons resident in the Borough were considered for teaching posts. One of my friends who applied was turned down because her home was 200 yards over the boundary. A little later Shrewsbury expanded, she re-applied, and taught in the town for over 40 years.

Another friend, a Methodist, ran into the snag that most of the village schools were Church of England and only employed communicants, but she got over the difficulty by being baptised and confirmed into that church. One of my neighbours told me that for years she had been head of a Shropshire Roman Catholic school. When she informed her Authority of her intention to marry a Church of England widower she was informed she couldn't keep her job unless he had become a Roman Catholic before their wedding. This made her so cross, she became a member of the Church of England and was a headmistress in one of their schools until retirement.'

SCHOOL BETWEEN THE WARS

Classrooms did not change radically after the First World War and children still faced long walks to school in country districts, no running water, no hot food and large classes of mixed ages and abilities. Gradually came improvements with the wider availability of public transport and the beginnings of the school meal system, though no doubt a grandparent had no trouble recognising the school of his or her youth in that described by a new generation of youngsters.

139

GETTING THERE

'I went to Rushbury Church of England school in the 1920s. From five years of age we walked the one and a half miles in all weathers; some children came from Longville or even as far as Wilderhope (about three miles). The road, then only a lane, to Rushbury from Heath Common was just made up of rough stones with grass growing down the centre, with mud and puddles on each side in the winter and we had no wellingtons in those days. When it snowed we just plodded through it with very wet feet and legs. I remember one winter it snowed all morning and Miss Strother, the headmistress, sent us home early in the afternoon. We managed to get about halfway up the lane only to find it blocked with a huge snowdrift, so we had to walk all the way back to Rushbury and walk an extra mile round through Wall. The big boys carried two of the little girls on their backs but by the time we reached the Heath Common the boys were so exhausted they had to leave the girls at Mrs Pitchford's farm and their parents collected them later.

What a difference in the spring and summer. Admittedly the lane was like a dust bowl but the hedgebanks were ablaze with flowers; primroses and beautiful white scented violets, ragged robin, cowslips and many more. The meadows too were covered with wild flowers – yellow rattle, the tiny blue milkwert, ladies bedstraw, quakergrass and the little purple orchids now, alas, gone forever. Then we used to take our lunch down to the packhorse bridge, or sit on the sunny bank under the rectory wall until the school bell called us to our lessons. The country lanes were also a haven for butterflies and birds. We used to find their nests and how I hated the boys taking the eggs for their collections.'

'Until I was ten I attended Lower Heath school under the headship of Mr R.B. Taylor. My father had attended the same school under the headship of Mr Bertram Taylor, Mr Taylor's father. The retired headmaster often walked over from Prees where he lived, to see that his son was doing his job properly.

I had a two mile walk each way but as there were up to 20 of us from cottages and farms on the way we were a lively group. I had a pair of red clogs and loved frosty weather so that I could strike sparks from the tarmac road. I also had an iron hoop and a stick to bowl it along with and that helped the journey along. After the two mile walk home at the end of the day, the dinner that had been kept warm in the bottom oven of the range was very welcome, the rim of congealed gravy round the plate in no way detracting from my enjoyment.'

'I started school soon after I was four and had a fair old trek to school, between three and a half and four miles. I well remember sitting in the grass on my way home because I was so tired.'

'Our school, Westbury Forest school, was about a mile and a half away across the fields. It had about 16 pupils when I started, aged between five and 13 years – and one teacher. Imagine trying to cope with that age range. We were taught the three R's well but when it closed down I was nine and I had been taught no history, geography etc. I supposed the poor woman couldn't cope with all that as well as the age range.

Because we were so far out in the country, if someone new came to the school they were treated like someone from outer space – we never saw any strangers. Our teacher didn't use a cane, her hands were her weapons. If anyone misbehaved she would stand behind them and box their ears from side to side.

The walk to school was wonderful in the summer with sightings of foxes, red squirrels, or orchids and all kinds of birds, but in the winter it could be horrendous. On the very cold mornings my mother would be up early and put potatoes in their jackets in the Aga to bake. Our "gloves" were always woollen socks (which my father knitted in the evenings) and we would each have a baked potato to go inside our gloves to help keep us warm.'

'Children going to school in Shrewsbury had a worrying time with the Smithfield and slaughterhouse being situated at Smithfield Road. The cattle, sheep and pigs were driven along the roads and often went berserk or decided to go the wrong way, with one of the cattle drovers taking off after them and the rest carrying on. When I saw a herd coming I usually dived in a gateway or ran back until they had gone past. This occurred every Tuesday and Friday. Along Coton Hill and under the railway bridge, the power station was also situated in Roushill and my father worked there. I used to call there for the accumulator for the wireless on the way home from the swimming baths after school. The slaughterhouse was opposite the power station and the noise was deafening, what with the noise of the large engines pumping away and the squealing of the cattle and pigs, especially the pigs, being killed.'

OUR SCHOOLS

'There were two teachers for about 50 pupils at Longville. The infants teacher took pupils to the age of eight, then the headmistress took

141

them on to school leaving age. The parson came in once a week to take the senior pupils' scripture lesson. We used to take sandwiches for lunch and a bottle of lemonade, though in the winter we could have a hot drink made at school, either cocoa or Horlicks. In the cloakrooms we had two taps and washbasins; this was rainwater. The boys used to fetch two buckets of drinking water from a well at the bottom of the village. Sometimes they would find a frog at the well and this would usually find itself in the girls' bucket of water. It used to cause quite a stir!

Most of the girls wore gymslips and jumpers or blouses and, as we did not have any heating, woolly vests, liberty bodices and fleecy lined knickers.

We had to do an examination every year before breaking up for the summer holidays; this would cover all the subjects we had worked on during the year.

The church and school worked very closely together. At some services pupils read the lessons and took the collection; it used to make us feel very important. The older girls would be allowed to help decorate the church for harvest festival and Easter and we would also take part in a service round the war memorial on Armistice Day. The highlight of the school year was the Christmas party held about a week before Christmas. We used to have a super tea, play party games and then Father Christmas arrived and everyone had a present off the tree and a packet of sweets and an orange.

In the mid 1930s big changes took place in the school, when all girls over the age of eleven were able to go to domestic science classes at Church Stretton. Every Thursday morning a taxi used to pick us up after assembly, and girls from Rushbury school went the same day. The boys went for half a day a week to carpentry classes, held in what was the old parish hall at Church Stretton.'

'The village school at Willey was built of local stone with a slate roof. There were two rooms, the infants room and the big room. Promotion from one to the other depended entirely on each child's ability. Water supply was pumped from a well.

The vicar was a VIP and if he entered a classroom everyone stood to attention. On Wednesdays he took assembly and gave religious instruction for about half an hour. Once a year an external examiner assessed this subject and the two best pupils were awarded a bible and prayer book.

The average number of pupils was 50, though once there were 75 on the register and the same two staff coped. The abilities of the pupils was very mixed, but problems were solved by the bright ones giving individual instruction to the dull ones, usually in the cloak-

142

rooms – rather unsavoury if wet coats were drying out there!

Subjects taught were varied and included sewing, especially patching and make-do-and-mend, woodwork for the boys, nature study and music.

Many children walked long distances to school in all weathers. One day the headmistress decided that cold water from the pump was not an adequate midday drink. It was arranged to buy a large kettle, milk was provided free by a local farmer and parents were asked for twopence each as necessary towards the cost of cocoa and sugar. The staple midday meal was sandwiches of bread and home-made jam, with a piece of home-make cake to follow. There were no sweets but a favourite tit-bit was cocoa and sugar in equal amounts wrapped in greaseproof paper. Some mothers thought this was unhealthy as it might produce gravel in the bladder! These children had dessicated coconut instead of sugar.

Red letter days came round annually. On May days the May Queen was chosen and crowned, the boys concocted a throne from chairs and sheets and tableclothes and all the children brought wild flowers. Sports days were held on the vicarage lawn and the girls wore their best dresses while the boys were suitably dressed in their best short trousers and hair oiled and parted. The races were very sedate and all were on their best behaviour. More important than the races was the excellent tea party which followed.

One special day was the day we saw the aeroplane. The sound of the engine was heard and, as this was an historic occasion, we were allowed to leave lessons and run into the playground, where we all waved to the pilot. The plane was a small low flying bi-plane and the pilot waved back.

Winter days were my favourite. We arrived at school covered in snow. There was a roaring coal fire to welcome us. Outer clothes were draped over chairs to dry, desks were drawn into a semi-circle around the fire and lessons began. Above all, we learned to overcome the elements and to persevere against adverse conditions.

Discipline was maintained in spite of well built brawny boys and the small slim mistress. The cane was old and splintered and kept in the desk. If the mistress lifted the lid a silence fell on the room – no one knew who was to be punished, probably for talking in class. or passing notes. If a boy was caned on both hands he became a hero. Minor offences were punished by half an hour's solitary confinement in the cloakroom.'

'The majority of the pupils in the 1920s travelled on foot to Loton village school. A few would maybe have a lift in a milk cart, which was transporting milk in 17 gallon churns to the local station, where it

School class before the war. Children were used to walking quite long distances unaccompanied in order to get to their village school. They were taught there from five to fourteen years – their entire school career.

was loaded onto the early morning train and sent to a dairy. From the area in which I lived, the milk went to Birmingham to Walter Cattell & Gurden.

Many school children tramped to school along cart tracks or across fields before reaching a tarmac road. There were no wellingtons in those days; a few children wore lace shoes but many wore black boots – both boys and girls. In winter time when lanes were deep with mud or snow, children reached the school with boots that were soaking wet and with mud up to their knees, not to mention rain-soaked coats. I remember the infants mistress would be kneeling on the floor of the clockroom to help the little pupils to remove their clothes and to scrape the mud from their boots. Clothing and footwear were then arranged along the huge fire guards around the large coke fuelled stoves, one of which heated each school room. During the course of the day the clothing was rearranged around the stove until it was dry, so that pupils set off on their homeward journey warm and dry.

Needless to say, there was a lot of illness among the children, and mortality was high compared with present day standards. There was no immunisation such as we have now and epidemics of scarlet fever or diphtheria were common place. In severe cases children were taken by ambulance to the isolation hospital – few people owned a car in those days. There were many cases of tuberculosis also, and each county would have one or more sanatoriums where a patient could spend as long as 18 months or two years. Not all cases were cured by any means.

During winter months I remember nearly every child seemed to have colds. There were no tissues or disposable handkerchiefs. Cotton or calico hankies were expensive and were often given as Christmas gifts. Many children arrived at school with torn squares of old sheeting pinned with large safety pins to the fronts of jackets and dresses. In some instances these were burnt and replaced with fresh "hankies"; others were carefully washed and boiled on washing day and used time after time.

I do not remember that we used any exercise books or even loose sheets of paper. Instead we had white chalks to write on small wooden black boards of which each pupil had one. We learnt our alphabet and tables parrot fashion – sometimes sung in a very singsong fashion.'

'In the school at Cruckmeole in the late 1930s we did spinning, dyeing from the hedgerows and weaving. I can remember skeins of spun sheep wool collected from the fields hanging on the railings to dry.'

'Some of us were sent to school in scratchy woollen combinations – you grew, they shrank. We wore clogs and pinnies and the famous liberty bodice with rubber buttons.'

'The boys wore hobnailed boots. These nails would fall out, so before the playgrounds could be used for physical exercises, races or games, the whole school would line up shoulder to shoulder and proceed slowly from end to end and back again picking up all the loose nails. The children then removed their footwear and ran in their stockinged feet. Few families could have afforded to buy gym shoes.'

'At Hookagate there were 120 pupils of all ages, but many left at twelve years and attendance was irregular. If an older boy pupil was really badly behaved, the then vicar of Annscroft was summoned – another boy cycled to the vicarage with a note. The vicar got his bike out and came to the school to cane the culprit in the playground.

In winter the school was very cold, with only one small coke fire for each room. The pupils were taken out for runs and walks to keep warm.

Fire drill consisted of the vicar blowing his whistle to evacuate the building. In a real emergency the chance of the whistle-blower being there was somewhat remote!'

'I remember some children at All Stretton having scurvy breaking out around their mouths because of vitamin deficiency. If by chance they had an orange they would practically eat the peel. They seemed to have a craving for it.'

THE NIT NURSE AND CHARITY

'The Nit Nurse was my personal dread. All the children lined up and she did a cursory search of each head. It was generally thought that if she took longer than the customary second or so, or if she spoke to you, then her search had been rewarded with a sighting of the parasites. A note would later be handed to the offending carriers to deliver to their parents. She always spoke to me because she knew my mother and always asked after her, much to my chagrin. I was mortified by the glances of my classmates and always complained bitterly to my mother but to no avail. She did it every time and I hated her more each time.

Children's garments were costly items and many were home-made. "Home-made" was a derisory term then. Most children at my school in Shrewsbury were reasonably well clothed but most garments were hand-me-downs – handed down and then handed on to another family. The general rule was one for play and one for best. Many children wore ragged, ill-fitting clothes and footwear often consisted of one pair of pumps whatever the weather.

The police often had surplus shoes, very heavy footwear characterised by a stud hole in the side of the shoe. These shoes were offered to children whose fathers earned less than £100 per annum. There must have been many whose father did not earn anything like that amount but both children and parents were too proud to admit it. I raced home to enquire if we came into that category and was greatly relieved to be told that we did not. Some children who had no suitable footwear just did not come to school when the weather was very bad.'

SIR AND MISS

'I remember the physical education inspector coming to the small country school at Tuck Hill in the 1920s. PE was called "drill" in those days. We looked forward to her coming because she brought her pet monkey called Bimbo with her.

The scripture inspector was also welcome because we had a half day holiday after he had tested us – I think it was a bribe to help us answer his questions!'

'We had a very pretty infants mistress at All Stretton and I remember the attendance officer kissing her behind the classroom door one day. She came out rubbing her cheeks and blushing and of course we children were taking it all in; we were highly delighted.'

'From a retired headteacher at Churchstoke village school comes this "gem". The daily milk supply, one third pint bottles for the pupils and pint bottles for the cooks, were deposited outside my classroom door. In order to collect their supply, the cooks had to pass through the dining hall and my room. This inconvenience had gone on for some time until a boy took it upon himself to take the bottles to the kitchen. One particular morning I was not very pleased with the performance of my class and I had to berate them soundly. At the mid-morning break this lad knocked on the kitchen hatch to deliver the bottles and it happened to be my wife (assistant cook) who opened up. Placing the bottles on the counter, he said, "He's naggy today. He's nagged and nagged at us all morning. He hasn't half given us a going over." Then looking up into her face he said, "What's he like at home?".'

SCHOOL MEALS

'From 1921 until she retired in 1955, Mrs Gertrude Duddell was joint caretaker, with her husband, of Coalbrookdale County High School. When they started the boys and girls were in separate schools but it became co-educational in 1932.

In addition, Mrs Duddell did some cooking. At first children would bring what they wanted cooking for their dinners, eg bacon and egg, bacon and tomato, egg on toast etc. They put their food on a plate with their name on a piece of paper. This was a great boon to the children who travelled many miles to school by train. Some came from Much Wenlock and further away from Longville, Rushbury and Wall.

In 1935 the school was one of the first in the county to have proper school dinners and as time went by Mrs Duddell built up a reputation as a very good cook. Many old students remembered her shepherd's pie, toad in the hole, queen pudding and "doormat" pudding. The latter was a flat sponge pudding baked in a rectangular tin which looked just like a brown doormat when it was cooked. Served with custard, chocolate or jam sauce it tasted delicious!'

INTO THE 1940s

'The children from Ackleton walked across the fields to school at Worfield, about three miles. In winter we were soaked by rain, in summer by the dew from the crops as there was only a very narrow pathway. We were referred to by some of the teachers as the Ackleto-nites.

I remember one morning when my brother was so taken by the sight of dewdrops on quaking grass sparkling in the sun that he picked a bunch and took it to the teacher. He was very disappointed when he arrived at school with just a bunch of rather dull grass!

At that time one left school at age 14. On the way home the big boys and girls would carry the little ones when they were tired. We were lucky, our aunt who was only four years older than my brother, and her friend had bicycles and sometimes we were given a lift to school on their carriers.

Mr Stanley Knowles, the headmaster, taught all of the children to write properly. There were no biros then but real nib pens and inkwells – I used to get ink all up my right forefinger.

There were six classes, Miss Thomes taught the babies, five year olds, to knit as well as other basic skills. There was a big dolls house and rugs and bedcovers to knit.

In the next class Mrs Brudnell taught us to embroider. A group of girls embroidered a tablecloth for a local lady and later Mrs B went to tea and said that the cloth was upside down, the reply being "I can't tell which side is which". I remember that cloth so well because I worked on it and when it was finished the lady brought a bag of carefully saved sweets for the girls who had done the embroidery – I was away from school and they didn't save me any. We also collected sheeps wool and made it into a rug on a loom.

Big girls were taught to cook and to clean house properly and the boys did woodwork and gardening. In the summer we had some lessons outside, we would sit in a big circle on our chairs in the playground and take turns to read. We had nature walks and outdoor painting lessons. The leaving age went up to 15. There were scholar-ships to Bridgnorth Grammar School. We scholarship people were very looked down upon in the early years but when it became necessary for everyone to pass an examination to attend the snobbery ceased.'

'During the Second World war Lilleshall Hall was used to house evacuees from Dr Barnardo's in London and Manchester. The golf course there was bombed as was the Big Wood at one point.

The village too was host to outsiders in the war years. The children of personnel from Cosford had filled up the schools in Albrighton and Tong so about 30 were brought to Sheriffhales. At first they were transported in army tenders, one of which knocked down the school gatepost. The newcomers brought new furniture but filled up the rooms to capacity. With the other evacuees from Smethwick adding to the problems, there was often friction between the local children and the outsiders but some friendships remain firm. Mr Dennis was the headmaster. He was very strict.

During the war years and in the following years the timetable was not that much different from the early days of the century. At eleven, however, one scholarship a year could be gained to go to Newport to the grammar schools there. Lessons at Sheriffhales consisted of prayers and scripture every day as it was still at that time a church school. Then arithmetic and daily chanting of tables followed. Writing with reading completed the three R's as well as grammar, punctuation and nature study. PE was exercises but there were some games, such as rounders, hockey, netball and football. In the playground could be seen whips and tops, hoops, skipping ropes, hopscotch and marbles. An old tin bath stood on end to serve as a house and some of the children formed gangs, mostly one sex versus the other. Stilts were made from ld tin cans and bits of string. The highlight of the year was a play performed by the children. Girls knitted dishcloths and vests and sewed samplers and cushions. They had a loom, too, on which were woven scarves. The boys did the gardening. In the grounds were two trees planted in 1936 to celebrate the coronation; an oak planted by the boys and a chestnut planted by the girls. Mr Dennis kept the cane out in the shed and used it when required but he would usually give a sharp rap on the knuckles with a ruler.

Later on the vicar fell out with the headmaster and the ensuing row meant that the school was taken over by the council.

The desks in school were still the all-in-one variety and the source of heat was still the three fireplaces. Tests were given each week and the winners were allowed to pick where to sit, thus the clever ones were always warmer than the rest! In the winter it was cold enough to freeze the ink in the inkwells. Lighting was by oil-lamp. The toilets were double seater buckets and were not favourably remembered by anyone!

There were still people poor enough to send their children to school in stockinged feet. The school used to provide wellingtons for them. Many children had to take time off school to help on the farm at certain times of the year. Two days off were allowed with a parental note, more with a doctor's note, so absentees were visited by the attendance officer. The boys were regularly off at potato picking time and children of either sex at harvest time.'

THE SCHOLARSHIP

There were two ways for children to be able to further their education at High School – their parents could pay the fees or they could win a scholarship. Pride in those who managed to do the latter was enormous, though until examination entry broke down the barriers, fee-paying students tended to look on scholarship pupils as a group apart.

COALBROOKDALE HIGH SCHOOL

'The school was a county high school typical of a number built in Shropshire just before the First World War. Girls form rooms etc were at one end – boys at the opposite. In the centre were the shared facilities – the assembly hall which was also used as a gymnasium, the science lab and the art room. These rooms acted as a barrier and it was truly girls at one end and boys at the other and never the twain shall meet. On the wall in the hall there was a plaque which read "1914–1918 These our school fellows died for England" and followed by seven or eight names.

Many pupils travelled to school by train and were known as "train girls" or "train boys". Again the sexes segregated themselves – boys stood at one end of the platform and girls at the other. On the trains, girls and boys never shared a compartment. The girls' uniform consisted of a navy blue gym tunic also known as gym slip, and a blue and white striped blouse. The gym tunic consisted of a yoke and the main part was really three box pleats. They were worn very short, well above the knees. Stockings were long fully fashioned. They were bought at Maddox of Shrewsbury and cost two shillings and elevenpence a pair. Maddox was a beautiful shop, quite high class; situated on the corner of High Street and Pride Hill in Shrewsbury – sadly the premises are now boarded up. Navy blue coats and navy blue velour hats were worn in winter and navy blue blazers and white panama hats were worn in the summer. Panamas could be scrubbed clean and one hat lasted all one's school days. Indoor shoes had to be worn, they were always flat heeled and had one strap and one button. On Prize Giving Days (Speech Days) white silk dresses were worn – they were worn again by confirmation candidates at the local church service.

Much homework had to be done – it kept pupils fully occupied in

the evenings. Many poems and sections of Shakespeare's plays and of the Bible had to be learned by heart. These have never been forgotten and still give pleasure. Homework was carried out by lamp light – finishing touches were executed on the train journey to school.

A favourite teacher was Miss Ruth Cubey – she taught Religious Knowledge, English Grammar and Junior Maths. She was strict and thorough and all lessons were a pleasure. Miss Cubey, to the delight of all pupils, was the first mistress to own and drive a car – it was a two seater Clyno. The boot of these cars opened up to reveal seats for two more passengers, who were, however, exposed to the elements.'

'In the spring of every year the headmistress of Rushbury school used to put forward names of pupils to take an entrance exam for Coalbrookdale High School. It says much for the then village school system that invariably one or two of the pupils nominated gained entrance and some won free scholarship places. The rail link from Craven Arms to Wellington provided transport, the first pupils being picked up at Rushbury station at 8.05am. Every station saw more pupils joining the train and at Buildwas Junction they were joined by those who had travelled on the Severn Valley line. Childlike, it was a great joy if for some reason the train was delayed as we then missed assembly and on the odd occasion class had even commenced!'

RADBROOK COLLEGE AND BRIDGNORTH

'When I was 13 I won a scholarship to go to Radbrook College as a junior boarder. This was a great experience and it was two years I have never forgotten. Only twelve scholarships were awarded each year and 24 had passed so we had to go to a Selection Day at Radbrook. We had a medical and an interview and I couldn't believe it when I was one of the twelve.

The morning started at six o'clock so this really got one used to early rising. As well as normal school lessons we were taught cookery, housewifery, laundry and pantry duties. We only had two visiting afternoons per month, one Wednesday and one Sunday and we had to write home each week. We went to church every Sunday morning, walking in twos in a crocodile. There were 24 juniors, twelve from the previous year. There must have been 200 students, who could come and go as they pleased; they were all paying, there were no student scholarships. The juniors used to have crushes on students.

Each Friday morning we had to line up outside surgery for our weekly dose of senna tea. Every morning we had PE outside before breakfast, hail, rain or snow. Three Wednesday afternoons and three Sundays each month (the others were visitors days when we were allowed visitors from two to four in the afternoon), Matron took us for a walk.'

'Winning an eleven-plus county scholarship was a rare achievement – about one in ten years at Tuck Hill in the 1920s. There was however a local "Grove" Trust Fund at Alveley which included Tuck Hill and one or two places were awarded every year at Bridgnorth Grammar School.'

152

THE WORLD OF WORK

ON THE FARM

Shropshire's rich arable and pastureland has supported generations of farmers and labourers, following in their father's footsteps through good times and bad. It could be a hard life, but it has left memories of times when labour was willingly shared at busy periods and life ran along time-honoured ways, from ploughing and sowing to harvesting and threshing. Into this century, labourers congregated at hiring fairs to offer themselves for another twelve month's hire – often the only break they had in the year's toil.

THE HIRING FAIR

'At Whixall the only holiday for farmworkers and dairymaids was New Year's Day. At the Gorby Market held in that week they could be re-engaged for a further twelve months or dismissed.'

'In about 1919 I was taken by my grandmother to see the Gorby Market in High Street, Wem, when farm servants were given a day off to come into Wem to receive their wages for the previous year, and to offer themselves for hire for the coming year. This applied mostly to men and I don't remember seeing any women.'

'On March 25th each year at Bishops Castle, if a man wanted to change his job, he would stand in the High Street signifying that he was free to take on other employment. Those needing new help would come along and inspect each man as to his strength and capabilities. If he liked what he saw he would give the man a shilling to clinch the hiring. If the deal fell through, the shilling had to be returned.'

'At the May Fair on 17th May it was hiring day at Knighton. All the workers would walk the street and wear something to denote the kind of work they were looking for, such as a tuft of sheep wool in their cap if they were shepherds. The farmers would choose who they wanted and would give the worker a shilling to hold an agreement. All the farm workers' holidays would be one week on May, then they would start their new job the following Monday.'

'Agriculture was the only industry at Weston Lullingfields – mostly dairy farming. This area extended to the Cheshire Plain and excellent Cheshire cheese was made around here. It was a rotation of commodities – the cows produced the milk to make the cheese; the whey from the cheese, after the cream had been extracted to make butter, was fed to the pigs; the pigs produced bacon and ham and made lots of very good muck which grew the grass to feed the cows to make the milk. I remember the pigs in the sties that joined onto the farmhouse fighting and rushing to throw coal into the battling animals, who immediately started crunching it and stopped fighting.

My father remembers taking the cheese to Nantwich to be sold, and during the Depression bringing it back home again. It was stored to mature in the farmhouse and some walls in the house are still salt damaged from the cheese and bacon. Cheesemaking on the farms died out when the local factories opened and the farmers just sold the milk.

The milking was done by hand and there was plenty of labour on the farm to do it. The milk was carried from the shed to the dairy on yokes on what we called 'bouks' and didn't the yokes hurt your neck!

The farms were worked with horses. As a child I had to lead the horses when we were carrying corn and their feet were very big and very close, but on the whole they were very gentle creatures. One old one, Captain, had the awkward habit of lying down in the shafts and going to sleep. In the way animals have of liking to stand on a high point, the horses used to stand on the top of the canal bridge and I would be sent to move them so the cows could get down the meadows to graze.

Corn grown mainly for animal feed was harvested with binders and before that, of course, with scythes. There is a field just below the canal bed called the Cobblers Meadow. It is so called because a local cobbler was boasting that he could scythe the field in a day, so the local workers bet him that he couldn't. He accepted the wager and the lads proceeded to lace the beer they provided him with Epsom Salts. It is said that he won his bet, without his trousers on!

I remember the farm having anthrax and the cows that died having to be burned, with the police in constant attendance.

The farm was visited by the saddler. A fire was lit for him in the saddle room where he spent a few days mending the harness and, with a little persuasion, boots as well. The stallions travelled the countryside to get the mares in foal and the groom spent the night on the farms, sleeping where he could find a warm corner.'

'There have been great changes with cattle. All our cattle were

155

Herefords and Shorthorns, then fashion changed to the Friesian cow for her milk and she was given the Hereford bull so that the male calf would have some flesh on it. The Friesian cow has held her place, but the bullocks are now mostly of continental strains.

The milking was done in the shippon. The cows were two to a stall and fastened with a chain and the milker sat on a stool with the bucket firmly between his or her knees. When the cow was milked dry, the milk was poured through a sieve into a large container, later into a churn when the dairies started collecting milk from the farms. The children of the family then went round the cows to 'drip' the last drop of milk from the cow; this is how we learned to milk. This last drop of milk was supposed to be very rich and creamy. When the dairies started collecting the milk it had to be cooled. This was done night and morning down a cooler in the newly built dairy. The milk ran down the outside of the cooler and into the churn. Inside the cooler the water made its way up and down to be saved in large tanks and troughs for the animals to drink. The milk churns belonged to the dairy.

Then came the milking machine. One man could milk three cows at the same time with help to carry the full bucket to the dairy for cooling. The churns were carried every morning and put on the milk stands ready for collection. Empty milk churns were put on the stand for the next milking. There were labels to fill up and fasten on the handles of the milk churn with your name and address, the number of gallons in the churn and then the total and whether it contained evening or morning milk.

Nowadays milking is quite different with milking parlours and many more cows being milked at the same time and the cows standing loose in a big yard waiting to be milked. They are housed loose and can help themselves to silage and their ration of meal is given to them as they are being milked. The milk is cooled in refrigerated tanks and taken away from the farm in a tanker.'

'My father first took me to market when I was eleven years old in the 1920s. Then a cow in calf cost about £17. I recall my father buying four cows. The owner asked £17 each for three of them but only £11 for the fourth. My father inspected them carefully and thought he had a bargain, but when he got back to our farm at Baschurch the transaction niggled him. Then another lad on the farm looked at them and said 'Open your eyes, gaffer, she's blind in one eye!'

In 1939 the first milking machine was installed at the farm. We had 14 cows then to be milked and new cowsheds were built, not milking parlours. Up to 1949 all cows had to be Tuberculin Tested. I can recall when 27 out of 29 cows aborted their calves.'

FOOT AND MOUTH

'In the early 1950s there was a foot and mouth epidemic. A vet had called at a farm near us in Cheswardine to treat a cow after he had been at an unaffected farm, and next day a Ministry vet came and shot it and told the farmer to bury it. The farmers asked me to help him – an experience I shall never forget. A week later the Ministry vet came and shot the rest of the animals and these were burned.

In 1960 there was another foot and mouth epidemic and it was confirmed at our neighbour's farm. They shot all the animals and one vet who came from there to us, wanted to see my cows. I refused to let him see them and he said I could not tell if a cow was ill so I told him where he could go to. He said he would be back in an hour with a policeman but I never saw him again. Five days later an older man called and asked me if I had been having trouble with one of their young vets. I told him why. He then asked me if he could look at the cows over the doors so I agreed and had no more trouble with them.'

AS BLUE AS WINBERRIES

'One Saturday at Baschurch my father told me to clean out the saddle room. One of the things I found was a bottle containing a blue liquid. There was no label as to contents, so I emptied it in the sheep-dipping trench. In due course the shepherd complained to my father that he couldn't bit make why the sheep were coming from being dipped 'as blue as winberries'.'

POULTRY FARMING

'On Christmas Day in 1922, young Bert Bradley of Bromfield, aged 13, having left his schooldays behind him, was now about to start his working life as poultry boy at a local farm. This meant having to leave his home and family to 'live in' at the farmhouse, sharing a bedroom with another worker.

On that first day he stood in the farmhouse kitchen, listening nervously as the housekeeper told him what his duties would be. Seven days a week, he would have to get up and start work at 5.30am and finish at 6.00pm.

His first job of the day would be to go to the field and bring in the horses, so that they could be made ready for their day's work. Then he would have to go and bring the cows to the cowshed for milking.

His own job would then start! He was responsible for looking after 200 chickens, 200 ducks, 200 turkeys and 300 geese and collecting the eggs. The first meal of the day for the poultry was indian corn, but the last meal was a mash. For this Bert had to carry several bags of the corn to a boiler standing out in the yard. This corn would be heated and made into a hot mash – 'The warmth of the hot food inside them makes them lay better,' explained the housekeeper.

In the summer the chicken sheds, which were on wheels, would be pulled by the horses to the stubble, after the corn had been cut and taken in. These houses would be moved to a different position every few days, with the poultry picking up the spilt corn.

Bert's meals would be eaten at the kitchen table, together with the other workers. His free time would be spent at choir practice and bell ringing – any spare evenings he was allowed to sit reading in the kitchen. His wages were two shillings and sixpence per week and the housekeeper explained that she would be keeping it safe for Bert, and after four weeks she would put it in an envelope and give it to the postman, who would then take it to Bert's mother! Bert could earn pocket money by collecting any eggs hidden around the farm, laid in inaccessible places; for these he would get a halfpenny per dozen. During the following year Bert was soaked to the skin many times, day after day, when standing out in the rain preparing the mash for evening meal. Snow, rain or hail, it made no difference. The boiler was never put under cover! When Bert had his 14th birthday, the farmer was informed by the labour union that he should pay Bert three shillings and sixpence per week and this would be increased every year. The farmer then told Bert that as he could not afford to pay such high wages, he must give him the sack! So ended Bert's first job. Such was life in those days.'

'I married a Shropshire man and still live at the same smallholding I came to as a bride in 1947. When we married my husband was a market gardener and I helped him with the crops which were in season. Although I had been brought up on a farm I did not find it easy picking potatoes, peas and runner beans, the latter not up sticks.

We also kept poultry which included guinea fowl and turkeys. Keeping poultry meant I had eggs to clean and poultry to dress. Then we were accredited, so twice a year the hens had to have a blood test which meant taking a spot of blood from under the hen's wing. This was done by a girl from the Ministry of Agriculture. If they passed we could sell the eggs to a hatchery for a higher price. The hens had to be free range and one hen always laid her egg under a rhubarb leaf in the garden. Our son, who was three, watched the hen and copied her squatting and cackling noise. One day as he did this I quietly popped an egg under him. I shall never forget his little face when he stood up and saw the egg. But he stopped playing his little game and I was sorry I spoilt it.'

'Farms at Hodnet in the 1920s were mixed enterprises and poultry, including turkeys, were reared on most farms. After corn harvest the turkeys were transported in their poultry houses to the stubble fields where they 'gleaned' their food and prepared for Christmas. It was a delightful task to walk on a late August evening to the stubble field to 'fasten up' the turkeys.'

'At one farm at Whixall which bred chickens in large numbers, the eggs were examined from time to time and any not developing properly were weeded out. Any considered edible were used for cooking while those too far gone were added to the lime wash used for painting the walls. One grandmother who had been in service there said, 'It was horrible when you were spreading this lime wash to see bits of chicken in it.' Goose wings were saved whole for dusting.'

THE FARMING ROUTINE

'Each year at Tilstock started with carrying out manure by horse and cart onto the fields. It was put into piles, then men would spend days spreading it with a large fork.

Then the ploughing – days of walking up and down after the horses. These were also stone-picking days, when all stones surfaced by the plough had to be removed because they would damage the machine when harvesting. When it was too cold or wet for other jobs, the men were busy hedging and ditching. Sowing was done by a man with what they called a fiddle, walking up and down the fields. Also at this time were sown turnips and mangold-wurzels for winter feed. The first harvest was hay. This was cut and left to dry, then put into stooks to be loaded later onto a cart. At the farm it was thrown through a pitch hole to the loft above the shippons for winter feed. The men worked until dark. As the corn grew, the men had the job of digging out docks and thistles. When the corn was cut it was dried in stooks. Taken to the farm, it was put in the bay ready for threshing. The winter days were spent grinding corn for feed. This was mixed with the turnips and mangolds when pulped.'

'Apart from the milking herd, there were herds of bullocks fattening in the sheds. The aim was to have them ready for the Christmas auctions, when the price was highest. Many owners relied on these sales for the rent – and paying the six monthly corn bill. High days for the farmers were the weekly auctions – women seldom went to these Smithfield auctions unless they were farming on their own.

Horse auctions were held once a month. The animals for sale would be fed and groomed by the waggoner, starting long before dawn. The horse's coat would shine like glass and the mane and tail were plaited with coloured ribbons. Then came the walk of some miles to Shrewsbury. A good sale made an exciting day.'

'In the 1940s in Meole Brace one of the Fox Brothers collected the pig's swill in an old horse-drawn bread van which had once belonged to Morris's of Shrewsbury. The van had candle lights on either side and at dusk he would drive past the house with the candles flickering and that awful smell of pig swill!'

HARVEST TIME

'Before the advent of the horse mower, the grass for hay was cut by hand scythes, often by gangs of itinerant workers. The gang which served Broseley was known as the Long Company and the man who led them, the best scytheman, was Jasper Griffiths. My father, as a small boy, followed them round the farm, fetching and carrying. He was given a small scythe and was taught to use it, acquiring in the process the nickname 'Jasper'.

The head man worked last in succession to the other workers and was thus able to set the pace. If the man working in front of him slowed down, he received a sharp tap on the heal from the pace-setter's scythe. This worked in turn right through the team. They scythed in a diagonal across the field and back, not round and round. Later they also turned the hay by hand and made it into cocks, which were carefully made piles of hay which would withstand a shower of rain and were later pitched onto waggons. When the corn harvest came they bound and stooked the corn and also came again at threshing time. The arrival of the horse-mower sadly threw these men out of work.'

'I was born in 1902 at Big Huntington in Ashford Carbonell. I can remember when corn was cut by hand with a sickle. An armful of the cut corn had to be picked up with all the heads lying in the same direction, a few stems were then withdrawn and wrapped around the sheaf and tied in a knot. The sheaves were then stood on their butts leaning towards one another, usually six to a stand. They had to dry in the wind and sun to hear three lots of church bells (three weekends). Sometimes if it was a wet season the grain would sprout in the heads.

Then came the reaper-binder, about 1920. This machine cut the corn, tied it in sheaves with binder twine ('farmer's glory') and ejected them ready for stooking.

When the corn was dry in the sheaves they had to be loaded onto a dray. This was a long flat cart with thripples back and front. There was an art in loading a dray. The sheaves had to be laid butts facing out. When the first layer was in place the next lot had to be placed in such a way that each layer was pinned down securely. The loader was also exhorted to 'keep your middle full'. The sides had to be built upright, no bulges to catch on gateposts or to fall off when the dray was manoeuvred around corners.'

'In the 1930s at our farm near Wentnor, we had only one field of oats and I can remember a man coming to cut this with a scythe. Afterwards we had a reaper and finally a binder, both drawn by horses. Hay harvesting entailed all the family's help. As soon as we came home from school we had to go into the hayfields. Father would cut the hay with a horse-drawn mowing machine, then it was all hands turning it with hand rakes, and after it was made it was raked several swathes together and cocked. If it got wet it had to be shaken well with a pitchfork, since it had to be really dry before cocking it. It was then lugged in to the barns with horse-drawn waggons. When the barns were full it was stacked and these had to be thatched with dried rushes in the autumn. The rushes had to be gathered and dried and fern or bracken was cut and harvested for littering down the animals in winter. Mangolds and swedes were grown for feeding the animals in the winter. These were put through a hand-turned cutter and mixed with hay that had been chopped up in a chaff cutter.'

'Farm work was almost inevitable for country boys. They worked hard for their four shillings a week. They learned to plough a straight furrow, spread farmyard manure with a fork, and sometimes pick heavy stones off the land. Some artificial fertiliser (nitro chalk) was spread by hand from a zinc container strapped around the shoulder.

Threshing the corn was a dirty, hard and dangerous job. The threshing box was towed into the stock or rick yard by the steam engine, to a position near the barn or corn stack. Firstly the steam engine usually had a fire laid in the front in the firebox and the boiler was filled with water, probably carried from the local brook or in a horse-drawn water tank. This was done the day before threshing. The next day the engine driver arose very early to stoke up his steam engine. A wide belt was attached to its driving wheel, then on to the pulley of the threshing box. When the steam engine started the belt went around like a mad thing to drive the threshing box. A 'feeder' man stood on top of the box and fed it with arms full of the harvested corn. This came out as corn one side, caught in a sack, straw on the other side tied in neat bundles from the binder, and chaff very dusty at the rear. Children often had the job of pushing the very lightweight chaff into a large sack and this was used in winter for animal bedding. To everyone around the noise was very loud, but pleasant – but the threshing box did groan when it was short of food! To stop the phenomenal show the engine slowed down and a strong pole was used to push the belt off the driving wheel. There were no safety officers in those days. Then, at the end of threshing, there would be a chase after the rats.'

'Threshing days were very hard days for men and women, the women having to provide so much food and if it rained the work went on and on. Men from neighbouring farms came to help and that's how it worked, everybody helping each other. Breakfast was a basinful of broth, bacon and egg and bread washed down with tea. At ten o'clock a basketful of bread and cheese and beer was taken out to the stack yard; strangely this meal was called lunch. Dinner was around one o'clock, a large meal of either lamb or pork or beef, with plenty of potatoes, swedes or carrots. Pudding was rice pudding with apple tart, or damson or plum pudding with custard. A favourite pudding was bread and butter pudding with some currants thrown in. Tea was greatly in demand as threshing was a dusty, thirsty job. Tea would be bread and butter with jam and cheese, jam tarts and slab cake. If the men in charge of the machine lived too far away they would stay the night. They would have supper with the farm workers of bread, meat and pickles.'

Even with machines like this thrashing box, a farming life could be very hard. Everyone in the family, including the smallest child, had their allotted tasks.

THE MOLECATCHER

'Mole catchers were hired twice a year to come onto the farms and set traps. The catchers would check their traps, and every mole that was caught, its tail would be cut off and this was then placed in a match box. At the end of the week, the catcher would present this match box to the farmer who would then pay the mole catcher a penny per tail.'

THE COMING OF MECHANISATION

'Many people assume that the changeover from horse-drawn teams on the farm to horse-power engines was a simple matter of putting the horse out to grass, putting a TVO (Tractor Vaporising Oil) tank in the cart shed, buying a tractor and persuading the waggoner to use it. It wasn't always as simple as that, as I remember from the coming of mechanisation to the farms around Picklescott. Tractors were in short supply and money was also needed for other things. Farmers never bought in those days unless they had the money in their pockets to pay for the goods. It was the inventive farmer who saw the positive aspects of mechanisation and improvised. As old Polly found the hills were getting steeper, Grandad gave her a rest from the heavy work of mowing, especially difficult on some of the hilly fields. He bought a horse-drawn mowing machine, which had a French Barnard engine on it. So Polly only pulled the machine which drove the long cutting knives.

Mr Shakeshaft from Underhill Hall was well known for his desire to make life easier on the farm. He attached a haysweep to the front of his sturdy Vauxhall car and swept the hay up into great heaps at the foot of an elevator, onto which the hay was forked and lifted mechanically to the top of the stack. The men then made the haystack and it was much easier than making hay cocks in the field, then loading each hay cock onto the horse-drawn cart and unloading them onto the stack. The haysweep was made of wooden tines with metal slippers on their points, and what the sweep left behind the wide heel rake picked up.

I well remember the fun and never thought of the danger of riding round the fields at Underhill in old Ford lorries without doors and with floorboards missing. These lorries did sterling work, being useful for all sorts of farm jobs. I particularly remember the hay harvest. We always seemed to have lots of people around working but having fun at the same time. Evans, who had always worked with horses, used to have us all roaring with laughter as he shouted 'Whoa' and 'Hold up' to the lorries as he sped between the rows of hay, which was pitched up onto the lorries as soon as he brought his mechanical charger to a halt. The clutches were a bit fierce as were the brakes, so the 'Whoa' served as a warning to those up on the load to hang on tight or risk sliding off the slippery load.

The lorries were used for hauling manure, for hay and the corn harvest. They carried the corn as well as the straw. If the back wheels were jacked up off the ground the lorry could work a pulley belt and operate the vicious whirring saw benches. The one Ford lorry was used as a muck spreader. This was achieved by taking an axle off a car, turning the prop shaft vertically and adding a table-like arrangement of slats. Not only could farmyard manure be spread from this contraption but lime and artificial fertilisers were also applied to the fields using this vehicle. It was never quite the same when the tractors came, together with the other specialist equipment. Sometimes tractors were shared between family farms. The early tractors often had problems and there were considerable variations in quality. The magnetos often developed faults – there would be damp getting into the casings, there would be only a poor spark or no spark at all. Tempers would become frayed as the non-mechanically minded operatives and the farmer couldn't agree on what was wrong. It was mainly a time of do-it-yourself repairs so the men quickly learned to understand their new machines. The old starting handles were vicious things and I've seen many badly bruised hands and arms. As the machine sputtered into life the handle would kick back and nearly take your hand off. If you were unlucky it would fly out, but you soon learned to get out of the way fast.

These machines were wonders for a while but we quickly got used to the new ways and didn't grieve for the times gone by when all work was done by hand or horse.'

IN SERVICE

The world of Upstairs Downstairs was for many girls the only avenue open to them of paid employment. This did not necessarily mean work in a big house on an estate, there were many more women who toiled in farmhouses across Shropshire, helping out in the house and on the farm, but for all servants the quality of life depended on the Master and Mistress.

MASTER WITH A BIG STICK

'My husband's grandmother spent her schooldays and early working years in the village of Tilley near Wem in the early 1900s. Her first job at the age of twelve was working at a local boys school where she cleaned the boots and shoes of the young gentlemen for one shilling a week. She later went into service as a housemaid to a family in Tilley and told us tales of how she had a half day off each week and the father of the family always waited with a large stick to be sure she was in by nine o'clock on that day, otherwise the stick would be brought into use.'

ON A COUNTRY ESTATE

'I remember my first sight of Loppington on November 18th, 1925: I was 15 and was about to take up the position of under-housemaid at Loppington House, seat of the Dickin family since 1820.

Rural Shropshire was a far cry from home in Castlefields, Shrewsbury, where I and my friends often went to the swimming baths and the cinema; the best seats cost fourpence! Loppington afforded no such attractions and, for some time, I had no transport to go elsewhere in my off-duty time, which was every Tuesday from 2pm till 9pm (in winter) and till 10pm in summer; and alternate Sundays from 2pm till 9pm. A period of extreme homesickness followed my entry into domestic service, although hard work ensured that I slept soundly at night.

My uniform was a blue dress, white cap and apron which was worn each day until 4.30pm when I had to change into a black dress, frilled cap and apron; I had to provide my own uniform which I bought with money borrowed from a relative. This was repaid at ten shillings each month from my monthly wage of £1 3s 4d. Once I had cleared this debt, I borrowed £4 17s 6d to buy a bicycle so that I and my new friend, the kitchen-maid, could get to Wem (and go to the pictures in Wem Town Hall). Sometimes I would cycle home to Castlefields on a Sunday; otherwise, I kept in touch with my family by letter.

I applied for this post through an agency situated near the Royal Salop Infirmary; I was engaged by Miss Dorothy Dickin, who interviewed me in Castlefields, and instructed me to say 'Miss' when addressing my employer. 'Below stairs' were: the cook, the house-maid, the under-housemaid, the kitchen-maid, the butler, two gardeners, the chauffeur, the gamekeeper, the cowman and the groom.

As under-housemaid, I rose at 6.30am in summer, or at 7.00am in winter, cleaned and lit the fires in the dining-room, small drawing-room and the library and kept the poker, tongs etc polished; brushed all the carpets using a dustpan and brush or a carpet-sweeper on alternate days; polished the wooden surrounds (no carpets were fitted); helped the butler wait at table if there were guests; was responsible for preparing the household laundry and the servants' laundry for collection each week by Mr Kitley, who came with a four-wheeler and pony. His wife did the laundry at their home at Rose Villa – now known as Spenford House. I remember how Mr Kitley would yell, 'Winifred, is that laundry ready yet?' More often than not I would reply, 'No, it isn't!' having been too busy with other chores. I also mended the household laundry and often had to repair sheets by 'putting sides to middle.'

'When I was 15 my mother accompanied me to a Domestic Agency in St Mary's Street in Shrewsbury, and I obtained a position as third parlourmaid at Cheswardine Hall, the home of the Donaldson Hudson and wife and three adult children.

There were 15 on the staff, four in the kitchen. Off-duty was half a day off per week and every other Sunday. However, there was nowhere to go except to bike to Market Drayton. The companionship of the other maids was a very enjoyable, we had nice bedrooms with carpet on the floor, and very good food – all better than our own homes – and £12 a year salary. The head parlourmaid was Violet Sharp, who was later concerned in the Lindberg Baby case.

I look back on my career as a house and parlourmaid with great affection – it taught me a lot. How to behave, to dress and to communicate. It gave me companionship and fun, and I saw lovely houses and a different way of life.'

'In the 1930s I went to work for the Squire and his wife as a kitchen-maid. My day started at six o'clock. My first job was to clean the coal range and light the fire to get the kettles boiling in time to take a cup of tea up to the cook at seven o'clock. Then it was lay the servants hall table for breakfast and cook whatever was on the menu each morning. I'd been there five years when war was declared and I joined the Land Army.'

'I was 16 when I left Wem to work near Oswestry. I felt sad to be leaving home but excited at going to work in a large house. It had been quite a struggle for Mother to provide my dresses and frilly aprons for afternoons. The house had a large staff – a butler, two footmen, a hallboy, a cook, a housekeeper, a lady's maid and four housemaids. The first housemaid had her own bedroom and I shared an attic bedroom with the others. We had our meals at a long table in the servants' hall and we sat in order of rank. The butler always carved. We had time off for church on Sundays and one afternoon each week.

As fourth housemaid I was paid £3 7s 4d each month. This included two shillings and sixpence for laundry and two shillings for beer! This I didn't drink so was able to put it with my savings. I saved hard to buy a bicycle, which cost me £8. Then I was able to cycle to Wem after lunch each Wednesday. We had to be back by ten o'clock and no one dared be late for the long straight drive was overlooked by the main rooms of the house.

After four months I became third housemaid. I stayed with the family for three years and then moved on to the house of a titled family. At my interview her ladyship remarked, 'I can see you sew well by the darn in your stocking!'. It was hard work in service but we were happy and very well cared for.'

WORKING FOR A FARMER

'I was in residential service in the late 1920s. I left school at 14 and sent straight into service in a farmhouse. I worked from seven in the morning to seven at night, baking, cheesemaking, poultry dressing, sausage making and so on. This was in addition to the normal cleaning duties, carrying fuel for fires etc – and all for two shillings and sixpence a week. But I also had plenty of good food, which would not have been so at home. Off duty was every other Sunday afternoon and an occasional outing, perhaps to the May Fair in Bishops Castle. I remember lighting the fire for the bakery oven one day, forgetting that the cat usually slept in there!'

'At the farmhouse where I worked at Wootton, there was a great long stone passage I had to get down on my hands and knees to scrub. The amount of brass to clean on a Friday was unbelievable. There was washing every Monday, milk utensils to be washed and sterilized, cooking every day and to crown it all you were either out weeding the garden or carrying water from the brook for the flowers. And all for eight shillings and one half day a week, from four o'clock till nine, and every other Sunday. Then you had to go all round the hens in different fields, shutting them up at night. I hated it and left after three months. I remember her saying 'If you stay here the summer you've got to stay the winter.' He used to ring a bell at five o'clock in the morning – it was over my bed and he rang it from his bedroom. If he didn't hear me about he'd get the broom and bang on my bedroom door. Frightened me to death.'

'Being the second eldest of six children, my mother had to leave school at 14 and find a way to support herself. In country areas the only option was to go into service. She was employed in the 1930s on a farm in the Cross Houses area as a maid to a family with four young children. On gaining her position she was delighted with her wages of three shillings and fourpence a week, after board and lodgings. This was more than her elder sister, who was only earning two shillings and sixpence.

Her work was general housework and helping to mind the children. She would rise at half past six and finish at half past ten or eleven o'clock. One task which remains in her mind is the blackleading of the kitchen range, which was done weekly. There was a brush to put it on, another one to brush it off, and then the range was polished with a cloth. In the afternoon she would take the children for walks. In the evening the children looked forward to joining her in the kitchen where she would play with them. Every third Sunday she had a half day holiday when she went home to see her family. After 14 months the opportunity arose at another farm in the area offering a wage of ten shillings a week. The work was similar but here she had the opportunity to serve afternoon teas at the tennis parties of which the family were fond.

At a further employment, where again she received a rise in wages, a uniform had to be worn. It was a blue dress and large white apron for mornings and in the afternoon she had to change into a black dress with a white frilled apron. After having her hair tied up in the morning, in the afternoon she could wear a white hair band. At this stage she bought herself a bicycle which was nearly new. Curry's of Mardol had some flood damaged stock and the bike cost £3 10s 0d.'

MINING, QUARRYING AND THE FORGE

Shropshire is famed, of course, as a cradle of the Industrial Revolution that changed the face of Britain in the 18th and 19th centuries. The descendants of the men who made that revolution possible continued to work in her coal mines and quarries, and in addition there are memories of the Dale Forge at Coalbrookdale, where so much began.

KING COAL

'In 1912 Ifton Heath shaft was sunk. I can see myself now, and all the kiddies around, standing watching the big steam engines carrying the chains etc to begin the sinking. I have lived to see the opening and closing of the pit and to me the village is poorer without it. Good old King Coal.'

'Annscroft was in a coal mining district and Father was the coal agent for the local colliery, Moat Hall. The pit was owned by Mr W. T. Shorthouse, who had a lovely house built in the village called The Laurels. On the other side of the road from the church was the coal wharf. When I was a lad in the 1910s it was a horse and cart which hauled the coal from the wharf; the pit had several. The pit shaft was about half a mile from the wharf across several fields. A tramline was laid to transport the tubs of coal from the pit head to the wharf. A horse called Curley pulled several full tubs and returned with the empty ones. In later years there was a youth with the train.

At the pit head there was an engine house for hauling the cage up and down. It was operated by steam, the boiler being fired by coal. A smaller engine house also operated from the same boiler. This engine was used to haul the tubs from the coal face to the pit bottom, by means of a wire hauser attached to a drum and run on jockey wheels down the shaft and along the pit bottom. I was told that the actual coal seam was only three to four feet deep and had to be hacked out by pick and shovel. It was then loaded by youths onto 'dans' (like a sledge) and hauled with a harness around their waists and a rope through their legs out to where the road had been widened to take the tubs. The quality of the coal was lovely. It would burn with immense heat and leave very little ash.

Eventually Mr Shorthouse sold the colliery to Mr Nicholas Fielden, who also bought out Hanwood Colliery. I was told that a road was driven underground between Moat Hall and Hanwood collieriers and the coal transported along the tunnel. As a result the wharf at Annscroft was closed down and the work transferred to Hanwood. The mine eventually closed down some time before the Second World War. The shaft was filled in and capped.'

'My father worked at Moat Hall colliery (near Annscroft). He began work at the colliery at the age of 15 in 1917. His task was to pull trucks of coal by means of a chain fastened round his waist. It was the practice for one boy to do this work for five miners who were responsible for paying the boy. The weekly wage for a miner in those days was 35 shillings per week plus five cwt of coal for every 14 days worked. It would cost two shillings and sixpence to have the coal delivered to the miner's home.

There was a coal wharf at Annscroft and a pumping station at Arscott. Moat Hall colliery was closed in 1934.'

'My father worked at Hanwood pit in the 1920s and 1930s. I've taken a little truck down to the wharf at Annscroft and had a hundred-weight of coal for elevenpence – hand picked beautiful stuff. If the miners worked twelve consecutive days they had five hundredweight of coal for drying their clothes. They used to get soaking wet from lying in water working. They would be walking home to Pontesbury, Asterley and Minsterley and we kids used to walk with them and get our faces blacked. They always wore the knees out of their trousers. A lot of them wore corduroys and they were patched and patched and that heavy and sticking out. In the severe cold weather they hadn't walked far and their trousers would freeze hard. They could hardly run if a council wagon stopped to give them a lift. We used to laugh at them and they'd take a swipe at us – poor old devils. It was hard work and a poor old place. A man did well to earn 30 shillings a week although some of the really good miners could earn £2, good money then. My dad wanted me to go to the pit to learn to be a blacksmith, but Mother said if I did she'd leave home!'

'Miners walked from Pulverbatch to Hanwood to work in the pits, then back again at the end of the day. The mine owner (Nick Fielden, born at Condover Hall) would give them a lift in his car, dust covered clothes and all, if he passed them on their way.'

'Parts of Little Wenlock were devastated during the Second World War and for a long time afterwards with open cast coal mining. The roads were a quagmire during wet weather, with lorries taking coal to Buildwas power station, and in dry weather it would be dust.'

THE PIT GIRLS

I can remember my grandmother, that was my Dad's mother, she lived in the Long Row at New Dale. When she went to the coal house for a bucket of coal she always returned carrying it on her head. When she was young she had worked on the local pit banks as a 'pit girl' carrying either coal or ironstone in an iron box on her head. Lots of the girls when they left school in her day went on to the pit banks to carry this stone, it was a terrible job for girls to have to do.'

'When girls left school in Dawley they hadn't very much chance of employment. Most of them had to work either on the pit banks or go as domestic servants. The pit girls would go down past my house here at about six o'clock in the morning. They always wore clogs and we could hear them pattering down because they always came down in groups. It was early mornings of course, and as they came they were nearly always singing; they were so happy although it was such laborious work, picking out the rubbish from the parts that were of value either as ironstone or small pieces of coal from the pit bank.

The pit girls picked out the ironstone and the small pieces of coal and then the penny stone went to form the pit mounds, many of which are still standing, although a great many too have been levelled and made into beautiful looking districts, with nice shrubs.'

THE CASUALTIES

'My grandfather was killed in the Barn Pits at Donnington in 1898. It was a very bad winter and they brought his body all the way from the Barn Pits to his home at New Dale in a horse and cart. My grandmother was left a widow with eight children to bring up.

Granny told me about a family called Frost who lived at No 1 Turners Row in New Dale. All round the village it was a mining area, and in the cellar of No 1 they stored the blasting material for use in the local pits. There were five children in the family and one day they were playing with matches in the cellar – four of them were killed in the explosion.

THE STONE QUARRIES

'My father had been employed in the offices of the Clee Hill Granite Company from the time he left school at 13 in 1896. In 1908 he was the sole clerk at a tiny office at Detton Ford near Oreton.

The stone from the Clee Hill quarries was sent to Detton by an aerial rope-way. Huge iron buckets on pulleys were filled with the stone and sent along the rope-way. As the full buckets went down, they pulled the empty ones up.

A light railway ran from Ditton Priors to Cleobury Mortimer with a siding adjacent to the rope-way terminal. Here the stone was tipped from the buckets into trucks, weighed on the office weighbridge and shunted onto the main railway line. Here it was dispatched for road-making all over the country. My father, wanting to give his young

171

sister-in-law a thrill, took her down to Detton from Clee Hill in one of the buckets on the rope-way. Just as they were nearly at the terminus, the lunch whistle blew, the rope-way ceased to function and they were left suspended over the river for an hour – by intention or accident he never knew!'

'I was born in the early 1920s on the side of the Brown Clee, above a small village called Blackford. Most of the land was owned, and still is, by Lord Boyne, whose seat is at Burwarton. The main source of work was at the stone quarries on the top of Brown Clee.

There were two quarries. One, called Gwilts Quarry, took its stone by road down in Clee St Margaret. The other, which was larger, was the Abdon Stone Quarry and their stone was transported by rail down a very steep incline into Ditton Priors. This was done by a never ending wire rope around a very big drum at the top, and as each end was fastened to the wagons, so the full wagon going down would pull the empty ones going up. This was a very dangerous job for the men working on the line as they stopped some of the wagons by spragging on the wheels. There were accidents and I had an uncle killed on this line.

The quarries finished in about 1936 and you will see in their place on Abdon today a set of radio towers which help to check the traffic on busy days.

A few miles south is another Clee Hill, called the Titterstone Clee, with a very steep road going over it from Ludlow to Cleobury Mortimer. There is a quarry here too, which is still working today. The stone is trucked by road. There used to be a railway running up to the quarry but this is now finished.'

'My family lived in a terraced house near the Dhu stone quarry on Clee Hill. No lorries in those days, the work involved manual labour and horsepower and I used to watch as, the workday over, the men and horses made their way home. The stone was in great demand for roadmaking and repairing, and the making of setts, beautifully shaped, was a specialised job for trained men. Other sizes of granite were used to make a base for roads being remade. There was a railway line running up from Bitterley bringing trucks to carry away the prepared material. The trucks also brought provisions for the shops in Clee Hill. They were delivered to a warehouse near the shopping area and then horses and carts conveyed the goods to the shops.

'My father was a quarryman and would walk from Pant over the hill to Porthywaen where limestone was quarried. He wore corduroy trousers, union shirts, a muffler round the neck, and a hessian sack bag draped diagonally around the shoulders, held in place with a 'bag pin'. This was similar to a kilt pin but much less substantial, and had to be replaced frequently because of rusting. He wore thick boots which were made watertight, either with dubbin or, more often, with goose grease. The cord trousers were tied just below the knee with string referred to as Yorks. Some of the explosives used in the quarry found their way to local wedding celebrations, when 'cannons' were let off.'

'Villagers in Bitterley remember how Clee Hill dominated their lives. Looming over the village, occasionally covered in snow or lost in fog, it was always part of the background. The sound of the quarry being blasted when the men stopped for dinner, and the trains coming down laden with coal regulated the day.

It was intended to build a railway line to carry stone from Titterstone to Ludlow from where it could be transported on the old GWR line, but the slope is so steep that an incline was built from Bitterley yard to the top of Titterstone and the weight of the full trucks descending pulled the empty trucks back up to the quarry.

In the 1940s or 1950s a Dr McGreggon from Clee Hill had been visiting a mother and baby at Bedlam at Clee Hill. It was a foggy day and he decided to follow the incline so that he would not lose the way. Unfortunately, owing to the fog, he did not see or hear the loaded trucks descending and so was fatally crushed beneath them. Nowadays the stone is transported by road and the incline and railway line lie deserted and unused.

The income of the small hill farmer was often supplemented by work in the quarry. Splitting and cutting the local dhu stone was hard work and very painful to the hands.'

'Until 1892 the whole of the Trefonen area was extensively mined for coal; however, stone quarrying continued until 1970 in the Nantmawr area of the village. Most of the cottages housed quarrymen, and mostly had smallholdings attached. The quarry had its own stables and smithy and the schoolboys used to steal rides on the quarry tracks coming down the incline plane. There was the constant noise of blasting rock and stone crushing. Now it is a small hamlet and one of the quietest places you could wish to find, with the whole area returned to the wild with badgers, many birds and thick with wild flowers.'

THE FORGE

'I was born at New Dale in 1906 where my Dad worked as a puddler at the Trench Forge. I can remember that he used to wear moleskin trousers on account of the heat from the furnaces, of course ordinary trousers would not have stood up to the heat. My mother used to make him a short vest to wear under his ordinary shirt because of the sweat; she used to make them out of a bit of flannel or winceyette. I can see my mother now washing those moleskin trousers in the wash house in the back yard, in the dolly tub with the wooden dolly; these trousers were of course too thick to go through the old mangles. Talking about the Trench Forge, my Dad used to tell me that they employed 'beer boys' to fetch the beer from the local pub in the Trench for the puddlers, as it was essential that they had plenty of liquid to replace that which they had lost due to the terrific heat in which they worked.'

'My grandfather worked for the Coalbrookdale Company, as did my father and myself. My father worked in a place they called the Back Shop and during the First World War I used to take his breakfast into the works. There were about six or eight men in the shop and most of them were making aeroplane cylinders. I often made a little core of one part as a boy.

At the age of 14, in 1919, I left school and went into the Dale Works. The boy whose place I was taking took me round the works and introduced me to all the different departments and the people who were in charge, though a lot of them I knew because I had been going into the works for a long time, taking in my father's breakfast. At one time I used to take my grandfather's. My first few days were taken up with learning the ropes, such as lighting fires. In the wintertime it was always my job to go and shut the shutters on the pool side of the shop, that was the Upper Furnace Pool.

I started in the pattern shop in the Upper Works. If anyone wanted anything fetching, or glue making or lacquer making, that was our job and we had to learn these things. My foreman used to tell me that you must watch what the men are doing so that in years to come you will be able to do it too, which was good advice.'

'My dad used to be a moulder in the Dale Works and I can remember him coming home and his shirt would be as wet as though he'd had a bucket of water over him. Sometimes when he took it off it would just part company, rotten with sweat.'

OTHER WAYS WE MADE A LIVING

Sometimes, the choice of employment was made for youngsters by their father, sometimes simply by circumstance and the need to work at whatever was available. The lack of transport meant that jobs had to be within walking distance of home. The following recollections give a taste of how some Shropshire people made their way in the world.

NO CHOICE

'My grandfather was born in 1871 and when he was nine years old his father bought the Naird Farm near Shifnal. Moving was a tremendous undertaking with only horses and carts to transport furniture and equipment. The cattle had to walk the 15 miles and Tom, my grandfather, had to drive them.

As the family of twelve children grew up their father decided their careers for them. They were given no choice. The farm would not support so many adults, so as each son reached the age of 14 he was apprenticed to a trade. George was appointed to succeed his father, although he did not enjoy farming, and Tom, who loved the land, was apprenticed to a grocer! It was assumed that all the daughters would get married, so they stayed at home and learned from their mother how to run a household.'

ON THE ROADS

'Some men around Longville in the 1930s were employed by the council as road workers. Some worked in gangs tarspraying etc and this was a job usually done in the summertime when the weather was warm. When a stretch of road was to be surfaced loads of chippings would be tipped in places on the roadside along with barrels of tar. They would then bring what we used to call a tar pot. This was like a big square iron tank with four iron wheels. Tar would be put into the tank, under which was a big fire box and a fire would be lit to heat the tar. When it was hot about three men working in a row would sweep a length of road with brooms to clean off dust and dirt, the hot tar would then be sprayed onto the road and then chippings would be spread over the tar out of a cart drawn by a horse. The tar pot was also drawn by horses as they were very heavy. The road would then be rolled with a steam roller.

All country roads also had what was called a lengthsman who would work full time on the same length of road, keeping open ditches and drains, and dealing with weeds and grass on ditch banks and verges. At night the roadman would lay his tools down on the roadside, turn his wheelbarrow upside down over them, and they would be there for him next morning.

WHIXALL BIBLES

'The 'Moss' at Whixall provided work for many of the villagers, who cut turf for their own fires and to sell. Children as young as eleven were involved with their fathers, and horses and carts travelled miles to sell the blocks of turf known as Whixall Bibles. Turfdiggers would burn off the top level of growth before digging a new area to get rid of any adders. Despite this, in fine weather families would picnic and pick cranberries at the edge of the Moss. The Whixall Moss Litter Co supplied the army with bedding for their horses during the First World War. During the Second World War part of the Moss was used as a bombing range.'

TIMBER

'One of the local crafts at Wistanstow was felling alder trees for making clogs. The men would cut them all out ready for a lorry to collect and take them to a factory to be finished off. The women always wore them in the cotton mills in Lancashire.'

'I remember a man coming into the Longville area in the 1920s. He lived in a little hut in a wood which was being felled and he was a charcoal burner. He would build the wood up into dome shaped piles, which would be covered over with earth to seal them. They would then be set alight and used to smoulder away for days. When they finished burning and cooled down, the earth would be taken off and the charcoal bagged up and sent away. This man also cut and roughly shaped piles of wood which went for making clogs.

Timber felling was carried out. All the hauling would be done with big teams of horses. If quite a large area of trees was going to be felled, a sawmill would be set up near the site so the horses could haul the timber straight from the wood to the mill. When part of the Wenlock Edge was felled in the 1930s, a mill was set up by Mr Sam

Spencer of Craven Arms at Wolverton Farm. The horses would be stabled at neighbouring farms.'

TAILORING

'I left school at 14 knowing how I wanted to earn my living. I wanted to be a tailoress. My father agreed to pay a small sum of money weekly for me to be taught the trade.

Two maiden ladies had a workshop in Wellington where they made ladies and gents suits, as well as exclusive ballgowns. The workforce consisted of eight workers and I was taken on as apprentice. I had to walk about two and a half miles to work.

The irons had to be hot by the time work started, which was half past eight, as every seam was pressed as soon as it was sewn. The stove was dome shaped and of cast iron. It had ledges round it on which the irons were placed, bottoms against the stove. At the bottom of the stove was a door which, when opened, allowed a fire to be built inside. Fifty irons could be warmed on this and they were in constant use. We had half an hour for lunch and, as the apprentice, I had to make the tea. Very often I didn't find time to eat my sandwiches. Work ended at half past five and home I walked. After

John Weaver earned his living as a tailor after losing a leg in a threshing box accident.

177

six months I began feeling faint in the morning and when the doctor saw me he said on no account must I continue the work. My mother put my notice in and that finished all my hopes of becoming a tailoress.'

'My grandfather was a tailor. He took this up because he had only one leg. He lost the other when he was ten years old by slipping on a threshing box. It was nearly off and the amputation was finished on the kitchen table at Common Wood. Thereafter, he wore a wooden stump with an iron ring round the base. Periodically, it went to the blacksmith for a new ring and he made a new pad for the top out of cloth from the shop. He did have one of the first new bendable artificial legs for his wedding, because he wanted to kneel. It had dozens of buckles and straps and must have taken hours to put on. He never found it comfortable and returned to the wood stump. We found it a few years ago at the family home and sent to Park Hall Hospital Museum.

The tailor's shop was at Ivy Cottage, a large room with an iron stove in the middle. Two huge wooden tables filled either side of the room and two Singer sewing machines were up the centre. Large irons, called 'ducks' were heated up on the stove. Enamelled bowls were on each board for water for pressing. Large windows went all along the side of each board and oil lamps hung from the ceiling – one over each board. Hanging on hooks were plaited strands of buttonhole thread ready for use.

Above this room was a large loft-type room. A wooden ladder staircase led up to it out of the shop and there were skylights in the roof. In the early days, this was used as a cutting room with my grandfather cutting out the clothes and passing them down rolled in bundles ready for making up.

Below, six men and two ladies were employed sewing. The men sat cross-legged on top of the table boards with a board resting across their knees and the women sat on the edge of the table board, rather like sitting side saddle on a horse. One lady did nothing but buttonholes and could do all the buttonholes in a pair of men's leggings in an hour – not bad for hand sewing. The other one mainly felled (hemmed) the linings in jackets.

Being a business, they did have toilets for men and women – the earth closet type. One was a two seater and the women's a three seater. My aunt's toilet was down the garden – the earth variety. The view was across open fields, but it was a long walk with a lantern on a cold night!

In the early days, people did not travel far, so delivering the clothes was not easy. Grandad took the orders to villages further afield by pony and trap, going to Bagley, Whixall, Wem and Ellesmere, etc. Some were sent by post, or people walked and collected them.

My grandad's name, appropriately enough, was John Weaver, and the house where they lived was called Weaver's Loft.'

BRICKMAKING AND BUILDING

'My grandfather ran the brick yard on Lord Brownlow's estate at Houghton, Ellesmere. As a child I often went there to watch the men and the traction engine at work. The large stones were taken out of the natural clay. This was put through moleskin rollers and cut to length with wire. The bricks were then put out to dry. Before they were covered with galvanised sheets I often wrote my name on the bricks. I also made little cups and teapots from small pieces of clay.

It could take up to 14 days for the bricks to dry depending on the weather. The baking was the trickiest part and Grandfather always did this himself. The bricks were placed in a large round kiln and the small doorway was bricked up. Three or four fires were placed on the outside and kept going for several days and nights.

All the clay was extracted before the Second World War and the brickyard has gone, but I wonder how many of 'my' bricks survive in the Ellesmere area?'

'My grandfather worked in the building trade. He was employed in the building of many houses in Church Stretton in the 1880s and 1890s, which was then becoming a holiday resort for the Victorians, including the building of the Longmynd Hotel. He worked on many buildings in Shrewsbury, including extensions to the prison, and was the builder's foreman on the construction of Radbrook College in the 1890s. In those days the workmen lived in lodgings near the building sites and only spent Saturday afternoons and Sundays at home, so Granny had to bring up her seven children practically on her own.'

BASKETMAKERS

'One family in Welshampton carried on the trade of basketmakers. They made chiefly large, shallowish baskets – the shape of large trays with a handle either end – and these were used by farmers and smallholders for work on the land. They used osiers because for the framework it was vital to have twigs that were strong yet pliable, and would bend without splitting. They rented osier beds not far away where they could be sure of a good supply.'

GETTING ABOUT

At the beginning of the century, if you wanted to get to work or school or the town for market, you walked or, if you were lucky, you travelled by horse or horse-drawn conveyance. Then the bicycle brought a new freedom, and the first cars appeared on Shropshire's roads. Those early bone-shakers have stayed in the minds of those who saw them and who drove them.

HORSE-DRAWN TRAVEL

'Up until the mid 1920s when cars became more common, private transport was by horse-drawn vehicles. Ladies drove governess carts or 'tubs' as they were known. The ponies were smart and pretty – tubs were roughly cube-shaped with rounded corners, one passenger occupying each corner. A more useful vehicle was a shandry. This was higher than a tub and the horse much stronger. A shandry could be used to transport goods such as bags of corn or tankards of milk to the milk factory or the railway station – milk was transported from country to town by rail. There was room for one passenger beside the driver and two more passengers could sit with their backs to the driver, facing the way from which they had come. There was also a low vehicle known as float – the horse pulling this was quite a heavy animal sometimes known as a half legged horse (half way to a shire). Floats could carry animals such as calves, pigs and sheep and other goods. There was no seat for the driver – he had to stand.'

'My mother used to tell me about the carrier's cart which went to Shrewsbury about once a week – eight miles away and all downhill. One day Granny went on the cart and suddenly the horse bolted and it was only Granny's presence of mind which kept the old carrier on the cart – she held onto him.'
'In the early 1900s there was a lady from Bromfield who used to go shopping in Ludlow in her donkey and cart and for a few coppers she would get whatever the cottagers wanted. One day her donkey

got out and was put in the pound (this was an enclosure beside the old bridge at Bromfield, where straying animals were kept till their owners paid for their freedom). She couldn't afford the fine so my grandfather and some of his friends went after dark and lifted the animal out and returned it to her.'

'The only public transport in my young days in Rushbury village was the train which ran three times daily except Sundays, from Wellington to Craven Arms. Only the very well-to-do had cars in those days.

Our nearest shop for food and general household necessities was two miles away so you were very careful not to run short of anything at particular times. Milk had to be fetched from the nearest farm. The nearest railway station was a mile away and as nothing was delivered everything had to be carried home. Our own mail was left with the stationmaster and we either collected or the engine driver threw it off the train near the house, giving us fair warning on the whistle when this was about to happen.

Eventually meat and bread were delivered first in horse-drawn carts and later in vans but many families were 'off the beaten track' and had to walk to the village or to the train to get supplies.

THE TOLL ON THE IRONBRIDGE

'When my husband was five years old he came on Christmas night in the family horse and trap from his grandparents' farm at the top of Madeley Bank. He was snug under the large canvas sheet lined with tartan wool.

They crossed the ironbridge and paid the old man who was still on duty on Christmas night although it was rainy and foggy.

They drove on over the railway crossing at the station with its dim gas lamps and past The Hairpin Bend and up through the brickyards and kilns glowing red in the mist, still at work. He remembers clattering home into the muddy yard and being hurried to bed with a hot drink while his father stabled the horse and put away the trap.'

THE FIRST CARS

'Before the First World War the first car in St Martins was owned by Captain Albeach of Plas Warren. It was high up, with big brass lamps. My mother would say 'Come on, the car is coming', and we would stand by the gate watching it go by. What a difference now!'

'A lady of the Churchstoke village remembers going to Newtown to buy her engagement ring. They bicycled so far, then hired a wago-nette at Montgomery. The wagonette took them to Newtown and after buying the ring they returned to Montgomery by train, then cycled home. The first bicycle she could remember was the 'penny-farthing', her brothers had one. They all had great fun trying to ride it in the stackyard so they wouldn't hurt falling off!

Among the first cars in our village were two Baby Austins, costing £99 each. We also remember a Chevrolet, a Buick and a Sunbeam which had a dicky seat on the back with enough room for two people to sit in. It had beautiful brass lights on it. Of course, no MOTs in those days, or driving tests, just five shillings we think, for a driving licence. We eventually had public transport in the village, the Mid-land Red Bus started coming through on its way to Shrewsbury.

Our first local service was started by Bill Hailstone. His first bus was a 14 seater and had bench seats up each side. You'd never find a service like his today, he would do shopping for you in town, take things to the cleaners and pay your bills for you. For these services he used to charge threepence. He would stop en route to have a word with a pal or take a message for you, nothing was too much trouble because time was not too important then. He may have been a bit late now and again but nobody minded. A journey from Churchstoke to Shrewsbury cost two shillings and threepence return.'

'When I was learning to drive at Withers in Shrewsbury, chiefly on Model T Fords, Sidolis used to leave their vehicles there and they all had Fords. The Model T had no self-starter, it had to be started with a starting handle at the front of the car. There was no gear lever and you only had three pedals. There was no accelerator, you had a throttle under the steering wheel. There was one lever on each side of the steering column, one for the ignition and one for the fuel. There was a hand-brake. When you took the hand-brake half off, the car was in neutral and right off you were in top gear. There were no batteries on them and the lights were bright according to the speed you were going. If you were going really slow round a corner, you had no lights.'

'Roads were of rough stone and country lanes just cart tracks; dry and very dusty in the summer, muddy and potholed in the winter.

One man remembered riding his bicycle from Alderton to Bas-church – instead of clouds of dust and rough stones, he had the thrill of seeing a steam roller working and even better the joy the riding his bike on that marvellous smooth surface.

In Cockshutt, everyone rushed out to watch a motor car driving through the village. Within a few years they were so commonplace that, in 1947, when the river Severn overflowed, one man was appalled to suddenly remember that he had left his car at a garage in Roushill. Surprisingly it was cleaned up and worked afterwards!

An aeroplane with engine trouble landed in one of my grandfather's fields at the Woodhouse, Shifnal. He was on his way to bring the vet to a very ill cart horse at the time. He spent all day with the pilot, absolutely fascinated. The pilot got his plane repaired and flew off. Grandfather returned home having forgotten to go to the vet. The horse died the following day!'

'The vicar was one of the first to own a car at Welshampton; it was a Trojan and we could always tell when he was coming down the village because the car seemed to make a rather loud 'chugging' sound. His gardener/handyman drove it, as I remember.'

'Tom Perkins at East Wall had an open tourer in the 1920s. He would meet us out of school and pile the car up with kids – clinging to the running board, even hanging on behind.'

'When I was 18 in 1925 we had our first car – a Humber with a soft hood. What a thrill, and after four lessons I was entrusted on the lanes.'

FIERY LORRIES

'One thing we children were frightened of were the Sentinel lorries which had a fire box underneath with a glowing fire. We could hear them coming as they gave a 'toot toot' on a whistle, and by the time they reached us we were over the hedge into a field.'

THE COUNTRY BUSES

The first country bus services, often started by local men who simply washed out the lorry they took animals to market in and put seats around the sides, are remembered with great affection – perhaps because they were so accommodating and friendly, and nothing seemed to be too much trouble.

'Grandad tells the tale of the Picklescott bus. Down on the main road, or 'down on the bottom' as he used to say, the trains ran regularly, but to get there you either had to walk to Leebotwood or Dorrington station or get a lift from someone with a pony and trap. An enterprising farmer, Mr Will Shakeshaft from Golding, used his lorry to take cattle to Shrewsbury Smithfield on Tuesday, then after some scrubbing and sweeping and putting in a few benches and some clean straw, took the wives to Shrewsbury Market on Saturdays to sell their produce. This was a vast improvement on the old arrangement of a long wearying walk with full, heavy baskets on both the outward and the homeward journey.

In later years Mr M. J. (Matt) Parry took over a similar mode of transport, but improved it by removing the cattle body and replacing it for the Saturday runs with a smart bus-like body with seats, which picked up along the route from Picklescott via Pease Lane, Wilderley and the Coppice Farm. The journey was smelly and bumpy, but the passengers, who led hard-working busy lives, caught up on the week's chatter before being deposited in The Lion and Pheasant yard at the bottom of Wyle Cop. They made their way to the Market Hall, set out their stalls, did their selling and their own shopping, having a cup of tea in Machins cafe, before heading down the Wyle Cop and back to the bus for home.

The journey home involved getting the bus up New Hall Bank and the Parish House Bank. Often the weary passengers left their baskets on the bus, got out and pushed. Sometimes the engine power was helped by harnessing up two carthorses and pulling the laden bus up the hill – the horses would be ready and waiting. It was not unusual for Mr Shakeshaft to have to harness the two horses to the front of the lorry and pull it round the yard on a cold morning to get it started.

At one time Mr Shakeshaft used to take a bus load of folk from the Picklescott area to the sheep sales at Bishops Castle. This was quite a day out. There was always lots to see, with a number of attractions as well as the sale. Bishops Castle having a good few public houses, it was a very popular place and the poor driver of the bus had a terrible job getting his passengers out of the various pubs and back onto the bus. His journey up the main street was a very slow one, with him jumping out at every pub and seeking out his passengers, often running the risk of losing some of those he had just gathered up from lower down the street.'

'By 1924 there were three bus operators competing for business in

Llansilin. They each tried to outdo the others by starting earlier and being the most obliging, being prepared to take live calves in a sack in the front of the bus. One lady remembers her husband happily taking aboard a large ram. Not such a happy occasion, though when he was filling up the rack which went round the outside at the top of his bus. It was customary to pile baskets with live cockerels (legs tied together!), pounds of butter and lots of eggs. One morning he was balancing one foot on the step to deposit a basket containing four dozen eggs when his foot slipped and all the eggs came tumbling out all over him. He just had to carry on and to face the amused remarks of stallholders in town who guessed what had happened. He also had to compensate the farmer to whom the eggs had belonged. Earning a living did not come easily in those days.'

'When the first bus came up to Lythwood, many people turned out to see it as it was covered – not like the open bus which only came to the Fox Inn. What a queue there was in The Square at Shrewsbury for the Bayston Hill bus, and there was often friction if the bus filled with Belle Vue and Meole passengers and was not able to accommodate Bayston Hill people – those left behind had to walk.

Sam was an Irish terrier. He belonged to Mr Nicklin who lived near Pulley Lane. On market days, Sam often waited by the Gravel Hole at the junction of Pulley Lane and Hereford Rod. The bus would stop for him and take him into Shrewsbury. When Sam had been there long enough, he would go to the Square and board the Bayston Hill bus. He was duly put down at his stop. Periodically the bus company sent a bill to Mr Nicklin for Sam's fares.'

'In the 1920s old 'Lishia', who had a pony and trap, took the villagers from Ashford Carbonell into Ludlow to do their shopping. A small field in the village known as Lishia's Orchard is named after him.

Later on, Yarranton's Bus Company from nearby Tenbury Wells served the village well for transport. These buses were driven by Fred and his wife and their three employees, Bill, Ted and Reg. All were friendly and helpful. If a villager was unable to go into town they would give the driver a basket and shopping list and while he was in Ludlow he would do the shopping and deliver it on the return journey, when he would be paid for the goods.

The school bus came into the village from Tenbury each morning and took the children and other passengers into Ludlow. It came back into the village at half past ten on its way back to Tenbury. It was back again at half past two on its way to Ludlow, to return again at four o'clock, so one could shop any day, morning or afternoon.'

ON THE WATER

Shropshire's canals and the river Severn once played a major part in the lives of its inhabitants, for work and for play. Whole communities looked to the canals for transport for goods and people, and their decline was never wholly compensated for by increased road traffic.

THE CANAL TRADE

'In bygone days, Weston Lullingfield's life centred largely around the canal and agriculture. A section of the canal ended at the wharf, now at the bottom of the main village; the canal is no longer in existence. It was intended that the canal went through to Shrewsbury and joined the Severn to transport goods to the south, but due to the cost of getting through the hilly countryside and needing too many locks the plan was abandoned. There is a glacial fault running through the land, a continuation of the meres at Ellesmere.

The village had a busy canal trade; barges brought coal for the farms and lime to the four lime kilns and cheese was taken back to be sold in the towns. There were also deliveries along the route.

My father and his brothers learned to swim in the 'cut', as it was called, and a lot of fun and games and fishing centred on the canal. My father says that he remembers skating along the canal all the way to Nantwich.

The chains for the Menai Bridge were forged at Upton Magna, taken by horse and cart to the wharf at Weston and shipped by barge to their destination.

A potent brew was made at The Canal pub which was greatly enjoyed by the bargees, who often stayed until their money ran out, causing a traffic jam in the canal basin. With the breaking of the canal banks further along the route and the subsequent drying up of the canal in this area, the pub was shut down.

The wharf warehouse, however, continued in use for some time. It was rented by Mr Jim Edge, who organised village dances there. He was the village carpenter and postman, and also ran the Sunday school. He took us on Sunday school trips, on the canal. The wharf later became a collecting place for churns of milk. The lifting crane for unloading the barges was removed during the war for scrap metal.'

'In the 1920s the section of the Shropshire Union Canal between Maesbury and Queens Head was much used. The latter was a busy little hamlet with a well stocked grocery shop, bakehouse, post office, garage, sand hole, coal wharf and two public houses, one especially used by the boat people.

The narrowboats used to bring flour and animal feedstuffs from Peates of Maesbury Mill. After unloading the boats would take on sand, which had been carried there on trucks on a small rail line from the sandhole, down a tunnel under the coal wharf, warehouse and road and onto the towpath. The trucks were pulled by a donkey, who would not take the empty truck back up the tunnel until he had had a titbit from the boatie. Peates had several lovely boats, all beautifully kept and well maintained.

Two lock-keepers used to look after this section of the canal. They had a small boat which they used when cutting back the reeds to stop the choking of the canal. The first lockhouse was about half a mile from Queens Head, the second more than a mile further on. Doctors and nurses used to have to walk from Queens Head in cases of illness or to deliver babies. I well remember a teenage boy falling ill with rheumatic fever at the second lockhouse. He had to be taken by the small boat pulled by his father, through the two locks to Queens Head where he was transferred by ambulance to the old RSI at Shrewsbury. Wildlife along this stretch of the canal was abundant, with herons, kingfishers, plovers, swans and coots, and the banks in springtime a mass of primroses. It was here I last heard the corncrake call, like grating a comb on a metal bar. Progress, however, was knocking on the door. It was during this decade that Sentinel of Shrewsbury brought out their wagons and Peates bought one. This was to be the death knell for the canal and the mule-pulled boats. Goodbye to the slow ways of life, peace and quietness. Hail to the noise and pollution on our roads.'

'In the 1910s my father only came home to Lower Frankton at weekends, as he worked on a canal barge fetching corn and various cargoes from Ellesmere Port docks to Newtown and Maesbury Mills.'

'The canal was an important means of transport for Maesbury village. Corn for the local miller was brought by barges, and coal and stone for roadbuilding also travelled this way. Large parcels for delivery to the shops in Oswestry came as far as Maesbury by canal and were

187

then taken the rest of the journey by horse and cart. The canal was officially closed in 1944.'

'My mother and father (I was born in 1914) remembered when the Newport Canal was used and the bargees used to anchor their boats in the canal basin and come into Newport to shop and drink. Nearly every other building in the High Street was an inn. The bargees lived permanently on their boats in a very confined space and the children rarely attended school, so few of them could read or write.'

'The canal played an important part in the life of Pant village. Many people including my father remember the barges of Mr Sam Owen bringing coal and other goods to the wharf at Pant. The boat was called The Five Sisters after his five daughters. There are many donkey paths coming down off the hill to the canal. There were canoes for hire (by the hour) by the bridge in Llanymynech. They were kept in Bob Wall's yard and Tommy Trevor's flat-bottomed boat used to dredge and repair the canal in Pant. When the canal was empty the flat shellfish in the bottom were always thrown back in. I can remember sliding on the canal but also watching skaters, we thought they were so grand, there used to be an inn by the canal called 'The Toad in the Hole', officially the Railway Tavern.'

TOM MORRIS'S BARGE HORSES

'There is a small pit mount on the edge of the farm near Willey, a pleasant place to picnic or birdwatch. However, it has a story hard to guess. The farm belonged to a certain Tom Morris whose initials are stamped into the oak fireplace surround in what was the old kitchen. he owned many horses which were used to haul barges on the river Severn, which in those days before the coming of the railway was the main artery of transport into and out of the local thriving industrial area.

However, the horses become sick and glanders was declared. he lost them all. They were shot and buried where the little mount lies. Without insurance and with no money to replace them, Mr Morris was ruined. The mount is now, 160 years later, covered by a beautiful grove of oaks.'

OUR RAILWAY

Before the Beeching cuts in the 1960s, the railway reached into every part of the county and the local station was part of the community, a busy place for goods and travellers. Though local riddles were often on the lines of 'Where is the Cambrian Railway mentioned in the Bible? God made all creeping things!', they were affectionate jokes and our railways are remembered with nostalgia today.

THE FIRST TRAINS

'My grandmother walked from Corve Dale to the top of Caradoc to watch the first train go down the Stretton valley.'

'The train at Stottesden was a mile and half out of the village. I did not see the building of the railway start but I can remember the track being finished. The men working on the railway used to walk to the local public houses daily and call at our home on the way back for a jug of cider which was free and home-made with the apples grown on our farm.'

PART OF OUR LIVES

'In my early days long distance travel was always by train. Our yearly outing was to Birmingham Goose Fair in October when the railway company put on a cheap excursion train. It left about nine o'clock and returned after the first house of the theatre. This is where we did our shopping for clothes, hats etc.

A horse-drawn brake came from Clun to Broome station twice a day meeting the trains to pick up passengers and parcels, and also to bring them to the station. Everything for Clun Valley came to the station. Fish came every morning about eight o'clock and was collected by the fishmonger from Clun with a pony and trap. Teams of horses and waggons started from up the Clun Valley about four in the morning to fetch coal. The horses were put in the stables in the station yard, fed and watered while the drivers went to the Railway Inn for their bread and cheese and beer. Some brought cider with them in a container which was fastened to the horse's collar. They then started the long trail back, about six or seven miles. Some of the hills were so steep they had to put slippers on the waggon wheels before going down, to stop them running away.'

'Baschurch station, now no more, was once the hub of activity. The train was used to transport people to work in Shrewsbury, children travelled to school and parcels were taken in the guard's van. People arrived at the station on foot, by bicycle and in Mr Miles' taxi. Some had season tickets, others bought their tickets from the ticket clerk. Rows of green tickets with the destination printed on them hung on boards. The waiting rooms had black horsehair seats, a large polished table and lavatories which needed a penny put in the slot to open a heavy door. There were chocolate machines, where for a penny the choice was Bournville or milk chocolate. In the winter there were glowing fires which the porter made up with shiny coal.

As well as passenger trains, goods trains called at the station. Churns of milk were lifted on and many packages. Sometimes baskets of pigeons were put in the guard's van. There was a late train from Shrewsbury which called at the station; people called it The Zulu – said to be because it started running during the Zulu War.

I have a vivid memory of the evacuation of Dunkirk in 1940. Our train was stationary in Shrewsbury, when a train came to a standstill on the central track. It was full of dishevelled soldiers who had been rushed up from the coast. Their uniforms were scruffy and they were unwashed, but they were very cheerful and shouted to us. Some threw French coins across to us. In hindsight, they showed a remarkable spirit.

Baschurch had a large goods yard where coal trucks were left. The local coal merchants came here to collect the coal. Households were definite in the type they wanted, Ifton coal and Cannock coal coming to mind. The area around the station was quite independent from the village. There were two shops, a public hall and an hotel called The Boreatton Arms. This was an unusual architectural design with turrets, but is no more.'

In 1924 my brother and I started to go to Wellington High School by train. The drivers and stokers fast became our friends and would urge us on as we ran, parallel with the train, along the adjacent road. The General Strike in 1926 meant there was no transport for a while and we walked the four miles to school and back again in the evening.

In the late 1920s and 1930s cars were gaining in popularity and the magical rate of travel was 60 miles an hour. Express trains reached this fantastic speed and I can remember being on the Wellington/Dawley road and persuading the driver of the car I was in to reach this breathtaking speed.'

WAR & PEACE

THE FIRST WORLD WAR

Even in peaceful Shropshire the hatred whipped up against the Kaiser and his men was fierce, though some came to realise that perhaps the ordinary soldiers weren't so terrible after all. The years of the Great War have left memories of hardship and suffering; soldiers on the move were a common sight and, though the country dweller was less affected than those in the towns, food and other commodities were scarce. There were also the forgotten victims of the war, a generation of women who had no alternative but to become 'dedicated spinsters'.

'T'OWD 'OMAN'S JED'

'When I was a child in the first decade of the century at Church Farm, Rushbury, people were still talking about the death of Queen Victoria. The news had come with the threshing machine men who came from Longville. 'T'owd 'oman's jed.'

There were no telephones. News was brought by the postman, or sent up the railway line. The daily newspaper came by post so it was always one day late.

But we all knew about the Kaiser and fears of a war. Once when the teacher at school asked us about the Kaiser a boy answered: 'He's cousin of our king and wants to be on his throne.'

Occasionally German bands came goose-stepping through the village, but my mother said: 'Don't give them any money, they're spying for the Kaiser.'

This must have been a regular Shropshire entertainment because the census of 1871 records six German musicians staying at the lodging house in All Stretton.'

'Mam talked about the beginning of the First World War. She remembered the Sunday when her brothers went into the army. She talked of all the young men going on the same day, and the village was silent and dead. After the war, pineapple was never served in grandma's house because uncle had been gassed and could not stand the smell of it.'

'My aunt's first job was as a maid at The Cottage on the Wrekin, owned by the Earl of Powys and run by Miss Byrrel. Apparently Miss Byrrel was a very good cook and The Cottage was famous for its 'duck dinners'. It had a dining room for about 50 people and another room large enough for about 200 or so. Besides my aunt another young girl was employed and a lad – who turned the bucket to make the ice-cream etc. She was working there during the hot summer of 1914 when Germany invaded Belgium and the First World War broke out. She tells of walking into Wellington to find out what was happening about the war, and being appalled by the sight they found in the Square in Wellington of exhausted men and horses resting as best they could before continuing their journey. They were the men of the yeomanry who had travelled from a camp in Nottingham to join up with soldiers in Shrewsbury, and they were in a very poor state.'

'During the war the army were guarding the conduit head water tower in Robald Lane which was the main source of water for the Shrewsbury area. My grandmother cooked their Christmas goose as they could not get it into their oven at camp. She did all the trimmings for them just as if they were at home and they said they enjoyed it very much and came singing carols in the evening.'

'About 52 men from Woore volunteered for service. Concerts were held to raise money for wounded soldiers and this was sent to the North Staff Infirmary to provide comforts. In December 1914 a concert held raised £8. A whist drive the same year made £11 16s 0d and this provided materials that were made into day and night shirts, bed jackets, mufflers, body belts and 112 pairs of socks.'

'My strongest memory of the war is of seeing soldiers marching past our schoolroom singing songs such as *It's a long way to Tipperary*. They must have been based at the big army camp on Prees Heath about two miles from the school.'

'Groups of soldiers were sent into the countryside during summer and autumn to help farmers with the harvest and potato picking. Anyone who had enough room had to billet them. We had two very nice young men who kept in touch for many years afterwards. Two of the big houses around Hopesay, Walcot Hall and Aston Hall, were convalescent hospitals for wounded soldiers.'

'I was born in 1911 and as I walked to school I passed a house which had a poster over a window of Lord Kitchener in full uniform. He seemed to be pointing his finger directly at me. Across the bottom of the poster were the words 'This has sent . . . men to fight for King and Country'.'

'In 1918 the Spanish flu raged through the district and there were many deaths in Madeley, my father being one of them. I caught it from him, but lived to tell the story. Death was not a stranger in many homes due to the terrible casualties in 'The War'. I remember the funeral of Captain Redding, who died of wounds after his return. In those days everyone drew their curtains as a sign of respect as the cortege passed; those at home came out to stand in silence as it passed, then joined to follow the mourners to the interment in Madeley churchyard.

Being a military funeral it was preceded by muffled drums and all mourners walked behind the coffin at a slow march. At the graveside they sounded the Last Post and guns were fired as a last tribute. The terrible tragedy of the war enclosed everyone in those last sad minutes.'

GETTING BY

'Food was very scarce. I was one of eight children and there were eleven of our family living at home. My mother would hear that they were selling dripping down at the old Shrewsbury infirmary, in the cellar. You had to get there early. We had our basin and if we saw any other children we ran to get in front of them. The cellar was down under ground and if we arrived and there were more than two people there it was no good; there was only enough for two people and it cost twopence. I got it very often and it was lovely, brown dripping with jelly – we didn't get enough meat to make our own.'

THE FORGOTTEN VICTIMS

'My aunt worked in a munitions factory during the war, which made poisonous gas. She was taken ill at work and the firm simply put her on a train home without anyone to accompany her. Some children looked after her. When she arrived at Wem a pony and trap had to be fetched to get her home. She only lived two weeks and she was only 20.'

'In August 1914 we broke up from school for the summer holidays and set off for our usual seaside visit – for a fortnight we thought. The next day came the shocking news that Britain was at war. My

194

A happy family portrait in Handlow at the time of the First World War, showing Marjorie Pratt with her parents and two sisters.

father immediately sent us to pack up all our things ready to return home to Shrewsbury, in case the passenger trains were withdrawn to leave the lines clear for the movement of troops and ammunition.

We returned to school to find there were to be no more cookery lessons and no more swimming lessons – the army had commandeered the baths. Then the army took over the school building itself and we were despatched to other premises. Both town and country girls had to take sandwiches for lunch, but what to fill them with was the question. Quite a number of Greenfields families had a chicken run in the garden, since eggs were a good standby. When a hen finished laying she was served up for Sunday dinner and gulped down with tears from the children who had fed her and gathered the eggs. Bread became more and more adulterated. It was said that horse chestnut flour was added; it certainly was very bitter. Flour was sieved to pick out mouse hairs and other foreign bodies.

Butter could be bought occasionally in the market but at a price. The grocer provided some margarine. After school we girls formed a queue at the Maypole shop (dairy produce). The queue would stretch right round to the Square, sometimes down the Gullet Passage, all waiting for two ounces of margarine. If you knew the policeman on duty, he might give you the wink to join the queue again.

Sweets were not manufactured, they only returned in 1919. We made 'chocolate' with cocoa butter and sugar. People gave up sugar in tea to make it into jam. We were all suffering from malnutrition – I was not the only girl who fainted in class.

The boys, our relations and friends, joined up. Some were of age, others, only 16, gave the wrong age. Those who had been in the Territorials or at public school were whisked off as officers. Peers and peasants were served alike as estates and farmers lost their heirs. Those young men who came back were shell shocked, gassed or wounded, and others were sent to Europe in their place – cannon fodder.

And what of the girls? Deprived of food, new clothes, proper shoes, boy friends, parties and kisses – all the fun and pleasures of adolescence and with no prospect of marriage or a family. They went out to work. Some went to colleges and teaching, many into nursing – both caring for other people's children, to whom they gave their motherly love and guidance. Others went into the Civil Service to replace the men. They became the 'dedicated spinsters' and held the schools and hospitals together between the wars and during the Second World War. Of all my contemporary friends, only one married young enough to have children. What a waste, and what a tragedy.'

THEY WEREN'T SO BAD

'In 1914 I can remember war being declared; we were all standing by the gate watching the Territorials marching to Copthorne Barracks, the women waving to them and calling the Kaiser all sorts of names.

Then it was 1918 and corn harvest, and one morning we heard that six German prisoners were coming to help with the harvest. All the women and children turned out to see them. The women had got brushes and mops in their hands. They were shouting and screaming at them and calling them murderers. The two soldiers who were escorting the prisoners told them to calm down and fortunately there was no violence. Mr Williams came to me and said 'I want you to go and lead the horses for them'. I was terrified but I went and they smiled at me which made me feel better. Mr Williams put them to work, two on the waggon placing the sheaves and the other four pitching them up. After a few minutes one of them came to me and asked me my name. I told him and then he introduced me to all the others, which surprised me as I did not think they could speak English. After that we got on very well. The second day they gave me threepence to go to the local pub for a pint of beer. This happened nearly every day – I used to have a drink out of the bottle and then fill it up with water; they never found out. After a few days they showed us photos of their families. The men were taking them to show their wives and before long the women who were shouting and screaming at them were giving them jugs of tea and cake.'

THE OLD WAR HORSES

'After the war, many coal horses were old war horses. A number was stamped across their teeth so that they could identified if anything happened to them in battle.'

HARD TIMES

Poverty and hardship were the lot of many in the depression years between the wars. The industrial areas of Shropshire faced the strife of strikes and lockouts, while farmers watched the value of their land and the market for their goods dwindle to practically nothing. It would be, tragically, another war which finally lifted the cloud.

A FAT SHEEP

'In 1926 there was a slump. A farmer could not sell a fat sheep for 26 shillings at the market in Ludlow, so took it home again.'

'There was a terrible slump after the war and the farmers had trouble selling their produce. Miss Florence Hamilton Russell of Cleobury

Court was very good and started a Co-operative Society to help. I married and moved away from the Burwarton estate soon after, but we returned in 1933 and I was appalled at the poverty. The hedges and gates were broken down and there was no money for paint or repairs. The farmers were living on rabbits and swedes, eggs and milk, with no sale for the produce until the Second World War.'

POVERTY AND PRIDE

'A family with three children were living in a two-roomed cottage near the canal at Whixall. The only bedroom was divided by a curtain, parents one side, children the other. The owner of the cottage lived in Whitchurch and when the rent was due the husband put his clogs on and walked to Whitchurch to ask for time to pay. He explained that he had a sow about to farrow and when the piglets were big enough to sell he would have the rent money. The owner refused to wait and the man had to walk back (about seven miles) and sell the pig at a great loss to himself.'

'There were usually more big families than small in those days, and the bigger the family the more difficult it became to keep them. In Wroxeter there was a charity which provided a jumper or pair of boots or shoes once a year to the poorer families, but none of the children liked having them because it was a sign of needing help. There was also a gift of half a ton of coal to poor widows once a year. One old lady who lived by us used to receive this and made it last nearly the whole year.'

'Money was in very short supply in the 1930s. Wages were very low for those in work, but there was no welfare for the unemployed, of whom there were large numbers. There was the dreaded means test. This meant an humiliating session in front of one's peers which invariably produced nothing and meant that few people applied for it, often because they were too proud to do so. Evictions were common in Shrewsbury, and one I remember vividly was of two elderly people who were left sitting in the road on their few possessions which had been removed from their home by the bailiffs. The workhouse would have been the next destination.

Moonlight flits were also common. We would wake in the morning to find that neighbours, who were heavily in debt, had disappeared. They only needed a handcart to carry their few possessions. Many of them made their way to the cities in an effort to find work.

However, there were entrepreneurs – out of necessity. One such was the rag and bone man. He came around at weekly intervals calling for his rags, bottles and bones. All these items were in short supply. Clothes were handed down until they were threadbare. Most bottles were returnable to the shop with a refund of a penny – a fortune! Bones, after being boiled to make stock and having the marrow removed, were buried in the garden as a fertiliser.

My mother kitted out four children, one husband and herself with hand knitted pullovers, jumpers and socks. She was greatly shocked to discover that my eldest brother had traded his newly knitted jersey with the rag and bone man for a balloon. She chased after the trader with a broom, eventually catching up with him several streets away. There was a confrontation and, after giving the benefit of her tongue, she did manage to retrieve the jersey.

A very cheap source of food in the 1930s were rabbits, and the skins were much prized by the rag man. We, however, would take these ourselves to the sorting depot, a shop in Barker Street, and collect twopence for each skin.

Another such entrepreneur was the scissor sharpener who called around weekly with his grinding contraption attached to the handlebars of his bicycle. Two leather belts from the grinder were attached, one to each pedal, and after the bicycle was immobilised with stabilisers, he would sit on the seat and pedal furiously to rotate the grindstone. He would then sharpen scissors, knives, tools and garden shears. I remember this poor, thin, weedy man vividly. He always looked as if he carried the worries of the world on his shoulders. He had a wife and eight children to support.

One day an incident occurred which had a profound effect on me. One lady was not satisfied with her sharpened scissors and demanded the return of her penny. The grinder offered to do them again but the woman refused. He was reluctant to return his hard-earned penny, and after some angry words he threatened to attack the woman with a pair of shears. The police were called and the man, his bicycle and machine were bundled up in the Black Maria. I caught a glimpse of his sad, despairing eyes and they haunted me for many months. I often wondered how his family fared afterwards.'

SMALLHOLDINGS FOR EX-SERVICEMEN

'During the 1920s the County Council bought part of Mr Boylin's farm at Annscroft and built five smallholdings complete with houses and farm buildings. These holdings were allocated to ex-servicemen and their families.'

STRIKES AND LOCK-OUTS

'During the time my parents spent at The Rodney pub there was a lock-out strike at the Coalbrookdale and Horseshay Works. Men arriving at the gates decided not to return home, but to await the outcome from the negotiations taking place inside. The weather being severe, they made their way to The Rodney, and threw stones at my mother's bedroom window, begging her to come down and let them inside to sit in the taproom. Having a very kind heart she did this, and lit a good fire and served them with halves of beer, the cost to be put on The Slate.

During the national Strike of 1926 there was great hardship in the homes of the strikers. Miners and railway workers would meet in The Shoes where a welcoming fire was lit in the taproom, coal being one commodity that was in good supply, due to the miners receiving coal as part of their wages. Many were glad to sell it to provide for their wives and families. Weekly pocket money for some of these men was a shilling; it bought a pint of mild beer, five Woodbines and a box of matches. Also a seat by the fire where they could sit for two to three hours in convivial company, away from the strain and stress of their homes. They sat on a curved settle, whose back made a shelter from the draughts let in by the opening and shutting of the door. Potatoes could be roasted in the hot ashes of the large iron stove, and sometimes a friendly butcher might provide a few sausages and a baker some stale bread to toast and dip in the fat. A game of 'Tippet' would be played endlessly, amusing anecdotes repeated, and stories from their past repeated.

At that time there was a general election, and a public meeting was held in the Anstice in favour of the Labour candidate, Miss Edith Picton Turbeville. This meeting was attended by no less a person than Lady Cynthia Moseley, wife of Sir Oswald Moseley, and also Miss Ishbell Macdonald, daughter of Mr Ramsey Macdonald, the future Prime Minister. Miss Picton Turbeville won the election, defeating the Conservative candidate by 300 votes.'

'The Strike brought great hardship into the district and my mother was asked to provide sandwiches for the children at the Wesleyan school who had walked some distance to school on very inadequate breakfasts, and were unable to return home for their 'dinners' which was the usual thing in those days.

I remember seeing Mrs Bert Jenks who was in the St John's Ambulance Brigade at that time, helping my mother with this task at our kitchen table. A large stale loaf of bread was rubbed into breadcrumbs and then mixed in a big bowl with a large tin of salmon to make it go further in the sandwiches. Kindly bakers gave the stale bread, and butchers and grocers donated other items. Milk was provided by Mr Poole of High Street. How long it continued I don't know. The much hated 'Means Test' came into force and great grief and humiliation ensued as a result.'

THE SECOND WORLD WAR

Once again, in 1939 Shropshire men and women faced the prospect of separation and danger. Soldiers were once more seen on the roads and trains, though this time they included the generous Americans who became the idols of many children, and women took a pride in the important jobs they undertook in the factories. The possibility of German spies working in Britain became, for one family, rather too close for comfort.

WAR IS DECLARED

'I was standing in my aunt's kitchen at Bromfield with my parents and relations listening to the announcement that war had been declared. The look on their faces and the race up the road to the church is still clear in my memory.'

THE RED CROSS TRAIN

'The Second World War came and village life changed greatly. A twelve-carriage Red Cross train arrived at our station in Hanwood and stayed there for a few years. With it came soldiers, a few of whom married local girls. As children, we were taken inside the train which to us seemed never-ending. It had beds, kitchen and living quarters for the soldiers. Every now and again, one would wake up and find that the train had gone but it was back again a week later. It was quite a while later that we were told that it had been taking wounded soldiers from Dunkirk and other places to various hospitals round the country.

There was a prisoner of war camp at Morda, first occupied by

Italians, then afterwards by the Germans. The prisoners were sent to work on local farms and in the quarries.

With the war over and the blackout lifted, it took a long period of time to get back to normal.'

SOLDIERS

'Before the war my family moved from London to Shavington, to live with my grandfather who was the stud groom at the Hall. We lived in a house in the stable yard.

In 1939 the Shropshire Yeomanry arrived. Officers were billeted in the Hall, but the poor unfortunate privates were given the lofts above the stables. There was no lighting, no heating and no beds other than camp beds, but, of course, plenty of mice and rats. The stable clock had to be stopped from chiming because it kept them awake at night but the villagers did not like this because wherever they were working they knew the time by the chimes and they complained bitterly – the clock struck again and the soldiers had to get used to it.

Shavington was a very small village and probably only 30 inhabitants suddenly had to accept another 200. The indoor tennis court at the Hall was turned into a concert hall with a stage and dances and film shows were held. The small chapel in the centre of the village held whist drives and I think that a small screen was pulled down in front of the altar. This chapel, along with the Hall and the dairy, were demolished in the 1950s.

Various British regiments were at Shavington during the war and towards the end the Yanks arrived. We children were never again short of sweets or gum.

'The Royal Shrewsbury Hospital South became a military hospital during the war. They had one or two convoys of wounded arriving in the middle of the night so all doctors, nurses and VADs worked many hours non-stop. If the patients had to have any painful treatment all the other men would call out 'It's better than pilchards!'. They had lived on pilchards for weeks! There were two wards of Italians and at Christmas they made beautiful nativity scenes.'

'The army stationed troops in Church Stretton during the war and being a small town this caused quite a stir. After the residents had come to accept the soldiers they realised that they could be very useful. Business improved in shops and hotels and a weekly dance was held. Some soldiers were employed as casual gardeners, although this proved disastrous in the case of the soldier who didn't know the difference between herbs and weeds and dug up the lot. The owner was not amused.'

BUILDING A SPITFIRE

'What did you do during the war?', occasionally my grandchildren
ask. I still feel a sense of pride when I answer with 'I helped to make
Spitfires'. It was in the early 1940s I had to make the decision to either
join the forces or do war work. I decided to try my luck at the latter
and got offered a job with the local firm of Sankeys. They did all kinds
of war work but assembling Spits appealed to me. The fuselage
engines etc were put together in Hadley, then they were despatched
to 'Castle Bromwich' to have the wings attached. It was a great thrill
to watch the planes grow from nothing. I was detailed with another
girl to rivet about nine operations, some in the cockpit and some in
the confined space at the rear. I remember thinking how small the
planes were, but so important to the war effort.

At last the day arrived when No 1 left the factory. We all watched
it loaded onto a huge lorry with trepidation. Some time afterwards it
came through the 'hush hush' channels that it would be flying over
for us to see one lunchtime. Although a lot of banter went on, we all
got a wonderful feeling of pride when it appeared at last. And now,
if I see a Spitfire at a show or museum, I still get a thrill thinking it
could have been one I helped to assemble all those years ago.'

THE SPY

'During the last war Cosford airfield was important to the war effort
and very interesting to the Germans. My husband worked as a porter
at the station there.

We lived in part of an old Georgian house near the church and had
two spare rooms. One day a very smart lady came with a little girl
and asked if they could lodge with us for the duration as they needed
to be away from London and the bombs. She said the little girl was
her granddaughter and showed me a photo of a young lady dressed
up in all her finery and said she was her daughter, who had been
presented at court. We let her have the two spare rooms and she kept
herself to herself and wasn't much trouble except for one or two
peculiar things. She had a lady friend who used to come and see her;
she would bring *The Times* newspaper and they would go into her
sitting room and stay a long time looking at it. One night I heard a
noise downstairs and went down to see her sitting at our kitchen
table with a lighted candle and the blackout pulled aside. I asked her
what she was up to and she said she couldn't sleep and was sorry to
trouble us and went back to bed.

She sometimes gave my husband a few shillings and tried to get
him to talk about Cosford and what went on there but he wouldn't

tell her anything, he was sworn to secrecy. My husband and I were very careful about the blackout but the warden said he had seen some chinks of light and we were fined £1. During the summer the lady said she would like to stay in Beckbury with us, but then she changed her mind and said she would take the little girl to the seaside for a holiday. The little girl wasn't very well and I thought rather neglected. She packed her bags and put labels on them and they were taken to the station. Later on we heard that she had changed the labels when she got to the station and then that she had been arrested and taken off to be interned on an island, I think it was the Isle of Man. Apparently, before coming to live with us she had stayed with some people in a farmhouse at Ryton and there had been trouble with the authorities and a light had been seen coming from the skylight.'

STRANGERS IN OUR MIDST

It wasn't long before bewildered evacuees began to arrive from Liverpool and other cities where they faced the threat of large scale bombing. In some cases it wasn't long before they were on their way home again – willing to risk any amount of bombs to get away from this alien environment, but others stayed and forged links which are still strong today. Other strangers came too, prisoners of war, Italian and German, to help on the land.

THE EVACUEES ARRIVE

'During the 1940s several evacuees from Liverpool were sent to Loppington; within an hour of arrival they had pinched all the fruit from the trees. Eight children were taken in at Loppington House where, intrigued by the animals, they each smuggled a piglet into bed! Footwear had to be provided as most of the children were barefoot; some of them were filthy and 'alive' with lice. Two teachers came with them and taught them in half-day sessions, alternating morning and afternoon with the village pupils.'

'We had evacuees from the poor part of Liverpool. They were poorly clothed, didn't know how to use a knife and fork and were not familiar with baths. We housed them at Bayston Hill, then the next day a number of their mothers descended on the village – we didn't know they were coming so no arrangements had been made for them. My brother and I filled sacks of straw for them to sleep on in a room at the back of the vicarage on the common. Some mothers brought their very young children with them and it was unfortunate these children were not used to using toilets!

The next day these mothers gathered outside the policeman's house demanding to be sent back to Liverpool. We were only too happy for them to leave as they all sat in the middle of the road outside The Three Fishes and refused to move until transport was provided, thereby holding up a convoy of troops.'

'My father was the billeting officer responsible for placing the evacuees from Liverpool in local houses. We had the two youngest boys aged about six and seven (they were not related). The youngest boy had two sisters placed on a nearby farm, but they were not happy there so we also ended up with them. Their teacher came with them and the local village hall was opened up and the teacher taught the youngest children there together with the young ones from the village. The others travelled by bus to the school three miles away. Slowly some of the children drifted back to Liverpool along with the teacher and then some more bombing brought more children. This time we had twins, a boy and a girl; they were very apprehensive but slowly settled down. After they had grown up the twins returned to see us and the older of the boys stayed in touch until his death but we never heard from the family of three.'

'Soon after war was declared a train arrived in Wem carrying little evacuee children from Liverpool. They marched in crocodile formation across the recreation ground with their cardboard gas mask containers across one shoulder and a brown paper parcel clutched in one hand. Homes had been found for them all – some with older people who had never had children of their own and whose homes were spick and span. Strange tales were to be heard during the next few days as a few of the children came from the very poorest districts of the city. Several refused to get into the beds; 'Only me Mam and Dad sleep in the bed. We sleep under it.' When the school reopened they attended it but as this was the 'Phoney War' period and no bombs were dropped, some of the children returned home.

Soon the Liverpool bombings commenced and urgent requests to return were made. At that time my mother-in-law had two boys and their sister living with her and after three nights of really heavy bombing, when the planes bound for Liverpool could be seen passing overhead with their heavy load of bombs, she was not surprised to receive a telegram from their mother asking if she and her youngest child could also come. An immediate reply in the affirmative was sent. The mother stayed for some time but left the little boy with her other children when she did return to her husband.

My mother-in-law had expressed her willingness to house a coloured child should one arrive – sure enough, along came Harold, later to be joined by his younger brother who explained that Harold's father was not *his* father but their mother belonged to them both. Somehow between all this there appeared Billy, a little ginger hair laughing boy with a face covered with freckles. He told us later that for the first few nights he had gone to the bottom of the garden and shouted as loud as he could, 'Mum, Mum, Mum, I want to come home!', and he had really believed that she could hear him.

My father-in-law was a local lay preacher and each Sunday morning and evening the whole household attended the Baptist church of which he was Secretary. Each night he would sit some of them on his knees and the others would gather around while he told them tales of Bobby and Billy and Bible stories. One night he was telling them of Jacob and his coat of many colours and one of them gasped out, 'Could he go in the street to play in it?' In the kitchen was a great round table around which they all gathered to play snakes and ladders and ludo etc, but their favourite game was 'Chapels', when they all took it in turn to play the part of the preacher. On one particular night it was Harold's turn and he had just said 'Thank you, God, for the hot water pipes (why, no-one knew) and for saving us from the bombs', when there was the sound of an actual bomb exploding. It was later found to have dropped near the Citadel near Harkestone Park.

One morning they were all rudely awakened by screams from Harold, 'Uncle Charlie, Uncle Charlie, the house is on fire!' and so it was. Harold had wanted to do something kind and helpful and had thought that if he could light the fire it would be a good thing to do, but he decided a little petrol would help things along. It certainly helped the fire. But my father-in-law believed that children were of far more importance than furniture and he looked to the motive behind the gesture and only a warning of the danger was given.

Each child's birthday was celebrated and special teas were also provided when mothers arrived at the weekends. The children stayed until the officials deemed it safe for them to go home.

'One of my many memories of Shropshire in wartime was 3rd September 1939 when the evacuees from Liverpool arrived by train. The Minsterley branch off the Shrewsbury to Aberystwyth railway line ran along the bottom of the garden of my home, Roseville, Pontesbury. That day the longest train that ever travelled that line arrived full of anxious looking children. There must have been about ten coaches and as the platform at Pontesbury station was only long enough for an engine and two coaches there were several along the bottom of our garden. The children to be billetted in the Pontesbury area were taken off and then the train moved on in stages to Minsterley where the rest of the children were to be billeted.

At school next day it was a scene of organised chaos with the many extra children and their teachers to be accommodated. Pontesbury school was large by Shropshire village school standards, but every possible space in the village was used for teaching: the church, two village halls and the five non-conformist chapel schoolrooms. I remember making a cover for my gas mask in the school room at the Congregational chapel.

In time life settled down again. Some of the evacuees only stayed a matter of weeks or months, but a few stayed for years and kept in touch with their war-time foster parents and have joined in the school reunions of the last few years in Pontesbury.'

ROMANTIC MANUEL

'In early 1939 we came to live in Shropshire which meant changing schools. Coalbrookdale was the nearest High School therefore I was transferred to it, much to their dismay. It happened to coincide with the time that evacuees were starting to attend the school. I was therefore considered to be an evacuee which didn't seem to be to my advantage. However, I made quite a few good friends. One teacher thanked me for bringing out some of the shy quiet pupils but asked me not to bring them out too far. I was a bit on the lively side and didn't take studying too seriously.

We had two Spanish refugees come to the school. The girl whose name was Carmen, spoke very little English. She was beautiful, slim, dark and rather remote. Everyone seemed to accept her and help her when they could. Her brother Manuel was another story. Talk about romantic, he pursued every female in sight. I was never a raving beauty but was still harassed by him. If I went to The Plaza Picture House (Coalbrookdale) he was often there. He'd slither into the seat beside me, if it was empty and start sweet-talking, at the same time trying to slide his arm round the back of the seat. I would sit tight against the back of the seat to curtail his manoeuvres, telling him to 'get off'. 'Oh, Betty be a good girl,' he'd coo. By this time my friend had usually arrived and he'd turn his attention to her, thank goodness. After I left school I hardly ever saw him. Years after, I heard a rumour that he was running a house of ill repute in London. Could it be true I wonder?'

PRISONERS ON THE LAND

'The war years brought visitors to Sherrifhales in the form of prisoners of war. The camp was built down the private drive to the Manor so the schoolchildren could see behind the school some of the preparations with the digging out of trenches for the huts. The Germans were followed in later years by Italians and finally by displaced persons such as Ukrainians. The Italians were popular with the girls as they used to whistle at them – they weren't so popular with the boys. The Germans were much better workers on the farms. The Italians were allowed out to Shifnal on a Saturday night, when it would be hard for locals to get into the cinema and the sweets in the shop opposite vanished with great speed. On their way back from work in the fields, the prisoners would share their rations with the children and talk to them.'

'During the war there were German prisoners at Worfield and they came out to work on the farms. On Mr Neal's farm one man was really a fisherman, one a farm boy far from home and the third was one of the ruling class and a real Nazi.'

'I can remember a POW from the camp at Annscroft removing his very wet trousers just as the local bus was passing. My father employed Italian POWs from the nearby camp at Sherrifhales. One of them was instructed to take a bag of clover seed out to a field and leave it under the hedge for sowing, then done by hand with a fiddle. He did, but emptied the bag and most of the seed blew away, to the fury of the sower who was usually a mild tempered man.'

'Italian prisoners were to be seen in Acton Burnell, where they lived in a small hostel guarded by two soldiers. In the daytime they worked on local farms and rode to work on bicycles unsupervised. They wore brown uniforms and were easily recognisable by the large coloured patches on their jackets. Some stayed on after the war and married local girls.'

DOING OUR BIT

With many of the men away in the forces, women had to undertake work normally done by men. The Women's Land Army was formed and quite a number of local women enrolled in this, tackling all kinds of work in the countryside. Others joined, for instance, the Women's Voluntary Service, or became Fire Watchers, patrolling the roads and lanes at night. Those men not eligible for service joined the Local Defence Volunteers, which became the Home Guard. Everyone, in short, did their bit.

THE HOME GUARD

'The Home Guard used to practise drill in the village hall at Tilstock, though with a chronic shortage of equipment. Rifles were in short supply and regularly the yard mop disappeared from its hook on practice night. They sometimes had war practice and on one occasion the 'enemy' were privy to all our positions and plans because the communications were telephoning to the 'other side' by mistake.'

'Once the Home Guard from Harmer Hill were out all night searching for parachutists seen descending near Tong Pool – after a fruitless search it was decided they must have been swans coming down.
A member of the Home Guard woken in the early hours was in such a hurry to dress that he unwittingly tucked the window curtain into his trousers with his shirt and brought the curtain pole crashing down when he attempted to run from his bedroom.'

'During the Second World War my father was a sergeant in the Home Guard and Mother was a morse coder for the Home Guard and the Searchlight Battalion that was stationed across the road from our house at Loppington. We were bombed quite often because of the searchlight.
I remember one night when we were being bombed, Mother had a lovely old dresser with her best plates on, and she ran out to stop the plates falling off. She wasn't bothered about the bombs, only her plates. I was put to sleep on a camp bed under the stairs as this was considered to be the safest place. One night Mother took a message on the morse coder that parachutes had been seen coming. So out

rushed the Home Guard only to find that it was a lot of swans coming in.

We took refugees during the war and I was unfortunate to catch diptheria. I went down in the February and didn't start to walk again until the November.'

THE LAND ARMY

'My family and friends had hysterics when I told them that I was joining the women's Land Army. I didn't know anything about farm life, I did know where milk came from but that was about all.

Arriving at Albrighton station, another girl and I were met by the farmer we would work for (Barbara was my friend for four years). The hostel was a big house at Badger Heath, it was great and the girls were friendly. 'Like to go to a dance?' one asked us. We were thrilled until she said we would have to bike four miles – we went to bed. It became clear to us that to get anywhere one had to bike. My first job on the Monday, dressed in overalls and hard black boots (oh, my feet), we were taken into a field, all green leaves – it was the first time I had seen potatoes growing. At five o'clock it was oh, my legs and back. Barbara and I were ready to go back home, we couldn't have managed to bike to Albrighton.

As the days and weeks went by we started to enjoy the work. I didn't get on with my first farmer (he was so rude) so moved to a very good farm, where the men were all from one family and very good and kind to us girls. My first Christmas the Boss told us to go for a Christmas drink at the house, we got a glass of milk and two shillings and sixpence, a lot of money in those days. The work was hard, with long hours in the harvest, beet and potatoes. I loved working with horses.

We had very good times, the RAF was not far away and there were good nights in the village pubs, where I met my husband home on leave from the navy.

Five years in the Land Army were some of my happiest days. I learned to play darts in one of the pubs and now I play for the WI.'

'Joan had already had five years experience in the Women's Land Army when she was transferred to Jimmy Lock's farm at Bomere: she had milked cows by hand and machine, herded goats, looked after pigs and been allowed to use some machinery (but never ploughed – that was exclusively men's work) but her extreme love was looking after horses. She was happy at Bomere Farm, living with a young widow, Betty, at Bayston Hill, and cycling to work every morning by 7am, past the nascent quarry, 'never take the cows past at 3pm'.

Bomere Pool was then just a beautiful wild place, reputed of course to be bottomless. Geese gathered in huge flocks there, and Joan remembers being ordered to crew a frail craft in order to trap some, and her fright at not being able to swim. But after a few months Jimmy Lock died, after first phoning his doctor to inform him of the fact, and Joan was transferred to Oteley Farm behind Percy Thrower's garden centre, where she milked and looked after the dairy, working in the sheds and fields afterwards. Farmer Mottram was not the easiest man to work for – he was old and crusty and found fault for seemingly no reason, and when Joan heard that Home Farm, Condover were looking for a land girl she moved yet again.

Joan still lived in Bayston Hill, paying her 28 shillings a week for board and lodging: not a lot nowadays, but then her wage was only

WOMEN'S LAND ARMY (ENGLAND & WALES).
RELEASE CERTIFICATE.
The Women's Land Army for England and Wales acknowledges
with appreciation the services given by

MISS JOAN HAY

who has been an enrolled member for the period from

JANUARY 1941 to 19TH JANUARY 1948.
and has this day been granted a willing release.
Date 19.1.48.   J. A. Preston.
                                    WOMEN'S LAND ARMY.

£2 10s 0d. The house has now gone, the lovely garden long since under concrete. There was no running water in the house, just an outside conduit which had to be unfrozen with boiling water in winter time, and a loo at the bottom of the garden.

Home Farm, Condover made no concessions to female sensibilities: Joan well remembers digging out the field corners where the plough was unable to reach, lifting and digging potatoes and beet cutting being the dirtiest and most back-breaking jobs. This large farm's work force consisted of Joan, a deaf mute of around 45 and one other man who worked from 7am to 5pm. In summertime Joan was often kept in the fields until night fell, and she entered in her diary of that time . . . 'he made me move 92 one hundredweight bags of corn from the lorry up the steps to the granary today, as he had to go to the cattle market'.

And yet there were happy times too. Joan enjoyed taking a pair of shire carthorses along the main road through Sutton Farm, past what is now Shire Hall, into the Abbey Foregate blacksmith, riding one and leading the other, and just the occasional car passing carefully.

It was at Home Farm that she met her first love, Allan, and after the episode with the bags of corn it was Allan who persuaded her to ask for a move, and move she did, this time to the Norton Farm and Stud Farm at Condover. Both farms were owned by Johnny Crow and managed by Ivor Faulkner. Occasionally she and Allan would go out for an evening – after a hard day's work the youngsters would cycle into Shrewsbury to see a film at the Empire or the Granada. She never remembers an air raid in this area, though there were plenty of German prisoners of war working on nearby farms. Norton Farm had eggs to spare for her to take to Betty – until then her midday meal consisted of peanut butter sandwiches, and her breakfast of fried bread and tomatoes: not exactly a protein rich diet for the long day's toil. Here Joan added bulls to her list of animal management: 'Old Bill' loved apples, and even on the day he slipped his ring while Joan was leading him past Condover Park gates he allowed Joan to drive him on to the farm.

'The first day I had to clean up the stack yard with a horse and cart – it blistered my hands. The rate of pay the first four weeks was eight shillings a week and we never got more than 25 shillings. I loved it. We were well equipped for the weather too, with a greatcoat, knee length breeches, stockings, shirt, pullover, denim dungaree overalls, wellingtons, a hat, and a tie with WLA printed all over it.

I used to get up early and get the cows in and help with the machine and hand milking, though hand milking made my wrists ache. Then we would have our breakfast after the cows had gone out and clean the milk utensils and scrub the dairy down. There were all sorts of jobs to get done. If I had time I would clean the horses out. There were six big carthorses and one morning the waggoner told me to open the gate and whistle them. All six came galloping up, the muck flying, and it quite scared me, they were so big.

Various jobs included pulping swedes and grinding oats for the cows. Cutting kale was another; you would go in the field with a sickle and cut these big thick leaves at the root, getting soaked as it was so wet. In the summer it was harvesting, hoeing swedes and mangolds etc and picking potatoes. Threshing the corn I was often on the box with the man who fed the machine, sometimes on the stack. I remember once feeling something running over me. It was a mouse gone up my trouser leg. I opened the zip at the side and he jumped out.

BOMBS AND CRASHES

'Schooldays over, my mother needed me at home and I joined various clubs, hockey in the winter and tennis in summer. Then, due, I think, to the death of a brother after a long illness, I became interested in nursing and joined the St John's Ambulance Brigade. Soon rumours of war were heard and our training intensified. I signed on as a mobile VAD and three days before war was declared was called up to a local hospital. I arrived with other volunteers immaculate in starched cap and apron and we were detailed to set up spare beds, which I should think had been in store since the last war by the look of them. We were far from immaculate by the end of the day! Next morning bus loads of patients arrived from Birmingham, evacuated in case the city was bombed. The seats in the buses had been removed and stretchers put in their place; some patients had only been operated on the day before and were in a sorry state on arrival.

'I was working on a farm in 1940 and there was one a anxious night when a string of bombs was dropped by mistake (the Germans obviously thinking they'd arrived at Tern Hill aerodrome), landing in a field close to the farmhouse. Early next morning the old cowman, with a hurried limp, rushed into the kitchen and excitedly told us a 'insanitary' bomb had been dropped in the Leg of Mutton field!.

'In 1943 a tragic accident occurred at the farm Bwlchyrhiw at Llansilin. A Spitfire plane was circling the Cynllaith valley for at least half an hour in the early hours of the morning. It is thought to have been on fire and the pilot looking for a landing spot. When it did come

213

down, it hit the farmhouse, set in fields with no other house for hundreds of yards. By another cruel twist of fate the residents, Mr and Mrs Williams, were sleeping in an unaccustomed back bedroom in order to air it for some expected visitors. The plane hit the roof and a huge beam fell right across the bed of the back room, killing the two occupants. Fortunately their two children survived.'

'A German bomber crashed about two miles from Acton Burnell. It was on a Sunday morning. I remember the local volunteer firefighters were called out to it; they came home looking like ghosts. I believe the plane was burnt up and all the airmen dead. No-one spoke about it afterwards.

We didn't have any air raids, only a few stray bombs dropped one night on the Caradoc, a hill not far from us. The noise was dreadful and we rushed out of our beds and stayed downstairs for the rest of the night. We were very frightened indeed. Every night blackouts had to be put up on all windows and if even a chink of light showed through someone would be at the door shouting 'Put that light out!' Lights on bikes had to be half covered with black paper. It is a miracle that we ever managed to see our way home in the dark. All the signposts were removed, and we all held identity cards with a unique number which I can still remember after 50 years.'

'The blackouts were fixed conscientiously every night, keyholes filled with paper and not a bit of light to be seen. German planes passed overhead regularly, going to Liverpool. On some nights the glow of fires could be seen 60 miles away. Three bombs were dropped at Marton and the whole village turned out next day to inspect them. I was out in the dark one night when the searchlight at Nibs Heath caught a bomber in the beam. The bomber retaliated by machine gunning the site. I was petrified.'

'The bombing of Liverpool went on night after night for a week or so and I would hide terrified under the bedclothes waiting for the planes to come back over Shrewsbury, praying they wouldn't drop any of their bombs on the way. I remember a land mine being dropped in the country outside and the house shaking. My father worked with the AFS (Auxiliary Fire Service) part time, and he was very upset when a young mother and her two children were killed on the Ellesmere Road when their cottage was blown to bits. They were the only casualties in the town during the war from enemy aircraft.'

'One incident which stands out in my memory was the day the glider crashed at Beckbury during the Second World War. It was on a

Sunday morning, my husband was changing into his uniform to go on Home Guard duties and he saw this thing ploughing across the field opposite our houses. He came downstairs to tell us then hurried off to try to help. It ploughed into Mrs Unitts' garden, coming to rest just outside her kitchen window and blocking the road for two or three days. There was no damage to the house but the garden fence was demolished. Apparently the tow rope broke; the pilot and his mate were injured but not too seriously I believe. The incident caused curiosity among the local people who came to see this large glider at close range. The gliders, towed by a Wellington bomber, were used to carry troops and were often seen overhead.'

'On 11th November 1944 I went into Much Wenlock cottage hospital to have my baby. It was a typical foggy November morning and when I arrived at about half past seven the hospital seemed exceptionally busy.

I was asked by the sister to hang on if I could as an American aircraft had crashed just outside Much Wenlock in a field up Bourton Bank and ambulances were bringing in the injured and dead. What a lot for a small hospital to contend with. I did hang on, until early evening when my daughter was born. Happiness for some, but, oh, the anguish for those American mothers yet to hear. Such is war.'

MAKING DO

Life went on, with the irksome restrictions of wartime and rationing to contend with. The stalwart members of the WI laboured over hundreds of jars of jam, in days when the connection had not become a joke and they were providing a much needed supplement to the ration.

TAKING THE HORSES

'At the beginning of the war all horses considered suitable were taken for the army. My father had three hunters and one of those was taken. She was a lovely mare and top price was paid for her, £60. Of the other two, one was too young and the other too old – much to my relief. However, I ended in floods of tears because the men said they would take my small pony as well! They were teasing but as a small girl it was terrible.'

RATIONING

Food rationing brought dried egg and dried milk. Tea, sugar, fats and meat were rationed, but in the country farm-produced foods were available and meat, rabbits and poultry added to a meagre ration. 'Drownding Mutton' sometimes appeared, after a sheep had 'fallen in the brook'! We smeared gravy browning on our legs to look like stockings. Dockets were needed for furniture and linen. My grand-mother took me to town and used her dockets to buy me two blankets at £5 each as a wedding present. Newly-weds scrounged furniture from their relatives or went to a sale.'

'Sometimes we used to be able to buy a tin of sausagemeat which came from America. There was enough fat in the tin to make the pastry and we used to look forward to sausage pie.'

'As the daughter of the keeper of the corner shop during the war I was a popular child. We didn't sell rationed goods, so whatever Dad found to sell, such as chocolate, sweets, biscuits and tinned goods, did not have to be kept for the rationed customers and so school friends hoped for a few extra goodies. Even my headmaster kept in with me in the hope of getting some titbits for our frugal school parties.

The shortages of everything stay in my mind. I recall hand-me-down toys, shoes, comics, clothes – almost everything. Anyone with spare beds had to take in boarders, usually workers directed to COD Donnington. Many came from London, from Woolwich Arsenal. Evacuees also were billeted in suitable homes; in Wellington they came from the Birmingham area. We had spare rooms but because of the shop did not have anyone billeted on us. Instead the local hotel used our spare beds for their overflow guests. Often these were the wives of Army officers from the camps around Wellington. I thought them very glamorous.

The shop was on the route of the convoys of lorries passing from the staging camp in Apley Park to the American camps at Atcham. I enjoyed being called 'kid' and 'honey' by the Yanks, climbing down from the trucks with their cigars and chewing gum to buy anything Dad could find them. I soon learned to say 'Got any gum, chum?'

Others from overseas who were glad of anything Dad could find them to eat were not, at first friends. However, many of the German and Italian prisoners helping on the local farms and businesses became just that. They made baskets, wooden toys and leather goods which Dad sold to give them some spending money. Henri was a doctor who went home to East Germany wearing one of Dad's overcoats and with one of my dolls in his pocket for a little daughter he hadn't seen for many years. We heard from him only once. Dad tried to trace him, but without success.'

When I walked down the road in Donnington eating an orange, I was an object of great curiosity. People were pointing at me and I could hear they saying 'Look, that girl is eating an orange!' I felt quite unique.'

'Men's woollen stockings were re-footed, the stitches picked up above the ankle. Clothing coupons had to be used to get the wool. Pillow cases and sheets were made from flour bags; four flour bags made one good sheet. Tablecloths and tea cloths were also made from these very good bags and they washed lovely and white. As we lived on the farm we had lard from the pig to make pastry with. Bacon gave off enough dripping to make cakes with, although dried fruit was scarce, though you could buy plenty of dates. We churned a little butter and mixed this with our margarine ration. Sugar was scarce but we used syrup and sweeteners to stew damsons and plums which we had bottled. Custard powder was off the market, but we made a lovely sauce with plain flour, and if it was stiff it was quite like blancmange if you coloured it. The worst of all was bread rationing which came late in the war. We had our own bacon, eggs, chickens, ducks and geese and caught rabbits which were much sought after by dealers from Liverpool.'

'During the war I worked on the farm and was asked to take the horse and cart to Morda Mill to fetch cattle feed. Not having driven a horse before I was a little nervous. When we got to the bottom of the lane the horse stopped at the milk stand. I told him to move on but he wouldn't budge, he thought that I was collecting milk churns, so I jumped down from the cart and led him on. He knew where the next stop was, off he trotted to the mill and pulled up at the door without any help from me.

Due to food rationing we ate very plain food, with lots of potatoes and vegetables which we grew in the garden. Dried egg was used in cooking. We had to queue up to buy food, only to find when it came our turn to be served there was nothing left for us.

We used to patch and darn our clothes, restyled our old dresses, and we bought cotton flour bags from the baker which we dyed and made into curtains and tablecloths. Many rag mats were made and given as wedding presents.

All our work was done by oil lamps and candles. How we managed to read, write and sew with such poor lighting was remarkable.

There was great excitement when a landmine was dropped in a field outside the village. Everyone made the journey to go and look at the huge hole in the field – nothing else there except this large hole. The war seemed quite near then. The Italian prisoners of war arrived and worked on local farms. Evacuees also came from Liverpool, some of whom still come back to the village every summer.'

VILLAGE LIFE

'In the Cressage area, the 505 Searchlight battery was billeted in a large house in the next village. The soldiers manned the searchlights in the surrounding countryside.

The first Christmas they were there the local WVS members organised a party in the village hall. Materials were provided by the Quartermaster and the local housewives made large quantities of cakes and sandwiches. Jellies and trifles were made in wash hand basins. Most weeks a dance was held in the village hall which the soldiers attended and some of them provided the music. Church parades swelled the congregation on Sundays.

Whist drives were held regularly to raise money for the Red Cross or to send comforts to the local men and women serving in the forces. After each one an auction was held and people paid quite a lot of money for things in short supply. A bag of sugar or perhaps half a pound of farm butter would make some bid against each other and raise the price quite high.

I remember going to the local bakehouse two evenings a week to hand out meat pies made for agricultural workers to supplement their rations.

Schoolchildren had a week's holiday in October so that the older children could help harvest potatoes in the fields. In the evenings and holidays I helped on the farm hoeing beet and stooking sheaves of corn. Another thing I did for the war effort was to fire watch at night in case cornfields were set alight by incendiaries dropped from planes on their way home after a bombing raid on Liverpool.

Once a week I helped at the Red Cross canteen in Shrewsbury, doing a night shift. Tiring work making endless cups of tea or cocoa, sandwiches by the score, and washing up. Soldiers passing through were glad of a meal or a sleep in a comfortable bed.

In our village a Pig Club was formed. In this way members could get meal to feed the pigs, which also devoured large quantities of kitchen waste. Members also helped one another when time came for killing the pig; joints of pork, ham, sausages, black puddings and pies and all the other pieces were a welcome addition to the ration.

Members of the WVS organized most of the social events in the village. They also arranged rotas for farm work by the women, the pie scheme and any jobs which needed to be done, such as collecting rosehips to make into syrup, knitting socks and balaclava helmets for the forces. Classes were arranged for making fur mitts out of rabbit skins and bedroom slippers from old felt hats.'

'The war started before I left school at 14 years. My first job at Stottesdon was at the vicarage; the vicar's wife kept rabbits, hundreds of them for meat. After that 30 Jersey cows arrived which we milked by hand, nice and warm in the winter but not so nice in the summer.

We had teachers from London staying in a cottage and they helped my father on the farm as he was in the Observer Corps and had to do day and night shifts. They especially liked working with the big carthorses. They adored my grandfather but could not understand him for months as he spoke a very broad Shropshire dialect with words such as 'oolerts' for owls and 'oonts' for moles.

The WVS and WI occupied the top floor of the vicarage for jam making. My father, Fred Yardley and others used to carry the sugar up three flights of stairs; quite a feat as it was in two hundredweight sacks. Also all emergency rations for the village in case of an invasion were there, hard biscuits and bully beef.

All sorts of black marketing went on at various farms, such as bringing a funeral hearse and mourners to pick up a dead pig.

The vicarage seemed to be the centre of the village in those days with the youth club and the vicar organising events for the war effort. He used to take the services and then get onto his tractor to help the farmers who were short of staff and he was a friend to all the soldiers stationed around at the searchlights. After the war everything began to change but we can look back and say they were not bad years living in the country.'

'Not being old enough to join up in the forces my friend, Rosalie Cotton, and I pulled an old handcart around Badger village collecting 'salvage' from each house. This consisted of used cans, meat bones (used to manufacture glue to make aeroplanes), and old rags etc. In Badger Hall huge nets were set up on frames and we threaded strips of hessian cloth in precise patterns to make camouflage nets for tanks and guns. Sometimes the colours were greens and browns for the war in Europe and sometimes sandy colours for the war in the African desert. We also rolled strips of white material for bandages. My mother and other women in the village knitted khaki socks and balaclava helmets for the soldiers. At home, when the enemy aircraft were overhead and my father out on night duty with the Home Guard, my mother and I would sit in the cupboard under the stairs if we were frightened. Only one bomb fell near Badger, in the fields between Badger and Burnhill Green, but we could hear the noise of the bombs falling on the Black Country and see the glow in the sky from the fires they had started.'

JAM AND THE WI

'During the war the National Federation of Women's Institutes, through the Produce Guilds of local WIs, organized the Jam Centres in the villages. The system was that all surplus fruit from local gardens was taken to the centres and, with sugar released by the Ministry of Food, local ladies with primus stoves and jam kettles made the jam. This was returned to the Ministry to be distributed under rationing to hospitals, shops etc.

Rhubarb in those days was always plentiful and was included in the jars of scarcer fruits such as raspberries and strawberries. Needless to say, apples were included with the blackberries picked from the hedgerows. The team of jam makers at Prees were of a wide age group, from 70 down to early twenties. We all wore hats! For three consecutive years Shropshire produced the largest quantity of jam of any county in the country, some 45,641 pounds in 1944.'

THE WELCOME HOME

'A Welcome Home party was held at Whixall in 1946. Eighty-nine men and women demobbed from the forces were each given £5 plus £1 8s 0d for each complete year of service. Dependants of those who died also had the same amount while two who had been POWs had an extra £5 each and so did the winner of the BEM.'

RATIONING WENT ON

'Between 1946 and 1951 I worked at the Co-op at Coalbrookdale and the rationing was still on. People would save their coupons up for something special. The books had to be marked for bananas and oranges, and coupons for tinned fruit and tomatoes. We would know when there was a queue outside the window that the lorry was at the other shop delivering the fruit.'

HIGH DAYS
&
HOLIDAYS

MAKING OUR OWN
ENTERTAINMENT

⟨⟩

Before the advent of radio and television, Shropshire's villagers and townsfolk made their own entertainment, taking advantage of the wealth of talent to be found in otherwise ordinary homes. The local hall was often the venue for plays and dances, eagerly awaited and appreciatively enjoyed as respites from work and day to day worries.

LIFE WAS NEVER DULL

'In the 1920s there came into Madeley Mr Richard Clarke, a former member of the famous D'Oyle Carte Opera Company. He went into partnership with Mr 'Dicky' Bowers and they converted an old chapel in Park Street into the Parkhurst Cinema. Incidental music from *The Gondolier*, *The Yeoman of the Guard* and *Iolanthe* brought to life many an exciting drama before the advent of 'The Talkies' in 1929, when we travelled by train from Ironbridge to Shrewsbury to see *The Broadway Follies* and *The Singing Fool*.

A large variety of entertainments took place in the Anstice, a beautifully constructed building for a small village like Madeley in those days. An impressive flight of stone steps led into a wide hall facing a sweeping oak staircase. On one side of the hall was a reading room with up to date papers and periodicals, on the other a billiard room. At the top of the stairs on either side were cloakrooms for the use of those attending balls and dances. In the ladies cloakroom was a very dignified elderly lady to hand out tickets for your coat and also to keep a warm fire burning brightly for those sitting out or not feeling too well.

Double doors opened into a large ballroom with adequate staging for either an orchestra, dance band or refreshments. On either side of the stage were changing rooms for visiting artistes. Large, floor windows lined both walls. An outside staircase led to a balcony with adequate seating for those wishing to attend the ball or dance but not to take part, just watch for a small token payment.

On the occasion of the visit of a group of 'Barn Stormers' I sat with a friend on the top row of the balcony to watch their performance of *The Murder of Maria Marten in the Red Barn* by William Corder. We huddled together in horror as the ghost of Maria rose from her grave to screech 'Guilty, William Corder, Guilty.' Other horrifying items were *The Man They Couldn't Hang* where three times the trap door wouldn't open, and the *Dumb Boy From Manchester* who having witnessed a murder was savagely beaten by the murderer, and left for dead, but managed to wriggle across the room and knock the telephone off its hook and dial the police. These items performed in the flesh were really terrifying because in those days none of us strayed far from home during dark winter nights, and nothing of that kind took place in the Gorge during our growing up.

We also had a visit from the Penstone family, who had just returned from touring South Africa with Jasper Maskylyn and his family. The highlight of their performance was for Mrs Penstone to be blindfolded, and to sit by a huge blackboard covered with numbers from 1–60. A member of the audience was invited to call out any number, she then called out all the other numbers without touching any one of them twice. Mr Penstone performed acts of hypnotism on local dignitaries in the audience, rousing shouts of raucous laughter from the audience.

There was a great deal of local talent available in the area and life was never dull. Black and White Minstrels dressed in Pierrot costumes staged concerts, all being local. Pageants of Empire were produced by Miss Elizabeth Fletcher and her Church Girls Guild, and dancing displays were given by Miss Nancy Briggs and her pupils, all over the area.

During the autumn and winter important balls were held at the Anstice, attended by everyone who could afford a ticket and a new dance dress and shoes, and for the men, if possible, full evening dress and black patent dance shoes. White gloves were compulsory, so as not to soil a ladies dress. Mr Jack Williams, Mr Fred Jenks and others sprinkled white powdered chalk on the oak floor boards, and then acted as MCs, having the authority to tap any man on the shoulder and order him off the floor, if not conforming with the accepted pattern of the dance.'

'Concert parties were formed in many villages, and in the two villages with which I was familiar, it was surprising how much local talent was to be found among the ordinary village people. Theatre visits were quite unknown to us until we grew up, and only then in our adult years did we go to the 'pictures'; these visits were definitely few and far between.

As an adult, I was privileged to live in a village, Acton Burnell, where for a number of years an annual pantomime was produced, all the cast being amateurs. This was produced by the lady of the manor, with much help from the RC priest of that time, and a local lady who was responsible for the music – the songs and dances. This

223

went on for a whole week, with evening performances and one matinee performance. The amount of local talent was quite amazing!'

'In the years before the war and again in the 1950s we had to make our own entertainment in Cressage as few people had cars to go further afield. Most weekends there would be a dance or whist drive in village halls or schoolrooms in the locality. Music for the dances was supplied by local talent – a pianist, violinist, drummer and maybe someone with an accordion. Concerts were great fun and many happy hours were spent rehearsing songs, plays and sketches for the big night. Costumes were made or borrowed, scenery painted and props made by a handyman. Great fun for all those taking part and good entertainment for the local people.'

'Although Highley was a poor village there has always been a deep community spirit and a camaraderie fostered by men working closely together and sharing danger in the mine.
Sports clubs have always flourished especially football, cricket and bowls. It used to be said that if you whistled down the pit-shaft, a footballer would emerge. Highley since the war has produced First Division footballers – Gerald Hitchens (Aston Villa and Milan), Stan Jones (West Bromwich) and Edward Hemsley (Sheffield United), who also played cricket for Worcestershire.

Rodington's Football XI in the late 1920s. Right up to the 1960s, Shropshire's villages could boast sports teams and many inter-village competitions were held.

224

A nonagenarian, himself a great sports enthusiast, told us that football between the wars was very well supported – the gate money on a Saturday afternoon usually amounted to £10, and since the entrance fee was only threepence, that represented 800 spectators.

The first tennis court in Highley was made on a piece of land at the back of the original vicarage. It was on a slope, which must have produced some interesting play! Other courts were later laid on the Welfare Ground and in a field near 'Springfields'.

Athletic meetings were held annually and attracted competitors from a wide area.

Whist drives and dances were very popular, and the latter often lasted until 2.00am. Ladies carried notebooks and various partners would write their names alongside the dance in which they hoped to partake. These 'date' dances were called 'Cinderellas'.

The Gothic Hall was a centre of social activity until it was burnt down on New Year's Eve 1928. Silent films were shown there – the owner's daughter played the piano for background music, while the owner himself often sang on stage. Often there would be ballroom dancing at the Gothic, or perhaps fancy dress dances. The local drama group was very active, performing such tear-jerkers as *East Lynne* and *The Sign of the Cross*.

Competitions for both children and adults were held regularly. You could dance, sing, recite, or do a comedy turn – like the man who sang comic songs with a sucking pig under his arm!

Games such as 'dunking' for apples or trying to eat doughnuts on a string were popular with children. The Plaza Cinema replaced the Gothic Hall.

The church and chapel also involved themselves in social activities. The church, for example, had its own string orchestra of about twelve players. They also ran two football teams, one of which was called St Mary's. The chapel had a team as well, and it gloried in the name the 'Prims' (Primitive Methodist).'

'The public hall at Baschurch seemed large, with fireplaces either side. The walls were dominated by large mirrors and at one end was a stage. This hall was well used for lantern slides, whist drives and entertainments. Visiting companies came, including The Soroptomists who were based in Shrewsbury. The hall would be packed. Local talent also took to the boards and I remember being a fairy in a school production. Dances were held and there was great competition over who should be Miss Baschurch for the Shrewsbury Carnival.'

'Of the entertainments at Llansilin village hall, chiefly remembered are the series of Drama Contests, the highlights of the years 1929 to

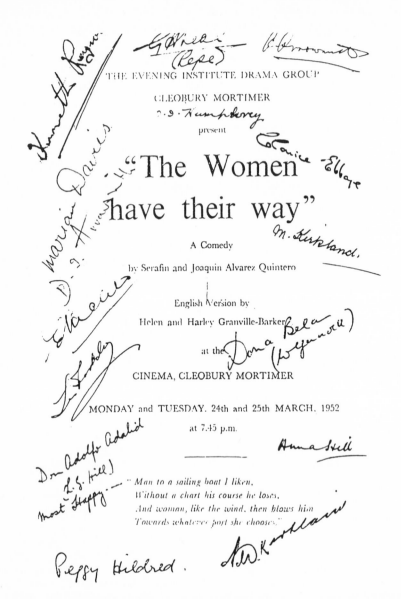

THE EVENING INSTITUTE DRAMA GROUP

CLEOBURY MORTIMER

present

"The Women have their way"

A Comedy

by Serafin and Joaquin Alvarez Quintero

English Version by

Helen and Harley Granville-Barker

at the

CINEMA, CLEOBURY MORTIMER

MONDAY and TUESDAY. 24th and 25th MARCH, 1952

at 7.45 p.m.

" Man to a sailing boat I liken,
Without a chart his course he loses,
And woman, like the wind, then blows him
Towards whatever port she chooses."

Every town and village had a wealth of local talent to call on for making their own entertainment. This is the signed programme of Cleobury Mortimer Drama Group Play in 1952.

226

1939. Contestants and spectators flocked from far and wide and plays were performed in English and Welsh on alternate nights, with a reduced price for a ticket to cover the lot. Money was very tight in those days but every effort was made to save in order to get to the renowned Llansilin Drama Week.

The hall was also opened for entertainment for 'the young men of the parish' and later for the men from away who were working on the pipeline which took Lake Vyrnwy water to Liverpool. Card playing and smoking were allowed, but not dancing or alcohol. Some sober pensioners of today do remember, however, getting dressed up and going by coach to the village halls of Llanrhaeadr and Llanyblodwel to take part in ballroom dancing!'

THE LUDLOW PAGEANT

'In 1934 a great event took place. Milton's *Comus* was to be re-enacted in the grounds of Ludlow Castle and among the 3,000 performers from the county, 29 came from our village, including ten children, among them my sister and me. I can't remember how we were chosen to take part but I have wondered since if it was that our parents could sew and thus make our sumptuous costumes. My own outfit was a simple affair of lemon cotton, long, right down to the ground. It had white trimming round the neck and a lemon and white cotton, square hat completed my ensemble. Remembering that we rarely went to Ludlow the run up to the actual performance was a wonderful time. For several weeks we had to make the exciting journey to town for rehearsals and when the actual pageant started on 2nd July 1934 our joy knew no bounds.

It was a grand affair. An orchestra of 100 musicians was in attendance along with a chorus of 200. There was a covered auditorium for 3,000 and seats, all numbered and reserved. Cheap day rail tickets to Ludlow were issued for railway stations within 100 miles radius at half fare.

It was an occasion I shall never forget; ladies and gentlemen, all beautifully attired, strolling around the castle grounds while horses and horsemen trotted around the castle green adding such grace and grandeur.'

'When, during the 1930s, a great pageant was held in the grounds of Ludlow Castle, local talent was recruited to play the parts of Ancient Britons. One was the famous Harry Rogers complete with coracle. The streets of Ludlow were freshly tarred for the occasion and it was a very hot day.

Weeks later my brother-in-law visited Harry at his house down in

'The Dip' by the Severn. He found him soaking his feet. 'What bist doing, Harry? he asked. Harry replied, 'I've got the foot rot' and proceeded to shave off that looked like large slices of black skin from the sole of his foot. 'That binner foot rot,' said Billy, 'That's tar!.'

OUT DANCING

'The school was the social centre at Edgton until the village hut arrived from Park Hall camp. Meetings were held there but the most fun were the whist drives and dances. Wet tea leaves were sprinkled on the floor during the whist to keep the dust down and were swept up before the dance began, but with the roughness of the wood and the wet patches from the tea leaves, no amount of powder put down to make it slippery worked. It always ended up with couples on the floor. My aunt, a mere 18 to 20 stone, was one, usually on top of someone. My uncle's foot went through the boards right by the stove at one dance – we laughed aloud about this at school the next day and got the ruler.'

'Just before the Second World War, local dances at Prees were held in suitable barns on local farms. One of these was Bostock Hall, in the loft above the short shippon, the one which faces the entrance to Top Yard.

There was no bar and these events would start at 7pm. Many practical jokes were played on people coming to the dance, such as a parcel placed in the road tied to a length of string held by a suitable person behind the hedge. When someone stopped and dismounted from his or her bicycle, the string was pulled and the parcel disappeared.'

'Concerts used to be held at my grandparents' farm in the granary, in aid of the chapel. The concert party came from Bishops Castle with a few locals also taking part. Not until I was 16 was I allowed to go to our local dances at Norbury which were held in a room over the old malthouse belonging to the pub, then housing hens. The hens must have wondered what on earth was going on above them because the room used to be really packed with people and we always had a live band and an MC to announce the dances, eg waltzes, quicksteps, foxtrots, the military two step, valettas and the Palais Glide.'

'Concerts and dances were organised at the public hall at Baschurch, with local talent taking part. The vet, a baritone, used to sing often, his favourite being *Keep the Home Fires Burning*. The station clerk was

228

a very good pianist, and, with three other instrumentalists, played at the dances. It seems that he almost made the piano dance, and kept 'The Gay Gordons' and the 'Highland Fling' going with the floor of the hall moving up and down with all the couples prancing about. When it was time for the quieter minuet, the pianist found it hard to slow down. Concert parties used to travel from village to village, and put on a show, which used to cost threepence.'

'During the war and for some time afterwards, I, my husband and two friends ran a small dance band consisting of piano, drums, saxophone and accordion. We played in most village halls in south Shropshire, for dances, social evenings and parties. We were not allowed petrol during the war as it was rationed so we often had to cycle several miles to dances, sending the instruments as best we could. Sometimes we sent them by train to such places as Bucknell or Bedstone, the organisers meeting them and putting them on the train next day. The army was very good and often helped out as they were allowed transport for recreation but could not carry civilians. I think people enjoyed our music, for older people still talk about Hamilton's Band and the good times they had.'

THE SILVER BAND

'Round about the time the colliery opened at Ifton Heath in the beginning of the century, a band was started by Mr Arnold Lovett. The band practised in the granary at Pit Farm and there were many local lads in it. They were resplendent in their uniforms of navy blue and red and they led all kinds of processions round the village, not least the chapel Sunday school Anniversaries, when they paraded into the chapels after the scholars and played grandly for the hymns. It is still going strong today.'

THE COMING OF RADIO AND TV

'The first person to have a crystal set in Longden was the vicar, and two evenings a week he would invite two couples to go and listen to some programmes. They had to listen through earphones. Children were not allowed!'

'We were the first in the lane at Acton Reynold to have a wireless set, but the old man next door didn't approve at all. Although he was keen on horse racing he would never come in to hear any of the big races and I'm sure he never believed the result until he read it in the paper.'

'We had our first wireless in 1925. It was a box with valves which lit up when it was working, and with a huge trumpet affair which produced the sound. It ran off a 'wet' and 'dry' battery – the 'wet' battery had to be taken to a man down the road to be charged and we had two batteries, one on and one at the chargers!

We had our first TV soon after the Second World War and as there were not many about at the time all the farm men used to come back all clean polished in the evening to see boxing when it was on, and it seemed to be on quite often!'

'Our first television set arrived in 1950, after we had had electricity put in and there was great excitement at switching on our nine inch set combined with a radiogram. All the neighbours were invited in to see the Cup Final and the Coronation in 1953.'

GOING TO THE CINEMA

'As we got older we would go to the cinema at Wem. The first three rows were kitchen-type chairs. These were what we could afford. Further back were the tip-up variety. A man came round once during every performance and sprayed everyone with disinfectant. We soon learned when to go to the toilet to avoid being sprayed.'

'We used to cycle to Shifnal on a Saturday night to the pictures. We could leave our bikes at Corsers cycle shop for a few coppers, and after an enjoyable evening at the cinema we would buy some fish and chips from Cottam's chip shop and eat them as we went to get our bikes for the homeward journey. These cost ninepence.'

'Although we were members of the Oakengates Salvation Army, my grandmother would take me to the Grosvenor Cinema in Oakengates just after the Second World War. I watched Laurel and Hardy, Abbott and Costello, Roy Rogers and Trigger, Charlie Chaplin, Lassie, the Bowery Boys and Ma and Pa Kettle. There were two houses and those with children usually went to the first one; the price, I think, was ninepence.

Talk about passive smoking – the air was blue from Woodbines, Craven A, Players and even Jet cigarettes. Babes in arms were taken along and it was not unusual to be watching a quiet scene and have it interrupted by a baby sucking a breast or bottle. The usherette would come round spraying the air with perfume – I don't know which was worse, the smoke or the perfume.

In Wellington there was a picture house called the Town Hall. One of its regulars was a very large man who had two seats made into one because of his size. When a cattle stampede was rushing towards him in a cowboy film, he would wave his stick and shout 'Whoa, whoa, get back, don't run over me!'.

SPECIAL OUTINGS

Outings were few and far between for most people, and many a child grew up without seeing the sea or travelling much beyond a few miles around his or her home village. Those that did arise were therefore all the more welcome and to be enjoyed at all costs.

TO THE SEASIDE

'Before the war the Salvation Army organised a trip from Oswestry to the seaside. My husband as a boy had no decent trousers to wear, so his sisters decided to make him a pair. They got an old coat, laid it on the floor and cut the shape around him. They then sewed the seams by hand. All went well until, at a stop in Llangollen, the children were given a trip on the canal. Don was impatient and jumped on board, ripping his seams. So there he was, wearing a skirt. His sisters went into the shop nearby and bought a penny packet of pins, and proceeded to pin them together again. The remainder of his day out was rather painful!'

THE BALDWIN-WEBB OUTINGS

'In 1931 the MP for The Wrekin was Col Baldwin-Webb and the Wrekin Conservative Party at this time organised the Baldwin-Webb Outings. Besides keeping the party in the news, they gave the constituents the chance to see parts of the country they would not otherwise have enjoyed. These outings were train excursions and people took advantage of them in their hundreds, flocking to their local railway station to board the special excursion trains. One year they visited the Military Tattoo in London, and a most spectacular sight it was. Meals were served on the train and appetites whetted for the next Baldwin-Webb Outing.

I remember two more of these great Shropshire outings. One was to the Isle of Wight with a beautiful view of the Needles, and the other, in 1938 was to the British Empire Exhibition in Glasgow with a sail round the Kyles of Bute. Col Baldwin-Webb, with his sister and agent, travelled to Glasgow by aeroplane, so they were there to welcome the Shropshire constituents when they arrived.

It was with a great sense of personal loss that we heard of the death of Col Baldwin-Webb. He was accompanying a large party of young refugees to Canada hoping for their safe evacuation during the Second World War when his ship vanished with the loss of everyone on board.'

SPORT FOR ALL

Cricket, football, tennis, pigeon racing, point to points – there was something for everyone's taste in Shropshire's sporting life.

THE VILLAGE TEAMS

'We had at Broome a cricket team, a football team, an airgun team, a table tennis team, a darts team, a dominoes team and a tennis team. Our airgun team won the Norfolk Cup three years running from 1909 to 1911, and the football team won the Blowers Shield in 1924; called Aston United, their jerseys were maroon and blue like Aston Villa.

We had two tennis courts and played matches with other village teams every Wednesday and Saturday when fine. We had a pavilion and provided tea to the visiting teams. It was all very friendly and hospitable.'

'There is a very good cricket pitch at Uppington and there used to be a good local team. My friend's mother used to do the cricket teas and I would go and help – mainly because I was sweet on the young man who did the scoring!

'Members of my family belonged to Wollerton Tennis Club in the 1930s, which was beside Wollerton Halt on the railway line. Saturdays were great days as we used to have lovely teas of sandwiches and cakes. In those days there were paraffin stoves to heat up the kettles to make tea. As a family we were keen on playing tennis at home and we spent a lot of time during the summer, mowing, rolling and marking out the tennis courts.'

'We enjoyed playing tennis and were fortunate enough to have our own tennis court at our home near All Stretton. My sister and I used to mow it and mark it out before we could play. We had quite a lot of tennis parties but that entailed preparing suppers. We also belonged to a tennis club, a journey of five miles on our cycles, and we played against other village clubs, usually on Saturday afternoons. Joining a tennis club was a good source of boyfriends, much to my father's disgust, as he thought having our own court would keep us at home!'

AT THE RACES

'The point-to-point races were much as they are today but with few cars. Horses arrived by train the previous day and were stabled locally overnight. The point-to-point course at Eyton on Severn has altered little in 60 years – except the size of the car parks. A popular rider of the day was Craig Tanner. Mr W. E. Downes of the Wheatland Hunt had a successful mare named 'Molly' and a Mr Sparrow of the Cheshire Hunt had a remarkable horse named 'Rara Avis' – in eight days he won four races.'

'I was born in Wroxeter and well remember the Eyton races that were held on Easter Monday. There was then only one race meeting a year and it really was a very exciting day for us. We used to sit on the wall at the bottom of the garden and count the cars going through the village to the races – there were very few cars on the roads then so it was something to see so many all on one day. We would then walk up to Eyton in time to see the races starting and were very intrigued to hear the bookies' calls.'

'Every year at Ifton Heath we looked forward to Bangor Races when a lot of coaches and traps went through the village. On the way back home the people would throw us coppers if they had had a good day. It was great fun.'

PANT HOMING SOCIETY

'Pigeon racing has always been popular at Pant. The pigeons were taken by train, but when they returned, the ring on their leg had to be taken to be put in a clock, which was by a five barred gate near the Powis Arms. If the pigeon was slow to go in the loft, it was known for it to be shot, so the ring could be taken off. A man was given a time allowance based on the distance he lived from the clock, and with so many houses it was possible to watch the progress of other competitors, and wives and mothers could shout encouragement as the men ran.'

THE MUCH WENLOCK GAMES

'The games were held every August Monday on what was called the Linden Fields or The Games Ground. Every kind of sport was competed for. The ancient game of quoits, the tilting of the ring, was done on horseback where competitors had to take a ring off a bar with a long pole as the horses galloped under the bar.

The only thing we didn't have was swimming because there was no swimming pool there. There was always a big carnival procession, led by a boy on a pony dressed as a Herald. Then came the Wenlock brass band, and of course the Town Crier, lots of decorated drays drawn by horses – the horses were dressed too with brasses and ribbons, then decorated prams and bicycles and lastly people on foot all dressed up hoping to win a prize. Then during the afternoon there was maypole dancing, the girls wearing old fashioned dresses and poke bonnets and the boys with baggy trousers, linen smocks and straw hats. What I am writing about is when I was a child about 70 years ago, but the Olympic games are still held today. I believe there was a short break during the Second World War, but it is as popular today as it was all those years ago. People travel from all over Britain to compete.'

SPECIAL OCCASIONS

Royal celebrations, recalled right back to the time of Queen Victoria's Jubilee in 1897, have been enthusiastically supported in Shropshire. There have been other special occasions too, such as the ending of the Boer War or the Festival of Britain in 1951.

234

QUEEN VICTORIA'S JUBILEE

'A great event in Dawley was the celebrations for Queen Victoria's Diamond Jubilee in 1897. At that time I was a scholar at Langley Girls School and the children from all the Dawley schools, which were of course, Langley, Dawley National, and Poole Hill, met on a big field down King Street and sang there. We all marched from our own schools and joined in this field to sing. We had a special hymn written for the occasion, but of course we always ended up with the National Anthem. During these proceedings my friend, who would be my partner in the procession, fainted and my teacher who was then Miss Deakin, came and stood by me. When we processed up the street, I was very proud to walk arm in arm with my teacher. After the procession we went back to our schools where we all had a very nice tea.'

THE BOER WAR

'My husband's grandmother remembered a huge bonfire being lit on a field in Wem in celebration of the relief of Mafeking in 1900. This song was sung during the Boer War:

> 'Lord Roberts and Kitchener
> Baden Powell and White,
> All went out to South Africa
> To make the Boers fight.
> And when the war's over
> How happy we will be
> We'll bring old Kruger to England
> And tie him to a tree.'

'To celebrate the end of the Boer War there was a dance in the Malt Kiln at Gobowen, now the Farmers' Union. Medals were given to commemorate the Coronation of Edward VII.'

'I can remember the ending of the Boer War in the year 1901, because a neighbour of ours at Dawley was a soldier who had fought in that war. On his return, the people in this district made such a fuss of him. I can remember that we made a garland of flowers and arranged it over the gateway leading to his house, which was the next house to mine. His name was Harry Poiser and on the day of his arrival after the war, the people in the district all congregated down there and then there was singing and such a fuss.'

CORONATION OF GEORGE V

'I remember the Coronation of George V celebration at Gobowen. We marched from the council school to the mission room with flags, or flowers on flag sticks. We had tea and sports in Pentrewern field, where the flats and Cornish houses are now. We also had mugs and royal blue-edged testaments given by Mr Bill Bowyer from the Hart and Trumpet. At night there was a dance in the mission room.'

'When George V was crowned in 1911 we had all kinds of games and sports on the cricket field behind the Kangaroo at Broome. The children then marched up to the school for tea and to have their commemorative mugs presented.'

QUEEN MARY

'HM Queen Mary (King George V's wife) used to stay with her brother the Marquis of Cambridge at Shotton, which Her Majesty considered was a 'glorified farmhouse'.

The best Queen Anne sheets were brought out for the occasions. Her Majesty insisted that her bed was in the corner of the room, with a screen surrounding it. The servants were instructed to curtsey if they met the Queen in the corridor and call her Ma'am – not easy when carrying jugs of hot water. When these royal visits occurred the local postman Mr Freeman used to act as a valet/butler to the Marquis.

Unfortunately one of Queen Mary's outriders was killed at Myddlewood when his motorcycle skidded on the ice. A waiting room was built at Yorton station for Queen Mary.

'I remember Woolworth's opening in Shrewsbury, when several children were sent by their parents to buy a bucket at the top price of sixpence. On their way home, coming over a railway bridge to Greenfields, they saw a big car, very grand, coming. It was Queen Mary who had been visiting her brother. So the children all jumped up and down on the bridge waving, with their new metal buckets clanking a greeting.'

'In the mid 1920s we were given a day off school to join the children from Hodnet school in lining the route for Queen Mary to pass through Hodnet. I was on the corner and the car went very slowly past and I had a good view of a very stately lady dressed in grey with the famous toque hat, pearls and a smile.'

JUBILEE AND CORONATION

'George V's Jubilee was celebrated in Wentnor, a mile away, with a tea party in a wainhouse for the children in the afternoon, followed by games and we were each presented with a Jubilee mug. The adults held a comic football match followed by a supper and dance.'

'The Silver Jubilee of George V and the Coronation of George VI in 1935 and 1937 respectively, were celebrated at Hodnet with a tea in the Lyon Hall and afterwards the gardens of Hodnet Hall were thrown open for all to enjoy. As I remember, it was fine both days. In the evening we repaired to Prees for their Grand Bonfire, which I think was part of the chain of beacons lit across Shropshire.'

'The Coronation of George VI in 1937 was a big occasion in Munslow. I wore a white muslin dress, made by my eldest sister, and red, white and blue sash. We ran races in our field and I won the little girls race – I don't think there was much competition. I remember having half a crown which my father kept for me but I reminded him frequently that it was mine. We had a marvellous tea in the buildings at the rectory and afterwards the grown ups danced. I shall never forget the excitement, although I thought my mother was very strange as I had never seen her dance before. An older sister was led onto the floor by the postman. It was all so colourful and strange and then I fell asleep.'

'A bonfire was lit by the Giants Chair on Clee Hill in 1937 when George VI became king. It was exciting to climb to the top to enjoy the fire but much more difficult to find one's way home to Bitterley in the dark with no landmark to follow.'

FESTIVAL OF BRITAIN AND THE CORONATION

'We celebrated Festival of Britain Year at Highley in 1951 with a huge bonfire, around which we sang with fervour, national patriotic songs. We were provided with song sheets but no musical instrument to help us on our way!

At the Coronation in 1953 we held street parties for the children, and had a week of activities, culminating in our first carnival, a most happy and successful event.'

'When the Queen was crowned in 1953 there were few TV sets around so we crowded with others into the front room of Mr Bert Ferrington, who lived in the blacksmith's cottage on the Hereford Road at

237

Meole Brace. It was a very small room and it got very hot and stuffy, but it was exciting and when we all stood up to sing the National Anthem it was difficult to sit down again as there was such a crush.'

THROUGH THE YEAR

Each year had its round of celebrations, from Easter to Christmas. Some have not stood the test of time, such as Empire Day on 24th May, once a red letter day in every schoolchild's calendar but now gone the way of the British Empire it celebrated.

EASTER

'There was an old custom in New Dale village which was carried out at Easter. It was called 'heaving'. I can only just remember it as a small girl, but my mother gave me all the details about it. On Easter Monday if the men saw any of the women in the village they would lift them up and on the Tuesday the women would lift the men up. The women would say 'It's heaving day today. I'm not going to fetch my bucket of water because so and so's up there, he'll lift me up'. But I think some of them went up purposely for the men to lift them up. It used to cause quite a lot of fun. I think this old custom had something to do with lifting Christ on to the Cross at Easter time.

Another old custom at Easter time that I remember was that most of the people in New Dale would nail a hot cross bun to their doors, and it would remain there until it crumbled away. It was supposed to keep all the bad luck away from the people living in that house.'

'It was customary for members, choir, and friends from Lords Hill Baptist church to meet in the Upper Works, Snailbeach in the afternoon on a Good Friday. They would walk around stopping at various places to sing hymns accompanied by Snailbeach Brass Band. Collections would be taken for church funds.

When they reached the Central Stores, Snailbeach, owned then by Mr Thomas Parry, he would supply sweets which the children would scramble for in his field.

On return to the chapel, tea was provided, for which I am sure everyone was ready. After tea was over and cleared away, the evening concluded with entertainment – usually a Service of Song, this being a story in words and song. A selected person would read the story in parts, the choir would continue with the story in song. This ended a most enjoyable day, well remembered by many.'

'The highlights of the year as children were Easter and Christmas. I remember when I was very young looking for little Easter eggs which had been hidden in the garden – a great thrill. We always had a boiled egg for tea which had been coloured by the cochineal added to the boiling water.'

'Good Friday meant a complete shutdown of all commerce in Shrewsbury in the 1930s. Nothing but essential services such as hospitals operated and even these were minimal. Traffic was still mainly horse and cart and this also would cease. It was a day for men to set their gardens and allotments, a fast-held believe that because it was a holy day, the resulting crops would be blessed and abundant. I suspect it was one of the few free days working men had to do the job. However, it was tradition and Good Friday was gardening day.

For mothers and children it was the annual trek to Haughmond Hill. Many Shrewsbury families did this journey along the canal from the maltings to Uffington, the canal being still us use, though quiet on a Good Friday. On reaching Uffington there was always a lady dressed in black from head to toe. She sat on a three-legged stool and sold lemonade at a halfpenny a glass. At Haughmond Hill scores of children climbed to the top, ate their sandwiches and played assorted games before the trek back along the canal in the evening. This custom had a long tradition, with religious connotations, but was even then dying out. With the commencement of the Second World War it, sadly, died out completely.'

MAY DAY

'A May Festival Committee was formed at Rodington and every 1st May the schoolchildren would perform intricate patterns with the ribbons around the may pole (after many hours of practice!) at the village hall. Then it was on a carrier's cart to the next village of Roden where the maypole dance was performed for the people in the convalescent home (owned by the Co-op estate in Roden for the Co-op's workers). This was always an exciting time for the children, and although I wasn't old enough to perform around the maypole, I was allowed to be a fairy and dress up in a white dress with wings and watch the May Queen being crowned! Unfortunately the May Festival committee folded in 1939.'

'Maypole Day in Shrewsbury was a lovely day. Preparations for this

Men in fancy dress at May Day celebrations near Shrewsbury in the mid 1920s.

would start a few weeks prior to the event. The maypole, made by the local men, would be a makeshift branch of a tree, planed till smooth and decorated with twigs. A small tricycle wheel nailed at the top and ribbons, usually twelve, would be attached. The youngest, prettiest girl (always a contentious issue!) would sit at the bottom supporting the pole, while the remaining girls clad in dresses made from crepe paper, would dance round it, hanging on to a ribbon. There was fierce competition for the best maypole from surrounding streets, but we were all rewarded with a glass of lemonade and a bun at the finish.'

'From Greenfields in Shrewsbury we went to the marshes in Berwick Fields (an old river bed) to pick may flowers to decorate the maypole, chose a May Queen and made dresses for the dancers out of crepe paper, different colours each year.'

'In Ludlow May Day was a great day when children danced around the maypole on the castle green. There was a May Queen and a fun fair.'

THE MAY FAIR

'The May Fair at Craven Arms was one of the social highlights of the year; I am remembering now those days, the 1920s and 1930s, before

240

the motorcar and television dominated our leisure time. The excitement began when we heard that the great steam engines towing their loads of fair equipment were on their way to our village; boys would press their ears to the ground, vowing that they could sense the vibration from the huge wheels of the engines some miles away. As soon as school was over we would rush to the fair field; normally we would go straight home from school, but not on those magical days of May. And there it was; it had arrived at last. The engines themselves were an impressive sight, massive, noisy, with gleaming nameplates and polished brass decorations, and the caravans were richly ornate with sparkling silver and brass and vividly-coloured glass. We would watch, fascinated by the speed at which the trailers were unloaded and the rides set up; the roundabouts, the helter-skelter, the chair-o-planes, the swing-boats, the cakewalk, the ghost train, the Noah's Ark; then there were all the side-shows and the circus tents to be erected.

The great day came, 24th May, and clad in our best summer dresses – the sun always seemed to shine for May Fair Day – we children would stand patiently at the front gate of our house waiting for our parents, content to watch the passing groups of people who walked from miles around to come to the fair. Some came by horse and trap, or horse and cart, or by the earliest of the motor buses or the occasional car, but most came by 'Shanks's pony'. All dressed in their Sunday best clothes, families of babies and children, parents and grandparents passed our house, but we never saw them from one fair day to the next. Older people have told me that they remember the hiring of farm-hands being a regular feature of the May Fair Day.

The fair ground was situated in the centre of our village, across the road from the main public house; the streets were lined with stalls of every description, but our favourite ones were those selling sweets. I remember the piles of brandysnaps, the multi-coloured gob-stoppers, the coconut ice, jelly babies, liquorice bootlaces, brightly coloured humbugs, and the ones I liked best, the cream pies; these were a wafer cup filled with a creamy mixture and topped with chocolate and coconut. All these were displayed uncovered but we didn't mind that at all. Then there were the toys, whistling birds on a cane, windmills and whipping tops, skipping ropes and spinning tops, bowling hoops and rubber balls; and of course the dolls with china faces and eyes which opened and closed. How exciting it all was for us children, making our way through the masses of people who thronged the streets, pushing and jostling with good humour.

Pocket money had been carefully saved for weeks and if we were lucky, donations would make it up to half a crown, a princely sum in those days when a halfpenny would buy you a bag of sweets. My favourite ride was the 'big cars' as we called them, spacious cars with three or four rows of seats all gloriously lined with crimson velvet material and with a shining brass bar to hold on to as the cars moved around and up and down at ever increasing speed. Most exciting of all the rides was the chair-o-planes, single seats into which you secured yourself with a thin chain; the chairs were then propelled at speed and at an angle high over the fairground and what a wonderful view of tent tops you got. The cake-walk was considered another very daring apparatus, really only for the grown-ups; you stood inside an enclosed drum which vibrated sideways and up and down, making it difficult to keep your foothold. I remember the feeling of horror when we children heard that a lady had broken her leg on the cake-walk.

The side-shows were a great attraction, from the boxing booths where the public was invited to box so many rounds with 'the champion' for a temptingly high money prize, the so-called wall of death, where a motor-cyclist rode round and round the vertical walls of a dome, and a motorist speeded round the walls in a tiny car with a tiger cub – no doubt drugged – clinging to the bonnet, to the freak shows. Misformed animals were exhibited, two-headed calves and three-legged sheep I remember, and sadly, misformed humans too; how we loved the dwarfs, and of course the 'fat lady' and the 'fat man'. There were the rifle ranges, the hoop-la stalls with gorgeous soft toys as prizes which we all wanted to win, but our hoops, if ever they reached the target, always seemed to fall over something we didn't really want. We always fancied our chances at the coconut stalls, but our shies never succeeded in dislodging a coconut. The roll-a-penny was good fun; here you won pennies to the value of the number of which your penny fell as long as it did not fall on a line. There was one stallkeeper who would give you seven pennies change for a sixpence, and we would chance the odd penny and save the six pennies for something else; I remember feeling most conscience-stricken in doing this, but it was a legitimate way of making a penny, and I'm sure the owner of the stall came out the winner eventually.

The fair stayed on a further few days, but for us the great day was over; all our money was spent, and it was with sadness that we watched the fair being packed up ready to move on to another village.'

'The first Friday in May was a special day at Bishops Castle. Everyone came to town and it was all the fun of the fair for us children. Miss Thomas, headmistress of the high school, tried to persuade us that it was not ladylike to go but I'm afraid that fell on deaf ears. While we were sampling the joys of the swings and roundabouts, the grown

242

ups were catching up with, in some cases, a year's gossip. The two teashops did a roaring trade. The Boar's Head, the Six Bells and the home-brew at the Three Tuns satisfied the men. Everyone went home happy and, in some cases, it was the horse who knew the way home.'

EMPIRE DAY

'On 24th May at Ludlow, the schoolchildren sang a little ditty:

> 'Empire Day, Empire Day,
> If you don't give us a holiday
> We will all run away.'

This meant half a day off school after the celebrations, to which the vicar, squire and parents were invited. Children entertained by showing their school work and singing songs from the National Song Book, patriotic songs such as *Jerusalem, Rule Britannia* and, of course, the National Anthem. In Ludlow the children marched through the streets to sing in the Square.'

'I went to Lea Cross school in the 1920s; we walked a mile and a half from Plealey. On Empire Day we had a half day off school and walked up to Hinton Hall. Col Head and his wife were the school governors. The girls would all dance round the maypole and we'd have a big tea party and the run of the parklands – it was smashing! Mrs Head and her three daughters would put down Treasure Hunts for us.'

'The highlight of the year was the tea party given by our local Women's Institute on Empire Day. All the children would line up in rows in front of the Union Jack and sing God Save The King, then they would march past and salute before going to the field nearby where they held all kinds of sports. Afterwards they would tidy themselves up and march up to the Hall where they were entertained to a marvellous tea.'

'On Empire Day the children from all the schools in Shrewsbury were marched through the town, waving little Union Jacks, to an assembly in the Quarry. A stage was erected to accommodate all the local dignitaries and the schools stood to attention in the front. There were numerous patriotic speeches, followed by patriotic songs, and the whole gathering was brought to a conclusion with a service led by, usually, the vicar of St Chad's. We were then formally dismissed and allowed the remainder of the day free.'

'School outings were unheard of when I attended school in 1931, so you can imagine the excitement when Empire Day (24th May) came around for this was the day out for us all. The whole school was mustered into the girls playground (we had two, one for the boys and one for the girls), we lined up in pairs and off we marched along two miles of country road to the home of a local retired colonel. What a day we had! We took part in sack races, egg and spoon races, wheelbarrow races and three-legged races. We also greatly enjoyed trying to eat a doughnut, suspended on a string from the branch of a tree, with our hands firmly tied behind our backs. What a mess we got in but how we enjoyed it all! Tea was laid out on long trestle tables in the park (it never ever rained for our day out) and we enjoyed sandwiches, jellies and buns before marching home tired and happy.'

OAK APPLE DAY

'On 29th May both girls and boys would come to school at Baschurch wearing oak apples, to commemorate King Charles II hiding in the oak tree at Boscobel.'

FETES AND CARNIVALS

'One of the most outstanding memories of my childhood is a village fete in which all the girls from the local Church of England school at Hookagate took part in what was undoubtedly the highlight of the fete.

In the weeks leading up to the fete (which was held in July 1935) plans were made to crown one of the schoolgirls as the Rose Queen. She would be attended by a Herald and four Maids of Honour. Voting papers were handed out to each child in the school and the girl receiving the most votes was duly chosen as Rose Queen, the girl with the second highest number being the Herald. To my utter astonishment and delight, although I was younger than the rest, I was chosen as one of the Maids of Honour. The other girls in the school formed part of the Queen's retinue, the four youngest being train bearers and two other little girls were corn bearer and flower girl respectively.

During the weeks that followed we practised at every available opportunity a number of country dances to be performed after the crowning ceremony. These included Rufty Tufty, Black Nag, Gathering Peascods – what lovely names! And then there was the great excitement of our dresses. The two women teachers and the headmaster's wife went to Birmingham and bought yards of cotton material which, with the help of one or two mothers, they made into lovely dresses. Only one of us had ever worn a long dress so one can imagine the joy of trying on the dresses. They were all made in the same style – a frill at the hem, armholes and neck with a fitted bodice and a full skirt. Four in lilac; four in rose pink; four in peach; the four Maids of Honour in white with a tiny floral design and all the infants class in pink with an identical floral design. We each carried a posy of flowers surrounded by a silver doily and wore a pretty headdress. I remember that the Rose Queen wore her sister's white wedding dress and had a gorgeous pink and silver train which, like the Herald's costume, had been borrowed from the previous year's Shropshire Historical Pageant.

The day of the fete arrived at long last. We dressed in the school and, fortunately, it was a fine day for we walked in procession from the school along the road to the house (Welbatch) where the fete was being held – a distance of about half a mile. What a beautiful sight it must have been to see all those little girls walking along that country road in their pretty dresses.

The Rose Queen was seated on her throne, surrounded by the Herald and the Maids of Honour on a dais on the large lawn in front of the lovely Georgian house. I can remember to this day the tingle of excitement as we took our places before what seemed to be a huge crowd of people. After the Queen was crowned by a lady from (I think) Meole Brace, we performed our country dances on the lawn. What a magical day it was!

I think back now and realise just how much hard work was put in by those teachers and their helpers – not only in teaching us the dances, but in making and fitting the dresses (about 30 in all) the headdresses and the posies. I sincerely hope that they felt they were rewarded by what must surely have been a very pretty scene on that country lawn, and in the pride of the parents who were present as well as the joy given to those young village girls. What a mercy it was a fine day. Just what would have happened had it been wet I can't imagine! A day never to be forgotten – by me at any rate. To my knowledge nothing like it has been attempted before or since in that locality.'

'One day in August at Bomere Heath was set aside for the Three Parishes Garden Fete. The prize specimens of the local gardens were displayed with pride and a large variety of home-made cooking and handicrafts were on show. Field sports were organised to please people of all ages, but the one that provoked most hilarity from onlookers was that of catching the pig with the greasy tail! The entrants were many and the shouts of the spectators offering encouragement could be heard for miles, but invariably the pig beat the field.'

'The highlight of the year at Tilstock was the Church Fete held on the vicarage lawn. The school children danced before a captive audience. Stalls selling everything were erected between all the usual games. Everyone was there. One particular year a village 'character' promised to help by running a stall. He said it would raise a lot of money, but kept it all a big secret. On the day of the fete, he put up a little round tent with a large placard saying 'Something Never Seen Before – Sixpence A Look'. People queued up, paid their sixpence and disappeared inside the tent. They emerged a little while later, having been sworn to secrecy. Village curiosity meant that lots of people entered the tent to discover before them 'a cow's tail' hanging. Indeed, it had never been seen before, it had always been seen behind!

Each August Bank Holiday the grounds of Tilstock Lodge were opened for another fete and horse show. People came from miles around. In the evening there was dancing on the lawn to the Whixall Prize Band. Proceeds from this fete went to the Nursing Association.

Another treat some villagers attended was Whitchurch Carnival. My dad borrowed a horse and open cart from his employer. The horse was stabled at the Bull's Head pub in Whitchurch whilst we enjoyed the delights of the carnival. After the evenings' torchlit procession, we would all meet up and climb back into the cart to return home.'

'The flower show was held on the rectory fields at Kynnersley in the 1920s. Children gathered grasses and wild flowers; these had to be named and there were prizes for the most varieties named. There were three-legged races, bowling for a pig, the greasy pole, coconut shies, fancy dress and numerous stalls, mostly of produce and homemade cakes and sweets. A silver band from a neighbouring village played popular tunes.'

'Every year there was a fete held on the lawns of Pitchford Hall by kind permission of Sir Charles and Lady Sybil Grant. One of the highlights was a fortune teller who was housed in the famous tree house. Some of the girls would make buttonholes and sell them. There would be a bran tub and races on the lawn. In the evening they would hold a dance in the village hall where there would be sandwiches and lemonade for sale made by the women from the village. No bars in those days!'

'I remember my mother allowing us to get up at five o'clock on the odd occasion to go to the showground on the day before the West Midland Show opened, to get lovely Jersey milk which the farmers gave away rather than throw away. The cattle, sheep etc were moved by road to the showground after being unloaded from the railway yards in Greenfields, so it was a great treat to see the champion bull etc walking along.

The Shrewsbury Carnival was a great event in our childhood up to 1939. It was held in September in aid of the Shropshire Hospitals. There were two parades from the Quarry and the evening parade was all lit up. The dancing troupes and bands came from all over the country to take part and there were lots of floats, all beautifully decorated. The Miss Shropshire competition was held weeks before and the final beauty chosen from all the entries from around Shropshire. They had their own special floats and their photographs were taken by a Mr Bryant, who had his studio on Castle Street and displayed them outside for every to see and judge which they liked the most.'

'Patsy Collins fair came to Oswestry for the March and May fairs. One girl went with her boyfriend without telling her Mum, but they went on the big wheel together and it got stuck with them at the top – so everyone knew where they were.'

CLUB DAY

'Baschurch had a Men's Club and a Ladies' Club. On Men's Club Day the men paraded through the village carrying a large banner. Then there was a service in church and afterwards a fair, with hobby horses, swingboats and coconut shies, near the public hall.

The Ladies' Club was formed in 1802 to help families in need; it was disbanded in 1975. The ladies paraded round the village with their banner, followed by older members carrying wands decorated with flowers. The junior members carried bunches of flowers. After the church service the procession went to Mrs Dawson's Room for tea. The wands and bunches of flowers were judged and prizes given. After this everyone went to the field near the public hall for the fair.'

'A great day in the village was the annual Summer Oddfellow's Club walk, when all the members and anyone else who cared to tag along would march from Clee Hill to Knowbury church behind my grandfather's brass band. With a huge drum in front, it must have been an awful racket! After church we would go to the club room at The Crown and sit down to a big dinner. Dad, although a child, was allowed in because his father was the band master. He looked forward to having the 'gable end' as he called it, of the huge suet roly-poly pudding. Afterwards there were sports in The Crown field and more music. I can remember such an event in 1922 with the women in skirts down to the ground and great big hats.

Gerald Portlock trained horses and dogs for work in the circus. About twice each year, dressed in a cowboy outfit complete with stetson hat, he would give an impromptu performance in Broad Street, Ludlow. Before 1950 there wasn't a lot of traffic and no-one seemed to mind a few minutes hold-up.'

HARVEST FESTIVAL

'Harvest Festival was a very important Sunday in the church's calendar. We had two services at Mainstone that day, at eleven o'clock and three o'clock. I so well remember the church being packed to the door on both occasions. We never had a harvest supper but we always had the traditional harvest goose for our dinner that day, with visitors from Bishops Castle and usually the vicar and his wife or the curate.'

HALLOWEEN AND BONFIRE NIGHT

'Halloween was an occasion which we found very exciting. My brother and his friend would get the largest swede they could find, and would hollow it out and cut eyes, nose and mouth on it and put a lighted candle in it, and stand it on the gate-post – hoping that the wind wouldn't get up too strongly, and spoil the 'funny face' which they had created.

Bonfire Night was also a busy night – in fact, the boys would be very busy for some time before 5th November, gathering rubbish, sticks and wood etc to make the bonfire, and all hoping for a fine night – so that it would burn well. The girls in the family usually tried to come up with a good 'Guy Fawkes' which was hoisted on to the bonfire and burned as we waved sparklers about. We didn't have any large spectacular fireworks in those times, not like children have today.'

ARMISTICE DAY

'At Wem in the 1920s we would all gather in one room at the school on Armistice Day, 11th November, to stand for two minutes silence – and silence it was, as all traffic came to a complete stop in those days.'

'The Armistice Day parade was always very well attended at Bas-

248

church. A parade was assembled outside the Boreatton Arms, consisting of ex-servicemen and women, Girl Guides and Ifton Heath Band. Mr Eric Dawson in dark suit, bowler hat and medals, led the procession. A large banner was carried behind him. A service was held at the war memorial, reveille was sounded and the names of the fallen read. Then wreaths were laid.'

CHRISTMAS AS IT USED TO BE

'In the 1930s it was very busy for us for a week or so before Christmas feathering and dressing geese, ducks and chickens. Some were ordered and collected from home at Wentnor, the rest my mother sold at Shrewsbury market, the old indoor market. They were packed in brown wicker baskets and taken by bus.

Mince pies were made on Christmas Eve so that they could be offered when the carol singers called. It was often Christmas Eve before Mother had time to marzipan and ice the Christmas cake. We hung a stocking up for Father Christmas and were thrilled next morning to find an apple, an orange, a sugar pig and a sugar mouse and maybe a few sweets. I remember having a brush, comb and mirror one Christmas. The postman came during the morning with the Christmas cards – you never had cards before Christmas Day, but not so many were sent in those days. We never had a Christmas tree or decorations until we were in our teens, though Mother would put some holly round the house on Christmas morning.'

'I remember the lovely Christmas parties each year for children who attended Longden village school, kindly given by Mr and Mrs Swire who lived up at Longden Manor. They would have a large fir tree taken up from out of the park and brought down to the Douglas Swire Memorial Hall. It was always beautifully decorated and underneath were the many presents. The girls were either given a dress or a nightdress and the boys had shirts or pyjamas. Each one had been made during the previous year by Nanny Sargent, who had been nanny to the Swires' children. She used to stand among the children with a pencil and paper, to take stock of the sizes of all the children ready for next year's party. We thought it was wonderful.

Also in the village every Christmas afternoon the village band would play carols at each house and five farms. They finally finished at about half past four. The bandsmen who lived out of the village and their families would then be invited to various houses to take tea, because in the evening the band would walk up to the Manor to play carols in the main hall while the gentry were having dinner in the huge dining room. Afterwards they would go into the servants' quarters, have a meal with them and play for the rest of the evening for dancing. Some of the younger members of the gentry would also join in the dancing and later on the men would play cards until the early hours of the morning. At about ten o'clock on Boxing Morning the band would leave the village to go to play carols at Exfords Green and Lower Common. Then they cut across the fields to Mr and Mrs Hobson's farm at Starrs Coppice, and then it was all up the common lane to arrive up at the Red Lion at opening time. After consuming about 27 different kinds of drink, they still found time for more in the evening, very tired but happy.'

'At Christmas time a party was held at Beckbury reading room (now the village hall). There was a huge tree, all decorated and every child had a gift. Parents had tea and sandwiches for sixpence and on leaving to go home, each child was given a bag containing an orange, apple, a few nuts and, best of all, a sugar bun.'

'The house at Lower Frankton was so cramped that during the Christmas holidays, when all the family were at home, my brothers and I had to sleep 'head to tail' – there were only two small bedrooms in the cottage. It was mostly pork, duck or cockerel for Christmas dinner, sometimes goose, but there were hardly any turkeys as they were difficult to rear. Those who were not very well off had a couple of rabbits.'

'Christmas was a wonderful time in the pub we kept at Broseley. The holiday was short – Christmas Day and Boxing Day only. The festivities began on Christmas Eve when the men had finished work and they changed into best suits. Carols were beautifully sung and plates of mince pies handed round. At midnight a dark haired man entered through the front door, bringing a piece of coal for luck. After a drink he left through the back door. The same performance on New Year's Eve. One fire at least was not let out during this time. On New Year's Day the holly was taken down and burned. Morris dancers came inside on Boxing Day and were most popular. It was a sacred, happy season for all.'

'Our next door neighbours at Loppington had eight children. They wore no shoes and slept head to toe. These boys, if their mother considered they had been naughty, received a stocking full of cinders at Christmas.'

'Christmas was always a lovely time after all the work of feathering and dressing the poultry. We always had goose with pork or beef, and there would also be pheasants. Mincemeat was home-made and small mince pies and large plate pies were made. About a dozen plum puddings had already been made in the big boiler. One of our treats at Christmas was home-made toffee. The house would be decorated with holly, mistletoe and Christmas cards. All the rooms had log fires burning and the oil lamps were lit.'

'At Christmas at Tilstock the old people of the village had a party with entertainment. The men were presented with a clay pipe and tobacco, the ladies with a caddy of tea.'

'In 1949, I lived in a small village on the Welsh Borders, without electricity, so Christmas was holly, mistletoe and painted cones, and a very 'modern' table lamp with mantle that gave a good light, and an open fire of coal and logs. The village and the hillsides were dark, except for a twinkle here and there, and lanterns around the stock. By Christmas 1950 we all had electricity, and what a difference that made! At that time it looked almost like the Oxford Street lights of today. I progressed to crepe paper twists of green and red. In the 1950s, when our sons were small, Christmas tree lights became available, and the multitude of baubles that we see today.

There were no fridges, so the poultry were fresh, killed and dressed in the week before Christmas with hopes that the weather would not turn mild! We did not have the selection of vegetables we see today. I recall the carrots, sprouts and a swede, as a gift from a local farmer, which certainly put flavour in the gravy! The bird was cooked in the oven on the range, and depending on its size, may have been cooked overnight.

Of course, the highlight of the weeks before Christmas were the numerous 'Feathered Whist Drives' in the various villages. Including of course the interval during which excellent refreshments were served, and all for two shillings and sixpence.

A younger friend recalls the wonderful toyshop on Wyle Cop, where her mother paid two shillings and sixpence a week all year towards their Christmas gifts. Phyl also remembers the shop where in her day it was a penny per week towards the cost of items, and all life's needs were available on the Cop!'.

'I can well remember some of the old customs which were observed in New Dale when I was a girl. On a Boxing Day the Morris dancers used to come round. They would be the youths out of the village, ten or a dozen of them, and they used to dress up in their mother's dresses and their mother's hats and black their faces. They would each have a broom stake, and they would dance around singing:

"Somebody's in the house of Dinah,
Somebody's in the house I know,
Somebody's in the house of Dinah,
Playing on the old banjo." '

'We had a big dance each New Year's Eve at Broome which was the event of the year. It was held in the school and a special sprung floor was put down and a popular band engaged. We liked to have new long dresses and if we had to cycle to the dance these had to be pinned up with safety pins to stop them getting in the wheels. When I first went to dances men had to wear white gloves and pumps. The ladies were given little cards with pencils attached so that the men could book you for the dances they wanted. They always said 'May I have the pleasure of this dance?' and took you back to your seat afterwards.'

'At Christmas the bellringers and men from the choir would come round singing. Mother would play the harmonium while the men breathed beer over her! Finches brass band would come round to play, sitting in the kitchen drinking beer and cider from the cellar. After a rousing chorus mother would not be pleased when they emptied their instruments onto the kitchen floor which would have to be washed!

We stood at the wicket gate between the farm and the church to hear the bellringers ring in the new year at St Peter's, and then the men stood on the top of the tower and sang:

"Give heed my heart
Lift up mine eyes,
Who is it in the manger lies?
Who is this child so young and fair?
It is the Christ child lying there.
. . .
While nations sing with joyous mirth
A glad new year to all the earth."

As the men made their way home, their voices rang round Rushbury, "Happy New Year".'

Index

254